Mechanisms

THE UNIVERSITY OF
WINCHESTER

Martial Rose Library
Tel: 01962 827306

To be returned on or before the day marked above, subject to recall.

Mechanisms

New Media and the Forensic Imagination

Matthew G. Kirschenbaum

The MIT Press
Cambridge, Massachusetts
London, England

First MIT Press paperback edition, 2012

© 2008 Massachusetts Institute of Technology

For information about special quantity discounts, please email special_sales@mitpress .mit.edu

This book was set in Garamond 3 and Bell Gothic on 3B2 by Asco Typesetters, Hong Kong. Printed and bound in the United States of America.

Library of Congress Cataloging-in-Publication Data

Kirschenbaum, Matthew G.
Mechanisms : new media and the forensic imagination / Matthew G. Kirschenbaum.
    p.   cm.
Includes bibliographical references and index.
ISBN 978-0-262-11311-3 (hc. : alk. paper)—978-0-262-51740-9 (pb. : alk. paper)
1. Mass media—Technological innovations. 2. Mass media and language.
3. Discourse analysis—Data processing. 4. Computer storage devices. 5. Data recovery (Computer science) 6. Gibson, William, 1948– Agrippa. 7. Joyce, Michael, 1945– Afternoon. I. Title.
P96.T42K567   2007
302.23—dc22   2007002121

10 9 8 7 6 5 4 3

For Kari M. Kraus
Who bears witness

Contents

Preface

> I hesitated
> before untying the bow
> that bound this book together.
> —WILLIAM GIBSON, "AGRIPPA"

william gibson agrippa. Type this string into any search engine and you will get dozens of hits on the electronic text of a 300-line poem by the bestselling science fiction author. "Agrippa" is a complex and multifaceted work—ekphrastic, elegiac, and autobiographical, about family, memory, and loss. Its central image is that of the mechanism, a trope that manifests itself as a photograph album, a Kodak camera, a pistol, and a traffic light, as well as in less literal configurations.[1] Explore a little further and you will find that the text, which dates from 1992, was originally published on a computer disk that came packaged with a limited edition artist's book with illustrations and etchings by Dennis Ashbaugh, also titled *Agrippa*. The pages of this book were supposedly treated with photosensitive chemicals that caused the images to gradually fade from view once opened and exposed to light; the electronic text of Gibson's poem, meanwhile, was encrypted so as to allow only a single

---

1. The best reading of "Agrippa" I know, particularly the poem's central trope of the mechanism, is Alan Liu, *The Laws of Cool: Knowledge Work and the Culture of Information* (Chicago: Chicago University Press, 2004), 339–348. Liu compares the work to Wordsworth's "Tintern Abbey" as a poem of authorial memory and autobiography, but with the serial discontinuity of the mechanism marking a major departure from a Romantic sensibility.

reading from the disk, the lines auto-scrolling up the screen and then gone forever—a 20-minute experience.

Of course the inevitable happened. Almost immediately, the text of Gibson's poem was "cracked" by hackers and posted to the Internet where it has remained in circulation ever since. It is questionable, meanwhile, how many of the accompanying artist's books were ever actually produced—certainly not the edition of 450 planned in the original sales prospectus. Gibson himself has claimed never to have seen a copy, despite the fact that he has apparently autographed one.[2] Continue exploring the history of this strange but affecting literary artifact and every assumption about it, other than its immediate presence on the screen in front of you, is called into question. Was the text's illicit dissemination online the point of the project from the very start, or did Gibson and the others originally imagine it as an irrevocably vanishing performance piece about the ephemeral nature of memory and media? Did the data on the disk truly employ an RSA encryption algorithm as was reported, a technology classified as a munition by the National Security Agency? (If so, it would have been all but impossible to crack for anyone without the aid of a supercomputer.) Is the text of the poem on the Internet even the same as the one that was on the disk? (Early press releases about the project had more consistently described it as a short story or even a novel.) What *is* certain is that in Gibson's "Agrippa" we have an electronic text that is volatile and ephemeral *by design*, which nonetheless turns out to be one of the most persistent and available literary artifacts on the Web.

The artist's book *Agrippa* is more elusive—far fewer people have seen a copy in person. It comes in a literal black box, a glossy onyx-hued receptacle made of fiberglass that supports the book in a nest of webbing and corrugated

2.   The copy at the New York Public Library (which I have inspected) is signed by Ashbaugh and Gibson on the flyleaf. In a February 2000 interview for the online *Ain't It Cool News* Gibson says the following: "[I]t's kind of an interesting question today as to whether or not any of these were ever really made. I don't have one—I've seen a photograph of one which I suspect to be either a forgery or a kind of dummy prototype that these guys in New York produced, and I don't know which." See http://www.aint-it-cool-news.com/display.cgi?id=5140. Scott Rettberg notes: "I had the chance to meet Ashbaugh a few years back. He told me that during the time shortly after the book was published, he and Gibson were suddenly inundated with requests for interviews, so many, he said, that they felt compelled to give each interviewer a different story about the project. Some of the stories were true." Online comment, http://www.otal.umd.edu/~mgk/blog/archives/000804.html#4147.

cardboard. The cloth-covered linen boards of the volume, distressed and arti-ficially aged by burn marks, in turn embed a floppy diskette containing the poem in a depression that has been hand-cut into the last fifteen or so ragged-edged leaves, laminated together to create a shallow well.[3] The interior of the book includes some forty-four pages printed in double columns with the lines of a nucleic acid quartet, a strand of DNA from (as it turns out) the *bicoid* maternal morphogen of the *Drosophila* or fruit fly;[4] the diskette, mean-while, contains the electromagnetically encoded text of the poem sheathed within its generic black plastic envelope. (Both serve to make *Agrippa* an early form of what we today call "codework.") As one turns the pages, the draw-ings, some printed with uncured photocopy toner, rub and smear—a book that cannot help but be remade in the act of reading.

We will seek to open many black boxes in the pages that follow. In late 2001, stories began circulating that a German firm specializing in data re-covery was using experimental laser scanning techniques to extract data from hard drives salvaged from the ruins of the World Trade Center.[5] Hard drives are black boxes, functionally as well as figuratively—shielded from trauma and sealed against external contaminants. Such precautions are essential be-cause in the nanoscale interval between the drive's floating read/write head and the surface of the platter even a dust particle would loom as large as a boulder and a collision with a foreign object would send the head careening across the surface of the disk like a meteor gouging terra firma with its scorch-ing impact. Apparently a suspicious spike in credit card transactions routed through computer systems in the WTC had been detected just prior to the planes striking the towers on the morning of September 11; investigators

3.   Peter Schwenger begins his excellent essay on the book by intoning, "Black box recovered from some unspecified disaster." See "*Agrippa*, or the Apocalyptic Book," *South Atlantic Quarterly* 92, no. 4 (Fall 1993): 617–626. My description refers to the so-called Deluxe edition of *Agrippa*; the book was also printed in a more vanilla "small" edition, though this was apparently cancelled with few copies finished. For more on the different editions, see James J. Hodge, "Bib-liographic Description of *Agrippa*," *The Agrippa Files*, http://agrippa.english.ucsb.edu/hodge-james-bibliographic-description-of-agrippa-commissioned-for-the-agrippa-files.

4.   For more detail on the DNA see *The Agrippa Files*, http://agrippa.english.ucsb.edu/genetic-code-item-d2-about/.

5.   Erik Kirschbaum (no relation), "German Firm Probes World Trade Center Deals," Reuters (December 16, 2001), http://propagandamatrix.com/german_firm_probes_final_world_trade.html, and numerous other online locales.

hoped that tracing the source of those transactions might lead to persons with advance knowledge of the attacks. While the story died along with many other post-9/11 conspiracy theories and wild goose chases, the techniques behind the data recovery were real. The German firm, Convar, maintains an image gallery of salvaged WTC hard drives in their press release area: they bear the marks of unimaginable stress and duress, scorched, scraped, and caked with primal grit and grime.[6] According to company executive Peter Henschel, "The fine dust that was everywhere in the area got pressed under high pressure into the drives. But we've still been able to retrieve 100 percent of the data on most of the drives we've received."[7] Clients were reportedly paying up to $30,000 to have their data restored. Thus the cold truth of modern data storage: given sufficient resources—that is, elite technical and financial backing—data can be recovered from media even under the most extraordinary conditions. This is a function not only of the hard drive's carapace-like shell (not unlike an aircraft's flight data recorder), but also the physical properties of the magnetic substrate in which data is embedded. (The technical term for the persistence of a magnetic recording over time is *hysteresis*.)[8]

These two episodes were my starting points in thinking about this book. Taken together they dramatize the complex nature of transmission and inscription in digital settings. On the one hand we have "Agrippa," an electronic text that must contend not only with its notoriously fragile digital pedigree, but which was actually *intended* to disappear from sight, yet is one of the most stable and accessible electronic objects I know. On the other hand is the extreme physical trauma of the World Trade Center collapse, yet electronic data emerges intact from its ruins. Both of these occurrences and their seemingly counterintuitive outcomes suggested to me that our current theories and points of reference for reckoning with electronic textuality were inadequate when parsed against what I had come to understand as the material matrix governing writing and inscription in all forms: erasure, variability,

6. These images are accessible from http://www.press.convar.com/default.asp?language=1.

7. Quoted in Kirschbaum, "German Firm Probes."

8. *Hysteresis* is defined by *Webster's Seventh New Collegiate Dictionary* as "a retardation of the effect when the forces acting upon a body are changed (as if from viscosity or internal friction); *esp*: a lagging in the values of resulting magnetization in a magnetic material (as iron) due to a changing magnetizing force." See http://www.lassp.cornell.edu/sethna/hysteresis/WhatIsHysteresis.html.

repeatability, and survivability.[9] *Mechanisms* is therefore a book about the textual and technical primitives of electronic writing and (by extension) other types of data recorded in electronic media.

In what follows, I have tried to write a different kind of book about electronic textuality, one that eschews top-heavy formalist or theoretical approaches to the medium and instead seeks to examine a number of specific digital writing technologies—and individual electronic objects—in their unique textual, technical, and imaginative milieu, thereby connecting to the new histories of inscription being written by such diverse critics as Friedrich Kittler, Lisa Gitelman, Bruce Clarke, Bruno Latour, Timothy Lenoir, Patricia Crain, and Adrian Johns.[10] *Mechanisms* is therefore a study of new media, but one that takes its cues not only from the digital edge but also from fields like comparative media, bibliography, textual scholarship, and the history of the book, or "book studies" as Jonathan Rose now calls it: "The problem with focusing on texts is that no one can read a text—not until it is incarnated in the material form of a book."[11] We cannot effectively address questions of literary history or interpretation, Rose contends, "until we know how books (not

9.   Similarly, Alan Turing notes "There are certain types of processes used by all machines. . . . These processes include copying down sequences of symbols, comparing sequences, erasing all symbols of a given form, etc." (63). "On Computable Numbers, With an Application to the *Entscheidungsproblem*," in *The Essential Turing: The Ideas That Gave Birth to the Computer Age*, ed. B. Jack Copeland (Oxford: Oxford University Press, 2004): 58–90.

10.   See Frierich A. Kittler, *Discourse Networks 1800/1900*, trans. Michael Metteer (Stanford: Stanford University Press, 1990) and *Gramophone, Film, Typewriter*, trans. Geoffrey Winthrop-Young and Michael Wutz (Stanford: Stanford University Press, 1999); Lisa Gitelman, *Scripts, Grooves, and Writing Machines: Representing Technology in the Edison Era* (Stanford: Stanford University Press, 1999); Gitelman and Geoffrey R. Pingree, eds., *New Media 1740–1915* (Cambridge: MIT Press, 2003); Patricia Crain, *The Story of A: The Alphabetization of America from* The New England Primer *to* The Scarlet Letter (Stanford: Stanford University Press, 2000); and Adrian Johns, *The Nature of the Book: Print and Knowledge in the Making* (Chicago: University of Chicago Press, 1998). Also see the essays in Timothy Lenior, ed., *Inscribing Science: Scientific Texts and the Materiality of Communication* (Stanford: Stanford University Press, 1998); Bruce Clarke and Linda Dalrymple Henderson, eds., *From Energy to Information: Representation in Science, Technology, Art, and Literature* (Stanford: Stanford University Press, 2002); and Jeffrey Masten, Peter Stallybrass, and Nancy J. Vickers, *Language Machines: Technologies of Literary and Cultural Representation* (New York: Routledge, 1999).

11.   Jonathan Rose, "From Book History to Book Studies," http://www.printinghistory.org/htm/misc/awards/2001-SHARP.htm.

texts) have been created and reproduced, how books have been disseminated and read, how books have been preserved and destroyed." Put another way then, "the computer" as a generic appellation is not adequate as a starting point for the kind of investigation of electronic writing I have in mind, any more than "the book," conceived as a stable and unvarying form, suffices for serious students of earlier periods of textuality. Here we will follow the bits all the way down to the metal.[12]

A mechanism is both a product and a process, and making *Mechanisms*—making it work—has taken me from the New York Public Library, the Folger Shakespeare Library, and the Harry Ransom Humanities Research Center at the University of Texas at Austin to the Charles Babbage Institute in Minneapolis, the Nanomagnetics Group at the Laboratory for Physical Sciences at the University of Maryland, and the Department of Defense's Cyber Crime Center, housed in an anonymous office park near Baltimore/Washington International airport. I have incurred a number of debts in this unexpectedly bilateral project, and it is my pleasure to acknowledge them here. Jonathan Auerbach, Kandice Chuh, Morris Eaves, Neil Fraistat, Lisa Gitelman, Katie King, Alan Liu, Bill Sherman, Martha Nell Smith, Catherine Stollar, and Noah Wardrip-Fruin all read large portions of the manuscript or read it in its entirety, and contributed important ideas. Nick Montfort deserves special mention and special thanks, not only for reading but for always being at the other end of an e-mail or an instant message and for first initiating me into the secrets of *Mystery House* over burritos in College Park. I am also indebted to my anonymous readers for the MIT Press, whose judicious suggestions and critique made the book that much better. Kevin Begos Jr., Michael Joyce, Patrick K. Kroupa ("Lord Digital"), and Alan Liu all intervened with critical data access at critical moments. Johanna Drucker, Neil Fraistat, Jerome McGann, Martha Nell Smith, and John Unsworth have each been there since the beginning or nearly so—I hope this book rewards their ongoing support of me in some small way. Professors Romel Gomez and Isaak Mayergoyz of the University of Maryland's Department of Electrical and Computer Engineering

12. The book can thus also be understood as an attempt at platform studies, described by Ian Bogost and Nick Montfort as the critical investigation of "the relationships between the hardware and software design of computing systems and the creative works produced on those systems." See http://platformstudies.com/.

patiently answered an English professor's questions about magnetic recording and arranged for me to visit their labs. Peter Stallybrass and Rogier Chartier's magnificent Technologies of Writing seminar, which I was privileged to attend at the Folger Shakespeare Library in spring 2005, became pivotal in my thinking about the project; my thanks to them, to my fellow students, and to the Folger for that opportunity. Supervisory Special Agent Jim Christy at the Department of Defense's Cyber Crime Center, along with staff members Ryan Vella and Nancy Meyer, accommodated my visit to what may be the country's premier computer forensics lab and shared what they could of their sensitive expertise. Virginia Bartow at the New York Public Library facilitated access to the NYPL's copy of *Agrippa*, and Darrell Hyder at Sun Hill Press dug out his typesetter's proofs for me. Elisabeth Kaplan of the Charles Babbage Institute at the University of Minnesota helped me make the most of a morning there. Catherine Stollar of the Harry Ransom Center at the University of Texas at Austin and Pat Galloway of the School of Information, faced with the daunting and unprecedented task of accessioning the 50 boxes of printed matter, 400 diskettes, and the odd laptop and whatnot of the Michael Joyce Papers, generously granted me complete access to the collection before it was publicly available. They both understood what I was after from the get-go, helped me navigate the material, and made my visit to Austin a success in every way. Thanks also to the outstanding staff of the Hazel H. Ransom Reading Room at HRC. My ultrawired graduate students at the University of Maryland keep me honest and keep me up to date: Jason Rhody, Tanya Clement, and Marc Ruppel each deserve special mention. Thanks also to everyone I work with or have worked with at the Maryland Institute for Technology in the Humanities (MITH), including Amit Kumar, Greg Lord, and Carl Stahmer. Despite the fine tunings of the many persons mentioned above, friction and flaws in *Mechanisms* are mine alone.

Versions of chapters were given as lectures and talks at the Washington Area Group for Print Culture Studies; the English departments of George Mason University, Miami University of Ohio, and the University of Minnesota; the University of Pennsylvania's History of Material Texts Seminar; and the School of Information at the University of Texas at Austin, as well as at meetings of the Society for Textual Scholarship and the Modern Language Association. I am grateful to my hosts and to the audiences at all of these venues. A shorter version of chapter 2 appeared as "Extreme Inscription: Towards a Grammatology of the Hard Drive" in *TEXT Technology: the Journal of Computer*

Text Processing (vol. 13, no. 2, 2004: 95–125). Individual passages in chapter 4 and elsewhere in the book appeared in earlier form in "Editing the Interface: Textual Studies and First Generation Electronic Objects" in *TEXT: An Interdisciplinary Annual of Textual Studies* (vol. 14, 2002: 15–52). This article was itself a revision of an even earlier dissertation chapter, a chapter that was my first attempt to write seriously about the ideas in *Mechanisms*. A few pages from chapter 5 have been online since December 2005 at *The Agrippa Files*.[13]

In addition to individuals, *Mechanisms* has been supported by a number of entities and institutions. The Graduate Research Board of the University of Maryland got me started with a stipend in summer 2003; I was a Resident Fellow at the Maryland Institute for Technology in the Humanities in fall 2003. The National Endowment for the Humanities awarded me a fellowship at an absolutely critical juncture in spring 2005, taking a chance on a project that must have seemed at the limit of their charter. The College of Arts and Humanities at the University of Maryland helped support my travel to the Harry Ransom Center. My deep thanks to all of them. Much gratitude is due Doug Sery, my editor at the MIT Press, for his early and unflagging support of the entire project—Doug's patience, attention, and goodwill are qualities for which I will always be supremely grateful.

Finally, I would like to express my appreciation to my parents Arlene and Mel, as well as the rest of my family and friends for their love and gentle distractions. My greatest debt of all, both personal and intellectual, is reflected—but not repaid—in the dedication.

A Note on Titles

The titles of both *Agrippa* and *Afternoon*, two works figuring prominently in this book, have been variously rendered by both their authors and by others. In the case of *Agrippa*, the situation is complicated by the work's multifaceted ontology—there are distinctions to be made between the artist's book, the poem, and the work as a conceptual whole. The title has often been capitalized (AGRIPPA), a practice originating with the original ASCII transcript of William Gibson's text. I do not do so here, but have instead adopted the convention of using italics to indicate either the physical artist's book *Agrippa* or

13. http://agrippa.english.ucsb.edu/kirschenbaum-matthew-g-hacking-agrippa-the-source-of-the-online-text/.

the total work—the book and the poem together—and quotation marks to single out "Agrippa," the written text Gibson authored. I have not, however, altered the title of the work as it has been variously rendered by others when quoting from secondary sources. *Agrippa* is a collaboration between artist Dennis Ashbaugh, author William Gibson, and publisher Kevin Begos Jr.

In the case of *Afternoon: A Story*, Michael Joyce himself both does and does not capitalize the first letter of each of the three words in the title; I have elected to capitalize them here, in effect normalizing the title, but I have respected his and others' variable local choices for purposes of quotation and citation. Likewise, Joyce has sometimes punctuated the title with a comma rather than a colon, and he has sometimes also imposed no punctuation at all. I have opted for the colon, except when quoting others verbatim.

A Note on *Wikipedia* as a Scholarly Source of Record

In several places this book references *Wikipedia* as a scholarly source of record, usually for some specific point of technical documentation. Information technology is among the most reliable content domains on *Wikipedia*, given the high interest of such topics among *Wikipedia's* readership and the consequent scrutiny they tend to attract. Moreover, the ability to examine page histories on *Wikipedia* allows a user to recover the editorial record of a particular entry, with every revision to the text date- and time-stamped and versioned. Attention to these editorial histories can help users exercise sound judgment as to whether or not the information before them at any given moment is controversial, and I have availed myself of that functionality when deciding whether or not to rely on *Wikipedia*.

Wikipedia itself, whose developers leverage their software's content modeling to expose document histories with a precision, transparency, and granularity unprecedented in printed publications outside the realm of genetic editions and textual scholarship, is a working example of the mechanisms I discuss herein.

Introduction: "Awareness of the Mechanism"

What we are trying to freeze is actually the present, which offers a highly distorted, fragmentary version of the past.
—ALEXANDER STILLE, *THE FUTURE OF THE PAST*, QUOTING AN EGYPTOLOGIST ON THE PRESERVATION OF THE GREAT SPHINX OF GIZA

Begin with a mechanism, just the kind you would expect: gears and comb-teeth wheels. The Recodable Locking Device is a mechanical construct for securing access to computer systems, developed at Sandia National Laboratories and described in a press release as the world's "smallest combination lock."[1] An instance of a broad category of technologies known as microelectromechanical systems, or MEMS, it consists of six interlocking code wheels, each about 300 microns in diameter. (By contrast, the diameter of a human hair is 100 microns.) Conceived as an alternative to software firewalls, which are inevitably vulnerable to software-based attacks, the Recodable Locking Device is an actual physical assemblage, ready to be embedded on a microchip where it can interact with computational functions. There are one million potential combinations, and should the wrong one be entered, the code wheels instantly lock and must be manually reset. According to the Sandia press release the Department of Defense regards it as "the first real technical advancement in information security that they've seen in a long time."

1. See http://www.sandia.gov/media/hacker.htm.

While MEMS devices operate on the micron scale, there is an even lower plane of technological development. MEMS are very small, but they are still indisputably objects in the world, accessible (with the aid of appropriate instrumentation) to the human senses. Their materiality is self-evident. But the physical sciences now have a way of naming the precise point at which the normal, observable behavior of matter ceases to be predictable and dependable, at least according to traditional models: science, in other words, can articulate the exact threshold between the material and the immaterial. That threshold is the nanoscale, where molecular structures are measured and manipulated at the atomic level, in billionths of a meter. The nanoscale is the place where the basic atomic properties of things break down—their "conductivity, hardness, or melting point" all become fluid and malleable, subject to renegotiation by "wave particle duality and quantum effects."[2] "A nanoscale wire or circuit," explain Mark and Daniel Ratner, "does not necessarily obey Ohm's law, the venerable equation that is the foundation of modern electronics." The reason is that Ohm's law, which "relates current, voltage, and resistance," depends on the mathematical assumption that a wire is something like a river, with electrons flowing in a broad stream; if the wire is only one atom in width, the electrons must negotiate it in strict linear sequence, and Ohm's law no longer applies.[3]

The nanoscale is now the venue for exotic writing techniques fusing inscription and fabrication. Here is one of those new textual scenes, far removed from the poet's hollow reed and rural pen but staining waters clear:[4]

Dip-pen lithography achieves its ultraprecision by placing tips coated with the material to be deposited—the pen's ink—within a few nanometers of a surface; a small water droplet condenses from the air and acts as a transport channel for the ink, allowing it to diffuse down to the surface.[5]

Mechanisms is not a book about MEMS or nanotechnology, but by beginning there we can think about inscription and fabrication—and the way techno-

2. Mark Ratner and Daniel Ratner, *Nanotechnology: A Gentle Introduction to the Next Big Idea* (Upper Saddle River, NJ: Prentice Hall, 2003), 7.

3. Ratner and Ratner, *Nanotechnology*, 7.

4. See William Blake's "Introduction" to *Songs of Innocence* (1789), lines 16–18.

5. Coire Lok, "Nano Writing," *Technology Review* (April 2004): 77.

logical processes such as dip-pen lithography dissolve the distinction between them—as situated on a three-dimensional coordinate axis of visibility, legibility, and instrumentation. Electronic textuality is similarly locatable, even though we are not accustomed to thinking of it in physical terms. Bits can be measured in microns when recorded on a magnetic hard disk. They can be visualized with technologies such as magnetic force microscopy (MFM), which is a variation on the scanning tunneling microscope (STM). When a CD-ROM is burned, a laser superheats a layer of dye to create pits and lands, tiny depressions on the grooved surface of the platter. The length of these depressions is measured in microns, their width and depth in nanometers. (The precise specifications, along with all other physical aspects of the disk and the recording process, are spelled out in a proprietary publication known as the *Red Book*, first printed in 1980 and licensed by Philips and Sony.) That CD-ROM drives are laser *optical* devices that *read* and *write* their data by interpreting patterns of reflected light offers an instance of a certain configuration of instrumentation rendering the physical phenomena of pits and lands both visible and legible (though not to human eyes), thereby restoring this post-alphabetic writing practice to recognizable registers of inscription.

In an essay on digital preservation, Kenneth Thibodeau, Director of Electronic Records Programs at the National Archives and Records Administration, offers a tripartite model for defining digital objects: first, as *physical* objects ("signs inscribed on a medium"—for example, the flux reversals recorded on magnetic tape); second, as *logical* objects (data as it is recognized and interpreted by particular processes and applications software; for example, the binary composition of a Word .DOC file); and third, as *conceptual* objects ("the object we deal with in the real world," such as a digital photograph as it appears prima facie on the screen).[6] By digital object Thibodeau means any "information object" (his term) whose ontology necessitates all three of these parent classes—physical, logical, and conceptual. The most powerful aspect of this model lies in its potential for interaction among the different classes or levels, which are capable of accounting for many of the unique complexities of new media artifacts. What appears to be a homogeneous digital object

6. Kenneth Thibodeau, "Overview of Technological Approaches to Digital Preservation and Challenges in the Coming Years," *The State of Digital Preservation: An International Perspective*, Council on Library and Information Resources, pub107 (2002), http://www.clir.org/pubs/reports/pub107/thibodeau.html. Subsequent quotations are also from this essay.

at the conceptual level (a database is Thibodeau's example) may in fact be a compound object at its logical and even physical levels, with elements of the database drawn from different file systems distributed across multiple servers or source media. "[I]n order to preserve a digital object," he writes, "we must be able to identify and retrieve all its digital components." The eminently practical concerns of specialists like Thibodeau have given rise to some of our best accounts of the ontology of digital phenomena and their relationship to more familiar forms of representation.

My reading of the critical literature on new media suggests that the field has focused primarily on the third of Thibodeau's three levels, the conceptual —that is, the phenomenological manifestation of the application or digital event on the screen—and only somewhat more recently, in the wake of mature formalist studies like Espen Aarseth's *Cybertext* and Lev Manovich's *Language of New Media* (both very different in their own right), on the inter-action between the logical and conceptual layers.[7] However much of my at-tention (especially in the first half of the book) will fall on storage, a category routinely elided in the critical discussion, presumably because the uses to which electronic data is put are seen as wholly independent of any particular mode of physical record.

Storage: the word itself is dull and flat sounding, like footfalls on linoleum. It has a vague industrial aura—tape farms under the fluorescents, not the flash memory sticks that are the skate keys of the Wi-Fi street. Yet storage has never been more important than it is now in shaping the everyday experience of computing, interactivity, and new media. Even a passing glance at technol-ogies like iPod or TiVo, both based on magnetic hard drives, should bring this point home. Like the vertical filing cabinets of a previous era, contem-porary information storage devices have distinct affordances that contribute to their implementation and reception.[8] Computers themselves were initially engines of prediction and prognostication (where will an aircraft be in the

7.   Lev Manovich, *The Language of New Media* (Cambridge: MIT Press, 2001) and Espen J. Aarseth, *Cybertext: Perspectives on Ergodic Literature* (Baltimore: Johns Hopkins University Press, 1997).

8.   The vertical file cabinet, which stored papers without folding them, was first devised by Edwin G. Seibels in 1898, working in his father's insurance office in Columbia, South Carolina. Paper records were previously stored folded, in floor-to-ceiling arrays of pigeonholes. Vertical fil-ing transformed standard business practices of the day.

sky such that a shell can be fired to intercept it), not recollection and storage; they only became so with the advent of the so-called von Neumann model and the somewhat later addition of random access disk memory, which enabled reliable real-time, nonsequential access to large reserves of information.[9] Storage is also a kind of imaginary, a focalized expression of the collecting impulse underpinning everything from the Web's myriad niche cultures (fan sites housing exhaustive MP3 archives of a band's live shows) to the global garage sale of eBay, which Steve Johnson has aptly referred to as an "infinite" storage system.[10] Crucially, storage today is both an accessory, something you hold in your hand or slip into your pocket (your iPod or memory stick), but is also increasingly disembodied and dematerialized as we approach terabtyte-scale disks where users are no longer constrained in their information retention by the capacity of their hard drives. Storage technologies will be a major element of this book because I believe we need to recapture their role in the cultural history of computing.[11]

Storage, along with transmission and computation (or processing), is also a primal media category for German theorist Friedrich Kittler. Yet Kittler's interest in storage is ultimately subsumed by his own idiosyncratic cosmologies and chronologies, in which storage, particularly of audio and visual "data streams," is part of a specifically modern zeitgeist (gramophone and film) that found martial expression in the trenches of World War I (which stored men in armed combat) before wireless transmission broke through the lines with the radio-equipped tanks of the German blitzkrieg two decades later (only to be defeated in turn, rock/paper/scissors-like, by computation, which broke the

9. Friedrich Kittler makes this same point about computation and prediction in *Gramophone, Film, Typewriter*, trans. Geoffrey Winthrop-Young and Michael Wutz (Stanford: Stanford University Press, 1999). See especially pages 253–263.

10. Steve Johnson, *Everything is Bad is Good For You* (New York: Riverhead Books, 2005), 196.

11. The extent to which storage, specifically the hard drive, can participate in a new media imaginary is suggested by the following passage from Hari Kunzru's recent novel *Transmission* (New York: Dutton, 2004): "Behind the walls of his secret garden, which existed not so much apart from as *between* the legitimate areas of the college network, his various experiments were still running their course, stealing spare processor cycles from idle machines, storing themselves in tiny splinters on dozens of hard disks. Together these fragments formed an interstitial world, a discreet virtuality that would efficiently mask its existence from the students and teachers doing their online business around about it" (27; emphasis in original).

"Awareness of the Mechanism"

German radio codes, thereby paving the way for the Cold War).[12] In ways that are not unlike those of Nicholas Negroponte or even Bill Gates, Kittler offers up a narrative of media convergence in which the original storage monopoly of alphabetic writing is now reinscribed as the universal ones and zeros of digital computation. This is a narrative that I find deeply unsatisfying, and indeed, much of this book is given over to the project of discovering the heterogeneity of digital data and its embodied inscriptions.[13] Despite having memorably claimed that there is no software, Kittler's attention nowadays has turned to chips and circuits, not to the contemporary storage devices that are the true heirs to his trinity of gramophone, film, and typewriter. The hard drive, whose visual resemblance to a turntable is not entirely incidental, therefore figures in this book as a way to read a contemporary storage device back into discourse network 2000.[14]

12.   See specifically Kittler's "Media Wars" in his collection of essays *Literature, Media, Information Systems* (G+B Arts, 1997), but also of course the two main works available in English, *Discourse Networks 1800/1900*, trans. Michael Metteer (Stanford: Stanford University Press, 1990) and *Gramophone, Film, Typewriter*. The introduction to *Gramophone, Film, Typewriter* (also offered with a different translation in *Literature, Media, Information Systems*) is perhaps the most compact and best-known summation of Kittler's positions.

13.   "Optical fiber networks" are the words which Kittler pronounces to open *Gramophone, Film, Typewriter*, and he proceeds to then articulate the narrative of digital media convergence. The most bracing counterpoint to this narrative that I know is Neal Stephenson's "Mother Earth, Motherboard," an epic travelogue of "hacker tourism" (his phrase) published in *Wired* magazine which consumes the bulk of the December 1996 issue. A kind of prelude to his subsequent novel *Cryptonomicon*, Stephenson travels from England to the Asian Pacific rim as he follows the laying of a deep-sea fiber optic cable, the Fiber-optic Link Around the Globe (FLAG). His account of the politics of the cable laying industry and the minute particulars of the cable itself is all that is needed to remind one of the nonvirtual realities surging through Kittler's bundled phraseology.

14.   Open the sealed case of a modern hard drive and even an untrained observer will note the resemblance to a small turntable, complete with platter(s) and spindle arm. This visual coincidence harbors deeper correlates. Like the phonograph, magnetic recording was originally intended to preserve sound, specifically speech. Moreover, magnetic recording emerged at almost precisely the same historical moment as Edison's phonograph: the American inventor Oberlin Smith articulated the essential principles in 1878 (a year after the phonograph debuted), and in fact corresponded briefly with Edison; Smith, however, never actually built a recording device. That was left to the Danish researcher Valdemar Poulson, who in 1898 captured the first

While *Mechanisms* aspires to speak directly to contemporary conditions of electronic textuality and the digital literary, its primary case studies are drawn from earlier decades of computing. They range from *Mystery House*, a piece of interactive fiction for the Apple II first released in 1980, to Michael Joyce's *Afternoon: A Story*—the first edition of which appeared for the Macintosh in 1987—to Gibson's "Agrippa," which was first uploaded to the Internet near the end of 1992. While the Internet itself was a real and relevant technology throughout this period, the network had not yet achieved its popular apotheosis, and the World Wide Web was still in its infancy at the time "Agrippa" was released (the first version of the graphical NCSA Mosaic browser was announced in early 1993). Equally important in terms of networked culture were bulletin board systems (BBS) and the colorful if insular scenes they spawned—an elite user would range freely back and forth across the thin membranes between the public Internet (including the nascent Web, as well as Gopher, USENET, and Bitnet), and the deeper pockets of networked connectivity that were the bulletin boards. Certain particulars of this network landscape will figure in my discussions of *Mystery House* and "Agrippa."

The eighties were also the first full decade of home computing. The personal computer was both anthropomorphized and gendered as *Time Magazine's*

---

magnetic recording on a length of steel wire. Poulson immediately set about developing a machine he called the telephonograph, which would allow people record and store a telephone conversation—in effect an answering machine. The telephonograph was never a commercial success (Poulsen's successor, the American Telephonograph company, tried to compete with Edison's phonograph for the market in dictation machines), but the basic principles of magnetic recording had been established. The next major advances came in the 1930s when several German firms, including BASF, introduced magnetic coated tape (first paper and then plastic) as well as a dependable recording apparatus (and made additional advances, including High Bias recording). The magnetophone, as magnetic tape machines were then called, was to prove an important tool for the emerging Nazi regime as well as the wartime German military. After the war the technology quickly migrated to the rest of Europe and the United States. With magnetic audio recording thus commercially launched, it was not surprising that the nascent computer industry began exploring magnetic recording solutions for its increasingly storage-dependant products. For more on the early history of magnetic recording, see Eric D. Daniel, C. Denis Mee, and Mark H. Clark, *Magnetic Recording: The First One Hundred Years* (New York: IEEE Press, 1999), particularly chapters 2–5.

"Man of the Year" in 1982. Disney's *Tron* was likewise released in 1982, literalizing the fantasies of the adolescents who thronged suddenly ubiquitous arcades during what is widely acknowledged as the "golden era" of video games (though by mid-decade the industry had crashed).[15] MTV went on air in August, 1981 with a straight-to-the-point shot of McLuhanesque pop, The Buggles' "Video Killed the Radio Star." Within the first few years of the decade VHS had won out over Betamax. Gibson's *Neuromancer* (written within sight of the glow of the coin-op arcades) was published in 1984, the same year the Apple Macintosh debuted (along with its famous Superbowl commercial with overtly Orwellian imagery created by Ridley Scott, himself not long removed from the set of *Blade Runner*, again 1982). At the other end of our time frame, *Wired* magazine, with a print aesthetic self-consciously designed to look like information, began publishing in 1993, the same year as the public release of Mosaic, the first graphical browser for the World Wide Web. There are several sound reasons to foreground this era in *Mechanisms*, roughly from 1980–1992. First, even the modest temporal distance serves to defamiliarize certain key cultural aspects of computing; for example, storage technologies and disk handling practices differ markedly from what is the norm today, as we will see. In 1981, the Apple II DOS Manual began by telling its readers that it would teach them "how to use the disk," an injunction that surely seems strange in the wake of two decades of ubiquitous and largely invisible hard drive storage. Second, the smaller storage sizes of physical media make some of the close readings and forensic explorations in the book practical. The *Mystery House* disk, which we will examine closely in chapter 3, is a mere 140 kilobytes. It contains 35 tracks and 560 sectors. It is therefore possible to study it in its entirety, as a complete artifact. A modern hard drive, by contrast, holds tens of thousands of tracks and sectors. While the techniques I will discuss are equally applicable in theory, the smaller file systems on 1980s-era storage media allow us to exhaust the physical spaces of the media and bring them into focus. It would be a mistake, however, to think size doesn't matter; we will also consider the ways in which user habits and activities change as storage media grow more capacious. The simple practice of creating subdirectories, for example, is relatively rare with file systems stored on floppies but commonplace, indeed essential, with hard drives. Finally, this work is

15. See Van Burnham, *Supercade: A Visual History of the Video Game Age, 1971–1984* (Cambridge: MIT Press, 2001).

intended (in part) to serve as a kind of primer on the preservation and recovery of digital literary history. Therefore I look backward to electronic objects whose distance from us is measurable not only in years, but also by palpable shifts in hardware, software, data standards, file formats, and other manifestations of materiality.

That last term, *materiality*, will be a watchword of the book. The questions I pursue here have their roots in a 1995 seminar with Jerome McGann on the subject of textual materiality and electronic editing. In what, I then asked, does the materiality of electronic texts consist? This has since evolved into a well turned question in the critical and theoretical conversation in the field, and a number of scholars have contributed their individual glosses to materiality and its seemingly counterintuitive application to new media.[16]

16. For example, according to N. Katherine Hayles, "The physical attributes constituting any artifact are potentially infinite; in a digital computer, for example, they include the polymers used to fabricate the case, the rare earth elements used to make the phosphors in the CRT screen, the palladium used for the power cord prongs, and so forth. From this infinite array a technotext will select a few to foreground and work into its thematic concerns. Materiality thus emerges from interactions between physical properties and a work's artistic strategies. For this reason, materiality cannot be specified in advance, as if it pre-existed the specificity of the work. An emergent property, materiality depends on how the work mobilizes its resources as a physical artifact as well as the user's interactions with the work and the interpretive strategies she develops—strategies that include physical manipulations as well as conceptual frameworks. In the broadest sense, materiality emerges from the dynamic interplay between the richness of a physically robust world and human intelligence as it crafts this physicality to create meaning." See *Writing Machines* (Cambridge: MIT Press, 2002), 32–33. Here we see Hayles placing her emphasis on what I would call forensic materiality ("the richness of a physically robust world") and its emergent interaction with what variously seems to be the artist's intent, the work's own autonomy, and its reception in a user or reader's cognitive faculties; missing, I would argue, is the computationally specific phenomenon of formal materiality, the simulation or modeling of materiality via programmed software processes.

The most elaborate and theoretically rigorous model of (again, forensic) materiality of which I am aware is Johanna Drucker's, in *The Visible Word: Experimental Typography and Modern Art, 1909–1923* (Chicago: University of Chicago Press, 1994). For Drucker, materiality is composed of "two major intertwined strands: that of a relational, insubstantial, and nontranscendent difference and that of a phenomenological, apprehendable, immanent substance" (43). This model is intended to advance the understanding that materiality inheres in "a process of interpretation rather than a positing of the characteristics of the object" (43). The basic contradictions apparent between Drucker's two "intertwined strands"—contradictions which follow from her

My own use of the term develops gradually (over the first three chapters) into a distinction between what I term forensic materiality and formal materiality. Understood in relation to one another, I believe this pairing allows me to accurately represent what the overall term materiality does and does not mean in an electronic environment. In brief: forensic materiality rests upon the principle of individualization (basic to modern forensic science and criminalistics), the idea that no two things in the physical world are ever exactly alike. If we are able to look closely enough, in conjunction with appropriate instrumentation, we will see that this extends even to the micron-sized residue of digital inscription, where individual bit representations deposit discreet legible trails that can be seen with the aid of a technique known as magnetic force microscopy. Less exotically perhaps, we find forensic materiality revealed in the amazing variety of surfaces, substrates, sealants, and other matériel that have been used over the years as computational storage media, and in the engineering, ergonomic, and labor practices that attend computation—everything from labeling a diskette, which situates electronic textuality amid other technologies and practices of writing (indexing and cataloging, longhand, adhe-

––––––––––––––––

premeditated commingling of difference and transcendence—are, as she acknowledges, necessary if the model is to adequately answer to the relational and contingent claims upon signification that would be advanced by a poststructuralist critique, together with the sensorium's phenomenological apprehension of substance and appearance as such: "The force of stone, of ink, of papyrus, and of print all function within the signifying activity—not only because of their encoding within a cultural system of values whereby a stone inscription is accorded a higher stature than a typewritten memo, but because these values themselves come into being on account of the physical, material properties of these different media. Durability, scale, reflectiveness, richness and density of saturation and color, tactile and visual pleasure—all of these factor in—not as transcendent and historically independent universals, but as aspects whose historical and cultural specificity cannot be divorced from their substantial properties. No amount of ideological or cultural valuation can transform the propensity of papyrus to deteriorate into gold's capacity to endure. The inherent physical properties of stuff function in the process of signification in intertwined but not determined or subordinate relation to their place within the cultural codes of difference where they also function" (45–46). Materiality, in this model, thus consists in a sustainable dialectic (Drucker's term) between relational and contingent social values as they are expressed through various ideologies and economies of production on the one hand, and experiential, physiological, ultimately *bodily* encounters with incarnate phenomena on the other.

sives, the felt-tip pen), to the contours of the keyboard and mouse that make their bodily marks felt in the ongoing pandemic of repetitive strain and white-collar work injuries, to the growing crisis of e-waste (the unsafe disposal and sweatshop recycling, often at third-world dumping sites, of hazardous but industrially precious components inherent to computing machinery). Not all of these will receive equal emphasis or attention in this book, but all can and should be understood as varieties of the forensic materiality I will extrude from the applied field of computer forensics.

Formal materiality is perhaps the more difficult term, as its self-contradictory appellation might suggest.[17] "Instead of manipulating matter, the computer allows us to manipulate symbols."[18] This point, basic to all aspects of computer science, comes in the opening lines of textbook on virtual reality and interface design. Nicholas Negroponte popularized the same distinction in terms of atoms versus bits. Unlike an atom, which has mass, a bit "has no color, size, or weight, and it can travel at the speed of light. . . . It is a state of being: on or off, true or false, up or down, in or out, black or white. For practical purposes, we consider a bit to be a 1 or a 0".[19] Bits are—in other words—*symbols* to be set and reset, set and reset, on again and off again, over and over again. Whereas forensic materiality rests upon the potential for individualization inherent in matter, a digital environment is an abstract projection supported and sustained by its capacity to propagate the illusion (or call it a working model) of *immaterial* behavior: identification without ambiguity, transmission without loss, repetition without originality.[20] Nonetheless, as we

17.   Late in the writing of this book I became aware of Paul de Man's use of the term "formal materialism," notably in *Aesthetic Ideology*, ed. Andrzej Warminski (Twin Cities: University of Minnesota Press, 1996). I do not intend my own use of formal materiality to imply any overlap with the particulars of de Man.

18.   Thomas A. Furness III and Woodrow Barfield, eds., *Virtual Environments and Advanced Interface Design Design* (Oxford: Oxford UP, 1995), i.

19.   Nicholas Negroponte, *Being Digital*, (New York: Knopf, 1995), 14.

20.   This conscious model of immateriality is usefully fleshed out in Lev Manovich's account of the constituent features of new media: its underlying numerical or mathematical ontology, its modularity (the "object-oriented" nature of much new media), automation (the subjection of human agency to various programmed or algorithmic processes), variability (the one-to-many relationship characterized by, say, the application of multiple stylesheets to a single source file), and its transcoding (the ability of a digital object to negotiate multiple layers in a computer's

will see when we look more closely at the operation of hard drives, computers are not flawless. Errors typically occur at the juncture between analog and digital states, such as when a drive's magnetoresistive head assigns binary symbolic value to the voltage differentials it has registered, or when an e-mail message is reconstituted from independent data packets moving across the TCP/IP layer of the Internet, itself dependent on fiber-optic cables and other hardwired technologies. All forms of modern digital technology incorporate hyper-redundant error-checking routines that serve to sustain an illusion of immateriality by detecting error and correcting it, reviving the quality of the signal, like old-fashioned telegraph relays, such that any degradation suffered during a subsequent interval of transmission will not fall beyond whatever tolerances of symbolic integrity exist past which the original value of the signal (or identity of the symbol) cannot be reconstituted. As John von Neumann pointed out in 1948 in his "The General and Logical Theory of Automata," digital computers could produce perfect results, "as long as the operation of each component produced only fluctuations within its pre-assigned tolerance limits" (294).[21] This, coupled with digital data's discrete, finitely differentiated ontology—*digital*, separated like the fingers of the hand—engenders the formal environment for symbol manipulation that is the reservoir for every function of a computer, from the workplace to the hot-wired edge.

Formal materiality thus follows as the name I give to the imposition of multiple relational computational states on a data set or digital object. Phenomenologically, the relationship between these states tends to manifest itself in terms of layers or other relative measures, though in fact each state is arbitrary and self-consistent/self-contained. A simple example is a digital image file. An image file is typically considered to consist of nothing but information about the image itself—the composition of its pixilated bitmap, essentially. However, the image can carry metadata (documentation as to how it was

---

internal architecture, as well as what Manovich sees as the interface between computational architecture and its various cultural "layers"). See his *The Language of New Media* (Cambridge: MIT Press, 2001), 27–48.

21.   John von Neumann, "General and Logical Theory of Automata," in *Collected Works*, volume 5: *Design of Computers, Theory of Automata and Numerical Analysis*, ed. A. H. Taub (Oxford: Pergamon Press, 1963), 288–328.

created, embedded as plain text in the file's header), as well as more colorful freight, such as a steganographic image or a digital watermark. This content will only become visible when the data object is subjected to the appropriate formal processes, which is to say when the appropriate software environment is invoked—anything from the "Show Header" function of an off-the-shelf image viewer to a 128-bit encryption key. At this point one layer of the digital object is artificially naturalized in its relation to the other, typically the original image which suddenly manifests extra, hidden, or special data. Formal materiality is not an absolute term, but rather one that tries to capture something of the procedural friction or perceived difference—the torque—as a user shifts from one set of software logics to another. It might also help to think of it as a way of articulating a relative or just-in-time dimension of materiality, one where any material particulars are arbitrary and independent of the underlying computational environment and are instead solely the function of the imposition of a specific formal regimen on a given set of data and the resulting contrast to any other available alternative regimens. (Formal materiality is perhaps also the lingering perception of some genuine material residue—however misplaced—which presents, like sensation in a phantom limb, when one cannot quite accept the exclusively formal nature of a digital process; for example, the vague sense of unease that attends me after leaving my desktop music player application on Pause for hours on end, something that would harm a physical tape system because of the tension on the reels.)

While it may seem tempting to associate forensic and formal materiality with hardware and software respectively, those associations should not be granted without question, not least because the lines between hardware and software are themselves increasingly blurred, as is manifest in so-called firmware, or programmable hardware, a contradiction in terms that literalizes the conceit of formal materiality at the very level of the chip.[22] Moreover, the

22. For example MRAM, or magnetic RAM, which is an alternative to, among other technologies, EEPROM, electrically erasable programmable read-only memory. The constituents of the latter name are themselves telling: the search for a stable, but also erasable—a variable but nonvolatile—storage medium has been a constant throughout the history of writing technologies, and we see it here in the parameters of erasable/programmable/read-only. This is the same technology used in so-called flash memory, popularized in the form of the keychain sticks that plug into a standard USB port. MRAM technology, by contrast, involves using thin slices of magnetic material to create the conditions whereby a microprocessor can be reprogrammed in response to electrical stimuli. By manipulating the magnetic polarity of the substrate—in

distinction between hardware and software as we know it today, though seemingly naturalized by the von Neumann model, is also a consequence of the various business practices that helped create and define software—a product without any industrial precedent—notably IBM's momentous unbundling decision of 1970, where the corporate giant, then under threat of antitrust legislation, committed to the manufacture and marketing of software as a commodity separate and distinct from the company's hardware (previously, clients buying a computer would have received programs custom-written for their needs as part of the purchasing agreement, a strategy which helped ensure something close to a monopoly).[23] Software's emergence as an industry commodity must be part of any calculus of its materiality, and this complicates any easy association with exclusively formal processes. Software is the product of white papers, engineering specs, marketing reports, conversations and col-

---

essence, each layer is a single "bit"—the behavior of all of the standard kinds of logic gates (AND, OR, NAND, NOR) can be emulated. This is useful because microprocessors are typically optimized for particular functions. The chip in a cell phone is laid out very differently from the chip in a digital camera. Interventions in the logical patterns of the chip at this level mean that the same physical processor can emulate any one of those special functions on demand. In one sense this inverts Turing's logic, since it is software functioning to reprogram hardware, rather than programmed software specifying a formal environment by way of internally consistent hardware components. In other words, an MRAM chip is a site of inscription. It is as if an ordinary erasable lead pencil was now being used to write circuits rather than the indelible ink of VLSI and other photolithographic processes. For a generalist's introduction to magnetologic gates, see Reinhold D. Koch, "Morphware," *Scientific American*, August 2005, 57–63. For the technical paper of record, see William C. Black Jr. and Bodhisattva Das, "Programmable Logic Using Giant-Magnetoresistive and Spin-Dependant Tunneling Devices," *Journal of Applied Physics*, 87 no. 9 (May 2000): 6674–6679.

23.   For a thorough discussion of unbundling and its significance, see Martin Campbell-Kelly, *From Airline Reservations to Sonic the Hedgehog: A History of the Software Industry* (Cambridge: MIT Press, 2003), 109–118. Kelly's distinction between a software "package" and a software "product" in this context serves to further underscore the mutability of software's status as commodity: whereas a "package" was a free entity provided by the manufacturer, "The term 'product' was consciously adopted by vendors to imply a new kind of software artifact for which the vendor took contractual responsibility for performance and reliability in exchange for license fees paid by users" (118).

laborations, intuitive insights, professionalized expertise, venture capital (in other words, money), late nights (in other words, labor), caffeine, and other artificial stimulants. These are material circumstances that leave material (read: forensic) traces—in corporate archives, on whiteboards and legal pads, in countless iterations of alpha versions and beta versions and patches and upgrades, in focus groups and user communities, in expense accounts, in licensing agreements, in stock options and IPOs, in carpal tunnel braces, in the Bay Area and New Delhi real-estate markets, in PowerPoint vaporware and proofs of concept binaries locked in time-stamped limbo on a server where all the user accounts but root have been disabled and the domain name is eighteen months expired.[24] Forensic and formal materiality are perhaps better brought to rest on the twin textual and technological bases of inscription (storage) and transmission (or multiplication), exactly those bases underpinning my earlier narratives of the survival of the WTC hard drive data on the one hand and the proliferation of Gibson's "Agrippa" across the Internet on the other. Forensic and formal materiality also accord with the fundamental duality of a mechanism as both a product and a process.

As all of the preceding must suggest, this book aspires to a strategic rhetorical intervention in the best tradition of forensic argumentation. The methodology for the book draws heavily from bibliography and textual criticism, which are the scholarly fields dedicated to the study of books as physical objects and the reconstruction and representation of texts from multiple versions and witnesses (sometimes collectively called "textual studies"). Given the origins of these methods in the study of paper and parchment, such an

---

24. This is evident from David A. Kirsch's heroic ongoing labors preserving the legal records and the marketing and business plans of failed technology startups from the dot-com era: http://www.businessplanarchive.org/. The archive includes the electronic records (e-mail, PowerPoint presentations, word processing documents, and spreadsheets rescued from corporate intranets and network share drives) from some 2000 Silicon Valley technology concerns, all of them now defunct. (Manovich would term this "history of the present.") Meanwhile, *net.ephemera* is a limited edition portfolio of documentation from a digital art exhibition at the Moving Image Gallery in New York City in Spring 2001, compiled by Mark Tribe of rhizome.org: "Net.art is made to be experienced online and is thus difficult to exhibit in physical spaces. *net.ephemera* approaches this problem by focusing on drawings, diagrams, notes, receipts, and other physical artifacts related to the making of net-based work." The portfolio contains photocopies of 25 pieces of printed matter, ranging from sketches and pseudo-code jottings on a legal pad to a USPS receipt ($7.45, paid with a credit card) for mailing items related to the show.

approach may seem odd or obscure. But in fact, textual studies should be recognized as among the most sophisticated branches of media studies we have evolved. As early as 1985, D. F. McKenzie, in his Panizzi lectures, explicitly placed electronic content within the purview of bibliography and textual criticism: "I define 'texts' to include verbal, visual, oral, and numeric data, in the form of maps, prints, and music, of archives of recorded sound, of films, videos, and *any* computer-stored information, everything in fact from epigraphy to the latest forms of discography."[25] But though recent years have seen a tremendous acceleration of interest (and much practical progress) in methods of electronic editing,[26] there has been very little consideration of digital media themselves from the specific vantage points of bibliography and textual criticism.[27] Rather, textual critics have tended to treat the computer mainly as a platform-independent venue for studying the artifacts of *other* media.[28] This is unfortunate, because I believe the contemporary textual studies community has furnished us with some of the best accounts we have of texts and textual phenomena.

Mechanisms is also, however, grounded in contemporary computer science, notably the applied field of computer forensics. With its emphasis on reconstructing and preserving digital evidence, computer forensics is the natural

25. Donald F. McKenzie, *Bibliography and the Sociology of Texts* (London: The British Library, 1986), 5. See also page 31 for another such reference. On pages 42–43 he relates the significance of Great Britain's 1984 Data Protection Act, which erected legal distinctions between digital and paper-based texts.

26. A very brief and selective list of important projects would include *The Electronic Beowulf*, ed. Kevin Kiernan, http://www.uky.edu/~kiernan/eBeowulf/guide.htm; *The Canterbury Tales Project*, ed. Peter Robinson, http://www.cta.dmu.ac.uk/projects/ctp/; *The William Blake Archive*, eds. Morris Eaves, Robert N. Essick, and Joseph Viscomi, http://www.iath.virginia.edu/blake; and *The Rossetti Archive*, ed. Jerome J. McGann, http://www.iath.virginia.edu/rossetti/.

27. One exception is D. C. Greetham's "Is It Morphin Time?" in *Electronic Text: Investigations in Method and Theory*, ed. Katheryn Sutherland (Clarendon Press: Oxford, 1997), 199–226. More recently, Adrian van der Weel has put forward this case in "Bibliography for New Media," *Quærendo* 35/1–2 (2005): 96–108.

28. This is, of course, the underlying argument of what may be the most influential essay ever written on electronic editing, McGann's "Rationale of HyperText" (1994): http://www .iath.virginia.edu/public/jjm2f/rationale.html. It is worth pointing out that as of this writing, all of the projects McGann describes in the hypothetical are now mature digital research enterprises.

counterpart to textual criticism and physical bibliography. Both fields necessarily treat their subject as material phenomena, and together they offer the basis for a theory of electronic textuality that differs markedly from existing approaches to the subject—precisely because textual criticism (which at least one authority, D. C. Greetham, has called "textual forensics"[29]) and computer forensics engage their respective media on their own terms. The book's "forensics" is therefore a theoretically and technically rigorous account of electronic texts as artifacts—mechanisms—subject to material and historical forms of understanding. It seeks to provide a corrective to certain commonplace notions of new media writing—that electronic texts are ephemeral, for example (in fact, data written to magnetic storage media is routinely recovered through multiple generations of overwrites), or that electronic texts are somehow inherently unstable and always open to modification (actually, a data file can be just as easily locked or encrypted, preventing any modification), or that electronic texts are always identical copies of one another (computer privacy advocates exposed that Microsoft's popular Word software embeds a code unique to each individual user's system in every document it produces).[30] By overturning these and other false perceptions, I attempt to move beyond the formalism and poststructuralism that has characterized much of the writing about electronic texts to date.

As much or more than specific authors and texts, this is a book that foregrounds specific technologies (the hard drive or magnetic force microscopy [MFM]), specific technological processes (hashing, error correction, and packet switching), software (hex editors, Storyspace, and the Concurrent Versions System), data standards (ASCII, JPEG, and SGML/XML), data structures (DOS's Volume Table of Contents), and approaches to digital preservation (porting and emulation)—in short, what Bruno Latour, himself an inveterate opener of black boxes, has taught us to call actants.[31]

29. See D. C. Greetham, "Textual Forensics," *PMLA* (January 1996): 32–51.

30. Mike Ricciuti, "Microsoft admits privacy problem, plans fix," March 7, 1999, http://news.com.com/2100-1040-222673.html?legacy=cnet.

31. Latour's actor-network theory is first delineated in *Science in Action* (Cambridge: Harvard University Press, 1987). Actor–network theory seems indispensable to developing robust theories of computational processes, where the human agent—the user—is only one participant in a long chain of interdependent interactions. As we will see when we look more closely at DOS, for example, the SAVE command marks the moment at which control over an electronic

I have constructed the book in two overlapping halves, like the figures of a Venn diagram. Chapters 1 and 3 develop my distinction between forensic and formal materiality, with the technology of the hard drive, the book's central example of a storage device, situated in between, in chapter 2. The second half of the book, chapters 3, 4, and 5, all offer close readings of individual electronic textual objects, specifically a bitstream disk image of the interactive fiction game *Mystery House*, the various versions of Michael Joyce's *Afternoon: A Story*, and the text file of William Gibson's "Agrippa," distributed across the Internet in late 1992. Chapters 4 and 5 also take up issues related to the longevity and survivability of digital objects in light of the forensic and formal properties of both physical storage media and networked transmission. (One of the key underlying assumptions in both of these chapters is that the practical concerns of digital preservation can function as vehicle for critical inquiry into the nature of new media and electronic textuality.) The chapters on *Afternoon* and "Agrippa" both also draw on significant new primary source materials, presented here for the first time in a scholarly discussion. *Mechanisms* thus breaks new ground in terms of access to recently available archival resources, themselves self-consciously situated here within the horizon of a particular work's transmission and reception histories. Throughout the book, methods and techniques of both textual studies (such as analytical bibliography or critical editing) and computer forensics (with its emphasis on the residual documentary status of digital inscription) are brought into play as the twin armatures on which the arguments rest.

Beyond the first chapter, which lays the conceptual and theoretical groundwork, the book's organization follows a more or less deliberate progression: from the close scrutiny of a physical storage device that is typically both unseen and little understood (the hard drive) to a digital construct that is actually a formal surrogate for an instance of physical source media (the *Mystery House* disk image) to the archival history of a piece of software and works created with it (Storyspace and *Afternoon*) to the reconstruction of an online

---

text passes from an organic author to an actor-network populated by the operating system, the disk drive mechanism, and the floppy disk. Theories of electronic textuality have tended to privilege the user, or the text itself, rather than these and other actor-networks, which are the fruits of "science in action" and "laboratory life."

transmission history ("Agrippa"). The following paragraphs discuss individual chapters ingreater detail.

Chapter 1 delineates the screen essentialism and accompanying medial ideology that the book argues has pervaded much of the critical and theoretical writing about electronic textuality to date, and it attempts to bring storage in the tradition of von Neumann computing (the most significant computational tradition of the twentieth century), where data takes the form of marks and physical inscriptions, to bear as a counterweight. The field of computer forensics is introduced, a field whose method and practice routinely contradict many of our commonplace assumptions about electronic textuality and new media, notably its supposed ephemerality, fungibility, and homogeneity. A forensic perspective furnishes us with two key concepts for an alternative approach to electronic textual studies: trace evidence and individualization. Ultimately electronic data assumes visible and material form through processes of instrumentation that suggest phenomena we call virtual are in fact *physical* phenomena lacking the appropriate mediation to supplement wave-length optics; that is, the naked eye. The forensic materiality of new media is thereby demonstrated by the bits and data tracks visible on MFM renderings.

Chapter 2, "Extreme Inscription," is an in-depth look at the specific writing and storage technology that has been central to computing in the last thirty years: the magnetic hard disk drive, or hard drive. The hard drive serves as the book's central example of what it means to consider storage media as a kind of writing machine. The chapter reviews the history of the hard drive and the significance of random access data storage to new media and the database logic articulated by Lev Manovich. I offer a detailed grammatology of the hard drive based on a technical and theoretical examination of the drive's basic operations—what I call a "machine reading," which takes an instrument or device rather than a text as its locus. Finally, the chapter considers the cultural logic of the hard drive: as storage capacities continue to soar the hard drive itself becomes ever more abstracted and removed from daily awareness, even while digital artists begin to construct a forensic imagination of the device and database projects like MyLifeBits make radical claims about the future storage of individual experience.

In chapter 3, "'An Old House with Many Rooms,'" I use a disk image of the vintage interactive fiction game *Mystery House* to conduct a forensic walkthrough, or multivalent reading, of an electronic object, a bitstream image of an original instance of 5¼-inch disk storage media. This exercise allows us to explore critical reading strategies that are tightly coupled to technical praxis, here including the use of a hex editor to inspect heterogeneous information once deposited on the original storage media. Doing so brings the distinction between forensic and formal materiality more sharply into focus, using the overtly forensically charged spaces of the original game to peek and poke at the content of the disk image (which includes the remnants of earlier, apparently deleted copies of other Apple II games). Ultimately the chapter attempts to locate what Jerome McGann once called the "factive synechdoches" of bibliographical knowledge within new media, while exposing a new kind of media-specific reading, new tools for critical practice (notably the hex editor), and relevant contexts surrounding personal computing in the 1980s. In the second half of the chapter I develop further examples of formal materiality by way of both image- and text-based data structures. Forensics is ultimately presented as a mode of difference or defamiliarization rather than as an attempt to get closer to the soul of the machine. This is the first of three case studies of electronic objects in the book, and at the book's midway point it completes the articulation of forensic and formal materiality.

Chapter 4, "Save As: Michael Joyce's *Afternoons*," takes as its point of departure the colophon to Michael Joyce's landmark hypertext *Afternoon*, which elucidates the numerous versions and editions of the work. Relying on materials newly deposited at the Harry Ransom Humanities Research Center at the University of Texas at Austin, the chapter offers a detailed version history of *Afternoon* itself in the service of a larger argument about the diachronic dimensions of electronic textuality. With its deliberately plural locution "Afternoons," the chapter attempts to reconcile the document versioning that is a hallmark of electronic culture with both the notion of the "version" in literary editorial theory and the cultivation of postmodern variability and instability in the critical literature about creative hypertext. The chapter suggests a scene of electronic textuality that is a hybrid of printed and electronic components, all of which are relevant to the project of versioning and all of which form their own contours amid the newly institutionalized spaces that are now the repository for Joyce's work as its versions are cataloged and accessioned for posterity. The chapter also offers the first detailed record of the development history of the Storyspace software underlying *Afternoon*, as well as a consideration of digital document practices that exploit the medium's capacity to capture the temporal and diachronic dimensions of writing and revision.

Chapter 5, "Text Messaging," completes the trio of case studies by documenting the publication and transmission history of Gibson's "Agrippa," offering, for the first time, an accurate account of the hack that delivered the poem to the New York City-based bulletin board MindVox, and the text's subsequent proliferation across the network. The point is to address the fundamentally social, rather than the solely technical mechanisms of electronic textual transmission, and the role of social networks and network culture as active agents of preservation. As soon as it was released onto the network, "Agrippa" simultaneously cemented its own prospects for longevity and initiated its ongoing dilation as a textual event, an event which continues to unfold even now with the recent release of a substantial body of archival materials on a scholarly Web site bearing the forensically-inflected title *The Agrippa Files*.[32]

Forensics itself is a Janus-faced word, by definition both the presentation of scientific evidence and the construction of a rhetorical argument. *Mechanisms* embraces both of these aspects. While it does not shy away from technical detail (or theoretical nuance), it is first and foremost intended as a practical intervention in the current discourse about digital textuality. As electronic objects begin to accumulate archival identities (by virtue of the libraries, museums, and other cultural repositories increasingly interested in or charged with collecting them), it will become essential to understand the nature of what is being collected and preserved, and where the most significant challenges of digital preservation finally lie. One underlying theme of this book is that those challenges, while massively technical to be sure, are also ultimately—and profoundly—social. That is, this book aims to show that effective preservation must rest in large measure on the cultivation of new social practices to attend our new media. These practices start with the habits of the individual end user, who can herself take active steps to document and protect their own content.[33] Many are perhaps now discouraged from doing so by the

32. Available at http://agrippa.english.ucsb.edu/, *The Agrippa Files* is the work of Alan Liu and a team of graduate students associated with the University of California at Santa Barbara's *Transcriptions* project. The site was prepared with the cooperation and assistance of *Agrippa's* publisher, Kevin Begos Jr.

33. This is the motivation behind Nick Montfort and Noah Wardrip-Fruin's pamphlet publication *Acid Free Bits: Recommendations for Long-Lasting Electronic Literature* (Los Angeles: Electronic Literature Organization, 2004). Also available online at http://eliterature.org/pad/afb.html.

perceived futility of the effort, one outgrowth of the medial ideology I detail in chapter 1: *None of this stuff is going to last, so why bother?* Feeding the forensic imagination is necessary for encouraging people to take responsibility for the digital objects they will create and encounter. One aching example: in a recent essay lamenting the evaporation of literary heritage into cyberspace as the result of routine correspondence among authors, editors, agents, and publishers now taking the form of evanescent email, the *New York Times Book Review* details the plight of the fiction editor for the *New Yorker*: "'Unfortunately, since I haven't discovered any convenient way to electronically archive e-mail correspondence, I don't usually save it, and it gets erased from our server after a few months... if there's a particularly entertaining or illuminating back-and-forth with a writer over the editing process, though, I do sometimes print and file the e-mails.... conceivably someone could, in the distant future, dig all of this up.'"[34] We can choose to take from this that e-mail is slippery and volatile stuff indeed, or we can choose to take from it that the systems people should stop automatically erasing the server every few months and that in the meantime more things ought to be printed and filed for posterity.

Likewise, in the realm of archives and curatorial practice, it will be important to insist that digital objects are no more homogeneous or self-identical than other artifacts, and that the relationships between individual digital objects (and versions of those objects) should be preserved along with the actual works themselves. Finally, critics and scholars of new media need to begin exhibiting critical habits that are more sensitive to the mature material conditions of new media. Here work must happen at the most basic level: for example, what does it mean to cite a new media object adequately? How do you distinguish between versions and builds? What do we need to know about the operating system? How much RAM is installed? Does it matter what graphics and sound cards are in the machine? And so on. This kind of information is routinely presented with product reviews on gaming sites or in the trade magazines, but it remains a rarity in our scholarship. If the readers of *Gamasutra* need this information but scholars still do not, we would do well to ask why they need it and we do not, and what critical assumptions we have operating in their place. (Unless otherwise noted, all electronic objects discussed in this book were viewed on a Dell Latitude ×300 Windows XP laptop with a 1.20 GHz processor and 632 MB of RAM, sound turned on.)

34. Rachel Donadio, "Literary Letters Lost and Found in Cyberspace," *New York Times Book Review*, September 4, 2005.

I conclude that new media cannot be studied apart from individual instances of inscription, object, and code as they propagate on, across, and through specific storage devices, operating systems, software environments, and network protocols; yet the forensic imagination of the book's subtitle is also conceived as a deeply humanistic way of knowing, one that assigns value to time, history, and social or material circumstance—even trauma and wear—as part of our thinking about new media. Product and process, artifact and event, forensic and formal, awareness of the mechanism modulates inscription and transmission through the singularity of a digital present.

1

"Every Contact Leaves a Trace": Storage, Inscription, and Computer Forensics

It should always be emphasized that physical facts are not less significant simply because the unaided eye cannot see them.
—ALBERT S. OSBORN, *QUESTIONED DOCUMENTS* (SECOND EDITION), 1929

Each diskette is a small (about 5-inch diameter) plastic disk coated so that information may be stored on and erased from its surface. The coating is similar to the magnetic coating on a recording tape. The diskette is permanently sealed in a square black plastic cover which protects it, helps keep it clean and allows it to spin freely. This package is never opened.
— *THE DOS MANUAL*, APPLE COMPUTER INC., 1980

Visibility itself is not a measure of inscription, modification of the substratum is.
—MARCOS NOVAK, "TRANSTERRAFORM" (UNDATED, ONLINE)

The most uncompromising statement on the materiality of digital media I know is a Department of Defense document labeled DoD 5220.22-M, the Operating Manual for the National Industrial Security Program.[1] Initially

---

1.   Available at http://www.dtic.mil/whs/directives/corres/html/522022m.htm as well as many other locations online.

published in 1991, it seeks to establish and standardize security practices for handling classified information at the juncture between government and industry. Some eighty pages in we encounter the Clearing and Sanitization Matrix, a table listing numerous varieties of magnetic and optical storage media together with DoD-sanctioned methods for removing data stored on each type. The options range from simple overwrites (recording random or arbitrary bits on top of existing information) to various levels of degaussing (using magnetic fields to neutralize the polarity of the magnetic media, thereby sanitizing it), to Option M, available for all optical and magnetic media: "Destroy—Disintegrate, incinerate, pulverize, shred, or smelt." Some sense of what this means in actual practice may be conveyed by the following colorful account, posted to a USENET newsgroup:

When I had to declassify disk drives in 1987, the NSA suggested that I take them out to the parking lot, and run them over with a tank. . . . I told him that the Pentagon parking lot had about 12,000 cars, but no tanks. His second choice was that we put the drive on top of a research magnet the Navy had. . . . I don't know what the field strength of that magnet was, but it had big warning signs all over the building. You had to take off everything metal just to go into the same room. The magnet consumed 186 volts at 13,100 amps. That's about 2.5 megawatts. We left it there for about a minute and a half. The field physically bent the platters on our 14-inch drive.[2]

The DoD's Clearing and Sanitization Matrix offers a bracing counterpoint to the first wave of academic writing on electronic textuality, with which it is exactly contemporary. While media scholars and literary theoreticians were feeling their way toward metaphors and neologisms designed to capture something of the fleeting quality of the flickering signifiers on their screens, bureaucrats at the DoD were wringing their hands over electronic data's troubling penchant for remanence—defined by an influential National Computer Security Center study as "the residual physical representation of data that has been in some way erased."[3] They were enumerating the relevant variables in a matrix while experimenting with a myriad of techniques designed to render

2. Posted by David Hayes to the comp.periphs.scsi newsgroup, 24 Jul 91 05:07:01 GMT, as "Re: How many times erased does DoD want?"

3. NCSC-TG-025, *A Guide to Understanding Data Remanence in Automated Information Systems*. Widely available online: http://crypto-systems.com/datarem.html.

discarded information invulnerable. Taken together, the academy and the DoD reveal two starkly different attitudes towards the textual condition of electronic objects circa 1991 (one year prior to the production of *Agrippa*) and ask us to develop an approach capable of accounting for the ways in which electronic data was simultaneously perceived as evanescent and ephemeral in some quarters, and remarkably, stubbornly, perniciously stable and persistent in others.

Stored Programs and Screen Essentialism

A document like the Clearing and Sanitization Matrix exists because of a particular tradition of computing: the stored program, which entails both physical and logical separation of the processing unit from a computer's memory, encompassing both data and instructions for operating on data—the literal stored program. John von Neumann's 1945 "Draft Report on the EDVAC" remains the single most influential and complete articulation of the stored program concept, even if it is not the sole progenitor. The Draft Report effectively dictates that there is no computation without data's representation in a corresponding physical substratum, the specifics of which very quickly get us into a messy world of matter and metal whose minute particulars seem conspicuously at odds with the equations and schematics dominating the rest of von Neumann's text: "[I]nstructions must be given in some form which the device can sense: Punched into a system of punchcards or on teletype tape, magnetically impressed on steel tape or wire, photographically impressed on motion picture film, wired into one or more fixed or exchangeable plugboards—this list being by no means necessarily complete."[4]

A year earlier John Mauchly, who worked with von Neumann at the Moore School on the ENIAC and who with Wallace Eckert would soon leave Penn to build the UNIVAC, had posited storing numeric data on "disks or drums which have at least their outer edge made of a magnetic alloy."[5] It is hard to think of such a scheme as "writing" in anything but the most generic sense— probably we are led to think in terms of materials science and fabrication

4. "First Draft Report on the EDVAC," http://www.virtualtravelog.net/entries/2003-08-TheFirstDraft.pdf.

5. Quoted in Paul E. Ceruzzi, *A History of Modern Computing* (Cambridge: MIT Press, 1998), 22.

instead. Yet, as scholars such as Frank Salomon have noted in their work on the khipu, the ancient Incan information recording device that stored data in knotted cords, the exclusive identification of writing with phonetic sign systems has been challenged in a number of quarters.[6] The magnetic storage

6. Frank Salomon, *The Cord Keepers: Khipus and Cultural Life in a Peruvian Village* (Durham: Duke University Press, 2004), 23–30. The crucial intervention is Geoffrey Sampson's, who in his book *Writing Systems* (Stanford University Press, 1985), elaborates a concept of the graphic sign known as semasiography to sit alongside of the glottographic systems of which the alphabet, where signs stand in for phonetic speech, is typical (26–45). However, any claim that data recorded on magnetic strips or other computer storage media is semasiographic writing must be immediately complicated by the fact that the data is not typically visible to the human eye, and if it is visible then it is not typically meaningful. In short, whether graphic or phonetic in its basis, writing is always defined in terms of communication, and the inscriptions in computational storage media generally fail to communicate effectively to a human being absent the aid of a mechanical prosthesis. As Winfried Nöth notes in his *Handbook of Semiotics* (Bloomington: Indiana University Press, 1990), however, "In cybernetics and systems theory communication is often the interaction between any two entities. Thus, Klaus (1969) in his dictionary of cybernetics defines communication as 'the exchange of information between dynamic systems capable of receiving, storing, or transforming information.' This definition of communication also includes processes of interaction between machines" (170–171). Thus there is a clear tradition of including machine processes in the context of communications systems. Other discussions of semiotics come to rest on the distinction between communication and signification. Typically the former is associated with intentionality, whereas the latter category, signification, is broader and encompasses nonintentional signals (Nöth 172–173). Umberto Eco, however, reverses the two: "For Eco, any flow of information from a source to a destination is a process of communication, even the passage of a signal from machine to machine" (Nöth 172). And there is yet another possibility. Rather than writing in the orthodox sense of semasiography or glottography (also known as lexigraphy), computer data inscription is more akin to the forms of symbolic numeracy found in practices of record keeping. Yet Salomon argues persuasively not only that writing has its origins in record-keeping tasks (as is well known), but that "the development of a writing system is nothing other than the practical case-by-case solution of social tasks which produces an emergent new data registry system . . . the record-keeping art takes shape around the social problems it solves" (28). In short, he posits a continuum rather than a break between writing and recording.

    In addition to whatever semiotic/cybernetic arguments one wants to entertain about the status of data inscriptions as writing, it is equally useful and important to juxtapose the prevalence of writing-related terminology in computer science practice. Even lay users routinely speak of reading and writing to and from a disk, and a disk drive includes an electromechanical instrument known as the read/write head. Are these metaphors or literal descriptors? Or else consider

Figure 1.1 Magnified image of a small portion of the magnetic strip on a Washington, D.C. Metro fare card after the application of MagView developer's fluid. Striated data tracks are most clearly visible near the top edge, perpendicular to the length of the strip. Photograph by the author.

devices envisioned by von Neumann, Mauchly, and others have become the preeminent information storage devices of our own day; indeed, so thoroughly integrated into our daily lives are magnetic recording media that we routinely embed them in an even older substrate, paper, so that a disposable printed card carelessly slipped into a pocket becomes the commodity token which admits me to my local transit system and debits the cost of my ride from a value recorded on the magnetic strip.

Though normally invisible to human eyes, the magnetic recording on such a card is indisputably an inscription, as is apparent after the application of aerosolized ferrite oxide, which makes the tracks and data patterns visible (see figure 1.1).

---

that "words" were a basic organizational unit in early data stores; a "word," according to Ceruzzi, was either an 11-digit number plus a sign, a string of 12 characters, or two 6-character instructions (23). If a computer scientist can speak quite literally about "writing" "words" without recourse to either glottographic or semasiographic writing systems, then quotation marks as I just used them are inappropriate and the definition of writing should be expanded to accommodate the phrase without them—just as the definition of "language" has expanded to include programming languages as well as natural languages without necessarily positing equivalences between them.

There is, of course, an obvious sense in which these marks and traces are meant to be machine readable and are here only incidentally revealed to the human visual field as the result of a rehearsed procedure. But it would be a mistake to think that the boundary between human and machine reading is always absolute or inflexible. The history of codes reveals a continuum rather than an absolute rupture between human and machine reading.[7] Early telegraph operators quickly learned to decode messages by listening to the sound of the receiver's mechanism rather than referring to the printed Morse it outputted. UPC symbols are legible to a trained observer. Punch cards can be manually deciphered and perhaps even more tellingly, their proper interpretation can be disputed, as vividly demonstrated during the 2000 election controversy in the United States. A computer forensics expert can visually inspect the patterns of magnetic tracks on a diskette treated in the same manner as the Metro card above and locate the starting points for the different data sectors. Still, all of these examples are admittedly specialized. Little wonder then that electronic writing's first generation of theorists turned their gaze toward the illuminated screen rather than the inscrutable disk. "[T]he simple, and possibly profound, truth," writes Xerox document scientist David Levy, "is that you can't see bits. You can't see them, you can't hear them, you can't touch or smell them. They are completely inaccessible to the human senses." Jay David Bolter puts it this way: "If you hold a magnetic or optical disk up to the light, you will not see text at all. At best you will see the circular tracks into which the data is organized, and these tracks mean nothing to the human eye."[8] The cathode ray tube was the implicit, and often explicit, starting point for most discussions of electronic textuality because it was only as bit-mapped fonts on the screen that electronic letterforms became recognizable as writing.[9] Critics such as Richard Lanham were quick to comment on the implica-

7. For an overview, see Charles Petzold, *Code: The Hidden Language of Computer Hardware and Software* (Redmond: Microsoft Press, 1999), especially chapters 1–10.

8. David M. Levy, *Scrolling Forward: Making Sense of Documents in the Digital Age* (New York: Arcade Publishing, 2001), 138, and Jay David Bolter, *Writing Space: The Computer, Hypertext, and the History of Writing* (Hillsdale, NJ: Lawrence Erlbaum, 1991), 42.

9. In fact, the early limitations of the Macintosh with its low-resolution VDT display were quickly enlisted by type designers such as *Émigré*'s Zuzana Licko—who began working seriously with the Mac within weeks of its debut—to provide the basic components of an electronic graphical identity. Licko says of this process: "I started my venture with bitmap type designs,

tions of desktop publishing and digital typography, noting that the creative control afforded by the font libraries and clip art galleries at every user's fingertips contributed to the breakdown of traditional distinctions between reader and writer while dramatizing the malleability of words and images in a digital setting.[10]

Nick Montfort has coined the term "screen essentialism" to refer to the prevailing bias in new media studies toward display technologies that would have been unknown to most computer users before the mid-1970s (the teletype being the then-dominant output device). One result, as Montfort discusses, is that an essential dimension of the materiality of early electronic literary productions like ELIZA and ADVENTURE is elided, since these works were historically experienced as printed texts on rolls of paper rather than as characters on video screens.[11] Thus one does not always need to look at screens to study new media, or to learn useful things about the textual practices that accumulate in and around computation. In their book *The Myth of the Paperless Office*, Abigail J. Sellen and Richard H. R. Harper employ J. J. Gibson's concept of affordances to evoke the raw, literal, physical materiality of different kinds of objects and media, especially paper: "The physical properties

---

created for the coarse resolutions of the computer screen and dot matrix printer. The challenge was that because the early computers were so limited in what they could do you really had to design something special. . . . it was physically impossible to adapt 8-point Goudy Old Style to 72 dots to the inch. In the end you couldn't tell Goudy Old Style from Times New Roman or any other serif text face. . . . It is impossible to transfer typefaces between technologies without alterations because each medium has its peculiar qualities and thus requires unique designs." See Rudy VanderLans and Zuzana Licko with Mary E. Gray, *Émigré (the Book): Graphic Design into the Digital Realm* (New York: Van Nostrand Reinhold, 1993), 18 and 23. What began as a material limitation in the medium's underlying hardware and display technologies was quickly accepted, adopted, and adapted as an integral aspect of the medium's aesthetic identity, an identity which has remained iconically intact and recognizable (think jaggies) even today, long after the technological base has shifted beyond the crude conditions Licko describes above.

10.   See Richard Lanham, *The Electronic Word: Democracy, Technology, and the Arts* (Chicago: University of Chicago Press, 1993), 3–28.

11.   Nick Montfort, "Continuous Paper: The Early Materiality and Workings of Electronic Literature": http://nickm.com/writing/essays/continuous_paper_mla.html.

Figure 1.2 Affordances of a 5¼-inch floppy. Photograph by the author.

of paper (its being thin, light, porous, opaque, flexible, and so on) afford many different human actions, such as grasping, carrying, manipulating, folding, and in combination with a marking tool, writing on."[12] For Sellen and Harper (a cognitive psychologist and a technologist respectively), affordances are all about possibilities for action, which determine how human beings interact with the physical things in their environment. Computer storage media also have their affordances, but as storage in general has become more capacious and less immediately tangible it is easy to overlook them. (USB thumb drives are perhaps the best example of a recent storage innovation whose affordances have changed the way we interact with data: they are small and lightweight but also rugged, more like an accessory or gear than the flatter, flimsier profile of media like CD-ROMs or disks, whose vulnerable surfaces must be sheltered.) Attention to the affordances of various kinds of storage media can reveal much about computing in different contexts, allowing us to reconstruct salient aspects of now-obsolete systems and the human practices that attended them.

This is a 5¼-inch "floppy" disk, a personal relic from my teenage years (figure 1.2). The Apple II computer with which this disk is compatible has

12.   Abigail J. Sellen and Richard H. R. Harper, *The Myth of the Paperless Office* (Cambridge: MIT Press, 2001), 12.

no hard drive. A program is loaded by inserting the disk in the external drive and booting the machine. In practical terms, this meant first retrieving the program by going to one's collection of disks and rummaging through them—perhaps they were kept in a shoebox, or stacked in a pile next to the computer, or in one of the many dedicated media containers marketed to the home computer enthusiast. Consider the contrast in affordances to a file system mounted on a hard drive: here you located the program you wanted by reading a printed or handwritten label, browsing like you would record albums or manila file folders, not by clicking on an icon. Written labels were therefore indispensable, their legible text standing in implicit counterpoint to the machine-readable markings on the magnetic surface sheathed within the plastic envelope to which the label was affixed. The label on this particular disk—handwritten, and placed over the manufacturer's label—indicates three different items: "Amort. Table" (amortization table, a tool used by accountants—why this would have been of interest to my fourteen-year-old self is beyond me now), "Matts [sic] Programs" (some programs I had written in BASIC), and (penned with an obviously different ink) "Koala Pictures" (Koala was a drawing utility—these were its data files). So on the same diskette we have, commingled, a freeware business application, programs I had written by myself and for myself, and the data files created by a commercial software package. The latter appears to have been added at a later date. This alone—the heterogeneous nature of the content, its incremental consignment to the disk—tells us something about the culture of personal computing at the time (which was clearly different from the affordances even of CD-Rs today.) In addition, we can see that a portion of the disk envelope alongside the label has been crudely cut away; in fact, it was attacked with a hole puncher. By mimicking the professionally cut write tab in a symmetrical location I double-sided the disk, signaling to the drive mechanism that the reverse side was also available for data inscription (to access the reverse side you would place the disk in the drive upside down). This was a common trick, and one I was quick to appreciate once I learned that disks had a finite capacity, that more disks were what enabled me to expand my software collection (primarily games), and that the money for buying new blank disks was to come out of my allowance. In this instance I can surmise that I double-sided this disk at some point well after its initial purchase in order to store the Koala picture files I was then generating with that piece of software (itself stored on a separate disk), hastily inking in an addition to the label which would allow me to locate them.

I am belaboring these details to make the point that as a teenage computer user I had unself-consciously worked with storage media whose material qualities were very particular but which differ markedly from what would be the norm today. Since even routine chores like disk defragmentation are performed far less frequently on the current generation of hard drives, storage has become ever more of an abstraction, defined only by a volume letter (on most Windows machines, "C"), a graphic hard drive icon, or a pie chart visualization of space remaining. Greater and greater storage capacity will only serve to further dematerialize the media as their finite physical boundaries slip past the point of any practical concern. Compare this to the kind of information preserved on the manufacturer's labels of floppy disks from the 1980s, emblems of a bygone inscriptive regimen: "Reliable and Durable" promises the label on one brand, "48 TPI" (tracks per inch) specifies another, and "Double-Sided/ Double-Density Soft-Sectored With Hub Ring" declares a third. This strange and alien cant was perfectly intelligible to me and millions of other home computer users, not because we were hackers or übergeeks, but because these specs defined the functional limits of what we could and could not do with a given piece of media in practical and palpable ways—in other words, its affordances.

A further contrast between screen essentialism and inscription or storage media is warranted, I believe, by the current state of new media studies in which the graphical user interface is often uncritically accepted as the ground zero of the user's experience. "We look through the interface unaware," writes Michael Heim in his *Metaphysics of Virtual Reality*, "as we peer through an electronic network where our symbols—words, data, simulations—come under precise control, where things appear with startling clarity. So entrancing are these symbols that we forget ourselves, forget where we are. We forget ourselves as we evolve into our fabricated worlds. With our faces up against it, the interface is hard to see."[13] Heim's experience here speaks powerfully to a technological sublime, a simultaneous ecstasy and oblivion immanent in our encounters with the virtual. But this "metaphysics," to use Heim's word (a metaphysics conceived, one suspects, amid the vertigo of Gibson's city lights

13. Michael Heim, *The Metaphysics of Virtual Reality* (New York: Oxford University Press, 1993), 79–80.

receding), is not finally symbolic (note that word's repetition in his text) but instead embedded within real-world technologies of production and design. Robert Markley, writing partly in direct response to Heim (in an essay that should be better known than it is), offers a prescient brute force disassembling of screen essentialism:

To ask what is on the other side of the computer screen is, in my mind, a crucial step in dissenting from this consensual hallucination. Behind the screen of my laptop lie silicon chips, a battery, microprocessors, and even what seem to be a few old-fashioned screws. It runs (now rather dated) software programs engineered originally in California and Utah. My access to the presumptive world behind the screen carries with it an effaced history of labor, of people building machines to design and to build even more sophisticated hardware and software. (77)[14]

"The imaginary realm of cyberspace," Markley concludes, "... is a fantasy based on the denial of ecology and labor, a dream that is also an apology for the socioeconomic power to bring together sophisticated technologies" (77). Markley's account is one of the few from this era to explicitly juxtapose the gaze of the end user with the unseen workers' hands—here literally screened from view—which are busy turning old-fashioned screws.[15]

Yet even in Markley's resolutely anti-essentialist hands, the screen still seems to slip into a synecdoche for "the computer" as a whole. What I have been attempting to accumulate here are thus a set of alternative access points for the study of computing, access points that bring storage, inscription, and engineering into the visible purview of what we think of as new media. But how did screens come to so obscure our view in the first place?

14.   Robert Markley, "Boundaries: Mathematics, Alienation, and the Metaphysics of Cyberspace," in *Virtual Reality and its Discontents*, ed. Robert Markley (Baltimore: The Johns Hopkins University Press, 1996): 55–77.

15.   Precisely this dynamic is explored in the 1994 corporate thriller *Disclosure*. The high-tech company that is the setting for the sexual harassment charges driving the film is showcasing a fanciful, fully immersive virtual reality environment with stunning visuals (or what passed for them at the time) as its next generation technology. Its current product, however, and the focal point for the plot, is a line of high-speed compact disk drives. As my colleague Katie King points out, here storage is made visible through the plot's attention to the manufacturing process and the associated industrial espionage. The climax of the film occurs when evidence of tampering with the drives is "disclosed"—on a big-screen TV—at a shareholders meeting.

A Medial Ideology

Jerome McGann has used the phrase "Romantic ideology" to describe the manner in which modern literary criticism of the Romantic poets has been characterized by "an uncritical absorption in Romanticism's own self-representations."[16] I believe electronic textual theory has labored under similar uncritical absorptions of the medium's self- or seemingly self-evident representations. While often precisely Romantic in their celebration of the fragile half-life of the digital, the "ideology" I want to delineate below is perhaps better thought of as *medial*—that is, one that substitutes popular representations of a medium, socially constructed and culturally activated to perform specific kinds of work, for a more comprehensive treatment of the material particulars of a given technology.

This tendency is already full-blown in Arthur C. Clarke's 1986 short story "The Steam-Powered Word Processor," which narrates the fictitious history of the Reverend Charles Cabbage (obviously a stand-in for the historical Babbage), vicar of the tiny church in Far Tottering, Sussex.[17] As Clarke tells it, the Reverend, weary of his obligation to produce varying sermons on the same theme twice a week, 104 times a year, contrives to build a device for automating the composition process. The Word Loom is envisioned as a combinatory machine for the manipulation of sentences (which it takes as the basic combinatory unit), and it is to be capable of outputting hard copy for the Reverend's use by way of something like a Linotype process.

The machine's database is the Bible and Cruden's Concordance, punched onto cards "at negligible expense, by the aged ladies of the Far Tottering Home for Relics of Decayed Gentlefolk" (932). Having solved the problem of data entry and beat Herman Hollerith to the punch (as it were), Cabbage (who we also learn enjoys a correspondence with the aging Michael Faraday) proceeds to other aspects of his design. The church's pipe organ becomes his chief inspiration: "He was convinced that an assembly of pneumatic tubes, valves, and pumps could control all the operations of his projected Word Loom" (932). But the reader quickly intimates that this ambitious enterprise is doomed from the start, Cabbage's novel solutions to problems of input, out-

16. Jerome McGann, *The Romantic Ideology* (Chicago: University of Chicago Press, 1983), 1.

17. In *The Collected Stories of Arthur C. Clarke* (New York: Tor, 2000), 930–934. All pages references are to this edition. Originally published in *Analog*, January 1986.

put, processing, and storage notwithstanding. On the day of its first and only public trial something goes awry—"Somewhere, in the depths of the immense apparatus, something broke" (933)—and the Word Loom is rent to pieces in a maelstrom of imploding machinery. All that survives today are "two or three gearwheels" and "what appears to be a pneumatic valve" in the possession of the Far Tottering Historical Society (932); that and, deep inside the British Museum, bound in a volume entitled *Sermons in Steam*, a single machine-generated page, badly printed and riddled with typographical errors. It is either a clever fake (we are told) or else it is "the only surviving production of perhaps the most remarkable—and misguided—technological effort of the Victorian Age" (934).

Of course no reader accepts this conceit, and it doesn't matter; the lesson is all about the folly of seeking to embed digital behaviors in an industrial engine. The Word Loom, which was to "weave thoughts the way Jacquard wove tapestries" (932; note the paraphrase of Ada, Countess Lovelace), could only succeed with the aid of new forces harnessed by Faraday in his work on electromagnetic energy, not the brass gearwheels of a Victorian mechanism. It is Cabbage's hapless lot to seek to pour new wine into a very old bottle. We, savvy readers and beneficiaries of the technology of word processing ourselves, are in on the joke and therefore understand that the story serves chiefly to underscore the radical break between electronic writing and earlier forms of textuality—a familiar and comfortable enough homily for old Cabbage to deliver in the end.

We can pick up the thread of the Word Loom just two years later when Umberto Eco, in his novel *Foucault's Pendulum*, contrives the kabbalistically named word processor Abulafia as the embodiment of a "totally spiritual machine" (24):

If you write with a goose quill you scratch the sweaty pages and keep stopping to dip for ink. Your thoughts go too fast for your aching wrist. If you type, the letters cluster together, and again you must go at the pokey pace of the mechanism, not the speed of your synapses. But with [Abulafia] your fingers dream, your mind brushes the keyboard, you are borne on golden pinions, at last you confront the light of critical reason with the happiness of a first encounter. (24–25)[18]

18. Umberto Eco, *Foucault's Pendulum*, Trans. William Weaver (London: Picador, 1989).

Already we can glimpse the particulars of our medial ideology: "Our best machines are made of sunshine; they are all light and clean because they are nothing but signals, electromagnetic waves, a section of a spectrum..." (153) wrote Donna Haraway in her famous "Cyborg Manifesto" (1985; that her words were also ironic strengthens rather than diminishes their medial impact).[19] Industry leaders may have grasped the appeal of this ideology even earlier than fiction writers or academicians. In 1982, four Bay-area entrepreneurs cofounded a new company devoted to network enterprise computing. They called it Sun.

By the mid-1980s, the digital sphere had assumed visual and material form as a definable and datable set of aesthetic practices; a recognizable spectrum of tropes, icons, and graphic conventions. This is the backdrop for the medial ideology I am describing. At stake is not whether such conventions for representing digital phenomena are accurate or correct to the formal ontology of information in an absolute sense, but rather the important fact that Western consumer culture had succeeded in evolving sophisticated and compelling conceits for depicting information as an essence unto itself, or more properly, information as a synthetic (at times even haptic) commodity. That the cyberspaces of both *Neuromancer* and *Tron* (as well as other cyberpunk productions such as the short stories in Gibson's "Burning Chrome" anthology or even the 1981 animated feature *Heavy Metal*) are artificial alloys derived of complex cultural skeins may seem an elementary point, but it is one that was often lost in the face of popular enthusiasms for virtual phenomena. A touchstone would be Michael Benedikt's anthology *Cyberspace: First Steps*, published in 1991, which collected the writings of many of the so-called digerati, the loose clique of artists and technologists who had emerged over the course of the previous decade.[20] Prefaced by Gibson, the volume contains fifteen essays, notable today for how literally some of them read Gibson's novels as starting points for actual research agendas in interface design and related fields. All of the essays oscillate between tacit recognition of the preliminary and tentative status of the actual technologies on the one hand, and a willingness to talk about cyberspace as though it were already an observable phenomenon on the other. Some contributors simply choose not to acknowledge this as an

19. In Donna J. Haraway, *Simians, Cyborgs, and Women: The Reinvention of Nature* (New York: Routledge, 1991), 149–181.

20. Michael Benedikt, ed. *Cyberspace: First Steps* (Cambridge: MIT Press, 1991).

issue; Marcos Novak, for example, does not hesitate to inform us that "The function of [cyberspace synthesizers] is to receive a minimal description of the cyberspace, coded and compressed, and from it to render a visualization of that space for the user to navigate with" (233). This is a reasonable enough description of the graphical Web browsers that would soon emerge, but one wonders if Novak didn't have something more fanciful in mind. In either case, he is assuming cyberspace is subject matter evocative enough for the reader to suspend disbelief and to benefit from a putatively sober description of a technology that does not yet exist. Other contributors are more circumspect, such as David Tomas, who asserts the following: "Although cyberspace has been popularized by Gibson's books, it is neither a pure 'pop' phenomenon nor a simple technological artifact, but rather a powerful, collective, mnemonic technology that promises to have an important, if not revolutionary, impact on the future compositions of human identities and cultures" (31–32). This appears a balanced assessment, yet it is clear that when Tomas talks about cyberspace as a "technology" he cannot mean technology in the sense of any specific hardware or software implementation—a meaning he hastens to jettison by preceding his reference to a "technological artifact" with the qualifier "simple" and by placing the whole of the phrase in parallel with the equally ineffectual notion of cyberspace as a "pure 'pop' phenomenon." Cyberspace, as it is invoked here, can only be a technology in the sense that the word itself— or more precisely, the idea of cyberspace—mimics the behavior of certain material technologies, functioning as a "powerful, collective, mnemonic"— or in other words, as a shorthand for a whole range of communicative agendas given depth and form by a shared aesthetic. This is what was reflected in *Wired*'s Teflon sheen when the magazine, self-consciously designed to *look* like information, began publishing in 1993.[21]

At the core of a medial ideology of electronic text is the notion that in place of inscription, mechanism, sweat of the brow (or its mechanical equivalent steam), and cramp of the hand, there is light, reason, and energy unleashed in the electric empyrean. Yet Clarke, Eco, and others among the first to write about word processors, both on and with their own home computers (such as Michael Joyce, whose experience we will examine in chapter 4), were not

21. Note also the remarkable visual consistency to the maps and renditions of cyberspace, both scientific and imaginative, on display at Martin Dodge's *Atlas of Cyberspaces*: http://www .cybergeography.org/atlas/atlas.html.

simply deluded or wrong. Indeed, what was *new* about the technology was precisely that it succeeded so completely in rendering the workaday labor of textual production *functionally* immaterial. Michael Heim successfully articulated an early intuition as to why. In his *Electric Language: A Philosophical Discussion of Word Processing* (1987), which precedes now better-known books by Richard Lanham, George Landow, and Jay David Bolter, he borrows the term "system opacity" from John Seely-Brown:

The types of physical cues that naturally help a user make sense out of mechanical movements and mechanical connections are simply not available in the electronic element. There are far more clues to the underlying structural processes for the person riding a bicycle than there are for the person writing on a computer screen. Physical signs of the ongoing process, the way that responses of the person are integrated into the operation of the system, the source of occasional blunders and delays, all these are hidden beneath the surface of the activity of digital writing. No pulleys, springs, wheels, or levers are visible; no moving carriage returns indicate what the user's action is accomplishing and how that action is related to the end product; and there is no bottle of white-out paint complete with miniature touch-up brush to betoken the industrial chore of correcting errors by imposing one material substance over another. The writer has no choice but to remain on the surface of the system underpinning the symbols.[22]

System opacity or black box: what was implicit in Eco's paen to dreaming fingers borne aloft becomes explicit in Heim: "Yet, in order to achieve such automation, *writing has to be removed from the element of inscription* and placed in an electronic element" (136; emphasis added). It is not that Heim is oblivious to the operations of his disks and storage peripherals; on the contrary, he insists that some basic understanding of how the computer stores and retrieves information is essential for even a novice user, else they will be duped by watching text scroll off the edge of the screen. But Heim conceives of this understanding pragmatically, as "a set of metaphors for making operational guesses at the underlying structure" (133)—not in terms of specific technologies. Thus in Heim's example, a user might imagine that two different versions of a document are saved in two different "places" on the hard drive (133–134). As

22. Michael Heim, *Electric Language: A Philosophical Study of Word Processing*, 2nd edition (New Haven: Yale University Press, 1999), 131–132.

Heim himself is careful to point out, "[t]his insight requires no awareness of the File Allocation Table (FAT) or the bits set for file identifiers on the level of machine-language bytes, nor does it require awareness of the tracking system on the disk drive" (134). Electronic writing thus becomes a friction-free "information flow" (133), an essentially symbolic rather than inscriptive exchange among a set of operational metaphors and the "electronic elements" on the screen. Later in this book, I will term this symbolic exchange formal materiality.

Meanwhile the academy had begun a conversation in earnest. In a chapter titled "Derrida and Electronic Writing" from the 1990 book *The Mode of Information*, Mark Poster described electronic textuality this way:

Compared to the pen, the typewriter or the printing press, the computer dematerializes the written trace. As inputs are made to the computer through the keyboard, pixels of phosphor are illuminated on the screen, pixels that are formed into letters. Since these letters are no more than representations of ASCII codes contained in Random Access Memory, they are alterable practically at the speed of light. The writer encounters his or her words in a form that is evanescent, instantly transformable, in short, immaterial.[23]

And one year later, in what may be the most influential critical study to emerge from this era, Jay David Bolter in *Writing Space* (1991):

Electronic text is the first text in which the elements of meaning, of structure, and of visual display are fundamentally unstable.... This restlessness is inherent in a technology that records information by collecting for fractions of a second evanescent electrons at tiny junctures of silicon and metal. All information, all data in the computer world is a kind of controlled movement, and so the natural inclination of computer writing is to change, to grow, and finally to disappear.[24]

Or George P. Landow and Paul Delany, also in 1991:

23.   Mark Poster, *The Mode of Information: Poststructuralism and Social Contexts* (Chicago: University of Chicago Press, 1990), 111.

24.   Jay David Bolter, *Writing Space: The Computer, Hypertext, and the History of Writing* (Hillsdale, NJ: Lawrence Erlbaum, 1991), 31.

So long as the text was married to a physical media, readers and writers took for granted three crucial attributes: that the text was *linear*, *bounded*, and *fixed*. Generations of scholars and authors internalized these qualities as the rules of thought, and they have pervasive social consequences. We can define *Hypertext* as the use of the computer to transcend the linear, bounded and fixed qualities of the traditional written text.[25]

The preceding accounts are not without nuance. In Poster, for example, who is in turn reminiscent of Eco, electronic writing is presented in relative and not absolute terms as compared to the pen or typewriter or printing press, and he specifies the computer's RAM as the site of the written act. Yet this very specificity makes the absence of storage all the more telling. Landow and Delany, interestingly, define hypertext first and foremost as the *use* of a technology, rather than a technology itself. Yet we still find a clear opposition between the expressive largesse electronic environments promise and textual stability which is relegated to "physical media," the presumed baggage of the Gutenberg galaxy.

We can continue to accumulate examples of a medial ideology, year to year. "[W]ith electronic text we are always painting, each screen unreasonably washing away what was and replacing it with itself," suggested Michael Joyce in 1992.[26] N. Katherine Hayles, in a widely read essay titled "Virtual Bodies and Flickering Signifiers" published a year later, puts it this way: "Working at the computer screen, I cannot read unaided the magnetic markers that physically embody the information within the computer, but I am acutely aware of the patterns of blinking lights that comprise the text in its screen format" (260).[27] Hayles, of course, fully understands the internal complexity of the symbolic transaction she is alluding to, noting elsewhere that the screen's "flickering signifiers" (as she calls them, after Lacan) originate as magnetic traces on a disk, which are then interpolated through binary machine language, compiler, application software, and so forth. The basic thesis Hayles goes on to develop, that signification in electronic environments involves "a

25. Paul Delany and George P. Landow, eds. *Hypermedia and Literary Studies* (Cambridge: MIT Press, 1991), 3. Emphases in original.

26. Michael Joyce, *Of Two Minds: Hypertext Pedagogy and Poetics* (Ann Arbor: University of Michigan Press, 1995), 232.

27. N. Katherine Hayles, "Virtual Bodies and Flickering Signifiers," in *Electronic Culture: Technology and Visual Representation*, ed. Timothy Druckrey (New York: Aperture, 1996), 259–277.

flexible chain of markers bound together by the arbitrary relations specified by the relevant codes" (264), effectively captures what most users experience as the basic phenomenological difference between analog and digital media (whether backspacing to correct a typing error or brightening an image in Photoshop). Digital signification, in this model, consists in an open-ended symbiotic exchange (or feedback loop) between computation and representation.

I believe that the close temporal proximity and occasional outright overlap in the passages I have been collecting point not to a transparent and self-sufficient account of the ontology of the medium itself, but rather to the emerging contours of a medial ideology. We see this best if we examine the dominant tropes and rhetorical markers. Speed and light (or lightning) are paramount: Heim's "electric language," Eco's "golden pinions" and "light of critical reason," Poster's "pixels of phosphor" and "speed of light," Bolter's "fractions of a second" and "evanescent electrons," Hayles's "patterns of blinking lights" and "flickering" signifiers, even Joyce's spontaneous "painting." This is consistent with the tropes that had already emerged in narrative and cinematic science fiction: the luminous, ray-traced aesthetic of *Tron*, or William Gibson's prose passages describing cyberspace in terms of "lines of light" and "city lights receding."

Recall Heim, for whom symbolic automation demands medial liberation: writing had to be "removed from the element of inscription" and placed in electronic form. With letterforms now "instantly transformable," we reach for the chiasmus of "fingers dreaming" and a "mind brushing the keyboard" (shades of Gibson's anti-hero Case and his Ono-Sendai cyberspace deck). We invoke adjectives like "flickering," "restless," "flexible," and their ultimate apotheosis, "immaterial." This medial ideology is precisely the same aesthetic to which *Agrippa* spoke so powerfully in 1992, with its then-contemporary meme of the viral, self-consuming text and the disappearing book. Screen essentialism becomes a logical consequence of a medial ideology that shuns the inscriptive act.

There are a number of important respects in which the theoretical debate has advanced considerably since the first half of the 1990s. The appeal to high poststructuralism forming the backdrop of many of the early accounts I have referenced has been abandoned, or at least its influence diluted. Espen Aarseth's *Cybertext: Perspectives on Ergodic Literature* (1997) emerged as the first major attempt to examine screen-level effects from the vantage point of their interaction with a text's underlying formal processes, leading to, among much else, a widening of the general purview of the field of electronic textual studies (video games, old school interactive fiction, and printed text machines such as *Choose Your Own Adventure* novels, the ancient *I Ching*, and Oulipean productions like Raymond Queneau's *Cent Mille Milliards de poèmes*).[28] N. Katherine Hayles, meanwhile, continued to refine her critical positions and has advanced what is probably the most extensive argument for materiality and embodiment against the backdrop of three recent books and a series of accomplished, media-specific close readings of printed and electronic texts alike.[29] In his widely read *The Language of New Media* (2001), Lev Manovich developed an extensive formal account of new media influenced by his background in film, but the book's most important contribution may yet be its advocacy of software studies, the serious study of specific software technologies as both historical and computational artifacts, a call that has also been taken up by Matthew Fuller.[30] Alan Liu's *The Laws of Cool* (2004), a majestic book whose fundamental frame of reference is as much the cubicle as the screen, locates its potential for a "future literary" within the cool enclaves of the Web nurtured by digital artists and corporate knowledge workers alike.[31] At an even more general level, new media studies has seen essential critical work on the politics of race, class, and gender;[32] the expansion into brand new areas, notably the

28.   Espen Aarseth, *Cybertext: Perspectives on Ergodic Literature* (Baltimore: Johns Hopkins University Press, 1997).

29.   The three books are *How We Became Post-Human: Virtual Bodies in Cybernetics, Literature, and Informatics* (Chicago: University of Chicago Press, 1999), *Writing Machines* (Cambridge: MIT Press, 2002), and *My Mother Was a Computer: Digital Subjects and Literary Texts* (Chicago: University of Chicago Press, 2005).

30.   Lev Manovich, *The Language of New Media* (Cambridge: MIT Press, 2001); see also Fuller's *Behind the Blip: Essays on the Culture of Software* (Brooklyn, NY: Autonomedia, 2003).

31.   Alan Liu, *The Laws of Cool: Knowledge Work and the Culture of Information* (Chicago: University of Chicago Press, 2004).

32.   For example, Anne Balsamo, *Technologies of the Gendered Body: Reading Cyborg Women* (Durham: Duke University Press, 1996); Lisa Nakamura, *Cybertypes: Race, Ethnicity, and Identity on the Internet* (London: Routledge, 2002); *Reload: Rethinking Women + Cyberculture*, eds. Mary Flanagan and Austin Booth (Cambridge: MIT Press, 2002); and Geert Lovink's *Dark Fiber: Tracking Critical Internet Culture* (Cambridge: MIT Press, 2003), and *Uncanny Networks: Dialogues with the Virtual Intelligentsia* (Cambridge: MIT Press, 2004).

white-hot field of ludology;[33] and the recent availability of essential basic reference tools such as *The New Media Reader* and *Information Arts*.[34] Yet for all of this activity, my argument is ultimately that we remain very much in the grip of a medial ideology, with many of the plain truths about the fundamental nature of electronic writing apparently unknown at a simple factual level, or else overlooked or their significance obscured.

In the next section, I introduce the field of computer forensics as a counterpoint. At the applied level, computer forensics depends upon the behaviors and physical properties of various computational storage media. For the theoretical observer, it is bracing to watch the forensic investigator run up against many of the same issues that have driven commentators in the realm of cultural and critical theory. While digital evidence can be instantly deleted it can often be just as easily recovered; while digital evidence can be copied perfectly (what we like to call a simulacrum), it can also be copied imperfectly, and in fact care must be taken lest it be copied incompletely; while digital evidence can be tampered with, it can also be stabilized and encrypted; while digital evidence can be faked, it can also be signed and algorithmically authenticated. In a very different climate from the anxieties of the academy discussed above, the forensic investigator employs a set of field procedures designed to establish an order of volatility for all of the evidence within his or her purview, clinically delineating the relative vulnerability and stability of data at many different points in a system's internal architecture. The irony is that while the protected internal environment of the hard drive is built to exclude the hairs, fibers, and other minute particulars of traditional forensic science, the platter inexorably yields up its own unique kind of physical evidence.

Computer Forensics

According to one definition, computer forensics consists in "the preservation, identification, extraction, documentation, and interpretation of computer

33. See Nick Montfort, *Twisty Little Passages: An Approach to Interactive Fiction* (Cambridge: MIT Press, 2003); Noah Wardrip-Fruin and Pat Harrigan, eds. *First Person: New Media as Story, Performance, and Game* (Cambridge: MIT Press, 2004) and Jasper Juul, *Half-Real: Video Games Between Real Rules and Fictional Worlds* (Cambridge: MIT Press, 2005).

34. Noah Wardrip-Fruin and Nick Montfort, eds., *The New Media Reader*, (Cambridge: MIT Press, 2003) and Stephen Wilson, *Information Arts: Intersections of Art, Science, and Technology* (Cambridge: MIT Press, 2003).

data."[35] Other definitions also emphasize the data's status as physical evidence.[36] Computer forensics is the activity of recovering or retrieving electronic data, analyzing and interpreting it for its evidentiary value, and preserving the integrity of the data such that it is (potentially) admissible in a legal setting. At a practical level this means working with hard drives and other storage media in the field and in controlled laboratory settings to locate files, metadata, or fragments of files that someone may or may not have taken active steps to expunge, and creating the conditions necessary to ensure that the data has not been tampered with in the process of its recovery or analysis. Precedents, case law, and statutes date back to the late 1970s, but computer forensics has really only emerged as a professional specialization in the last five to ten years. There are now a number of textbooks on the shelves, growing numbers of specialized software tools (some retailing for many thousands of dollars), specialized hardware like self-contained drive imaging units, and elite corporate training programs. The most advanced computer forensics, however, undoubtedly happens not in commercial settings but through government agencies like the FBI, the NSA, the National Center for Computer Security, and the U.S. Department of Defense's Cyber Crime Center. Computer forensics in fact transcends the investigation of so-called cyber crime (such as identity theft) to claim a much broader purview. As the textbooks unfailingly point out, the search and seizure of digital evidence has become a routine part of many criminal investigations. The BTK Killer is an example of one recent high-profile case where computer forensics furnished the major break: Dennis Rader was identified and apprehended after residual data on a floppy disk he sent to a local TV station allowed authorities to pinpoint the computer where the disk's files had originally been created.[37] Likewise, popular awareness of computer forensics has grown through the popularity of television drama and genre fiction. Nor is its purview limited to desktop computers and laptops. One government lab I visited prides itself on its ability to retrieve and analyze data from the full spectrum of electronic devices: pagers, cell

35. Warren G. Kruse II and Jay G. Heiser, *Computer Forensics: Incident Response Essentials* (Boston: Addison-Wesley, 2002), 2.

36. For example, Eoghan Casey, *Digital Evidence and Computer Crime* (Amsterdam: Academic Press, 2000), 4.

37. As was widely reported in the media, for example, here: http://abcnews.go.com/WNT/story?id=539702&page=1.

phones, personal digital assistants, GPS units, digital watches, game consoles, digital cameras, magnetic access cards, programmable appliances, automotive chips, and more.[38]

The most relevant forensic science precedent for computer forensics is the field of questioned document examination, which dates back to the end of the nineteenth century. It concerns itself with the physical evidence related to written and printed documents, especially handwriting attribution and the identification of forgeries. Questioned document examination also bears some resemblance to the academic pursuits of analytical and descriptive bibliography (which emerged in an organized fashion during roughly the same years), but the forensic enterprise subjects the myriad physical implements of writing and inscription to a degree of scrutiny that might give even a hardened bibliographer pause. (Handwriting identification as it is practiced by a forensic expert is not to be confused with graphology, the more dubious practice of deriving personality traits from the appearance of an individual's handwriting; this approach was explicitly rejected by the earliest texts on document examination, including Persifor Frazer's *Bibliotics, or the Study of Documents* [1894, itself now largely discredited] and William Hagan's *Disputed Handwriting* [also 1894].[39]) The questioned document examiner is almost

38. On April 21, 2005 I visited the Department of Defense's Defense Cyber Crime Center (DC3 for short), located in an anonymous office park near Baltimore/Washington International airport. I was received by Special Agent Jim Christy, the director of the lab, who began his career as a computer crime investigator with the Air Force in the 1970s. In conversation with Christy, a genial and engaging host, it became clear that the lab's two biggest challenges were the sheer volume of incoming data, and maintaining its accreditation in the face of constantly changing software. In terms of volume, a typical case might involve analyzing a hard drive with 80 GB of data. This is the equivalent of 1,360 file cabinets or 34 million pages of written material. Much of the investigation is automated, with technologies such as data mining and visualization playing a growing role. But the core of the analysis must be performed manually. In a typical year, DC3 might handle a volume of data that would fill 15 miles of physical file cabinets. This number will only increase. As for accreditation, each new generation of forensic software has to be vetted in order for any evidence it yields to be legally admissible in court. Keeping abreast of the accreditation process is a significant drain on staff and resources given how quickly software in the lab evolves through new versions and releases.

39. Even Sherlock Holmes, author of a "little monograph" on the dating of documents, was not above the temptations of graphology: "'Look at his long letters,' he said. 'They hardly rise above the common herd. That *d* might be an *a*, and that *l* an *e*. Men of character always differentiate

always concerned with a document in its physical entirety. To quote Ordway Hilton, a contemporary authority:

Not only must these examiners be able to identify handwriting, typewriting, and printed matter, but they must be able to distinguish forgery from genuineness, to analyze inks, papers, and other substances that are combined into documents, to reveal additions and substations in a document, and to restore or decipher erased or obliterated writing. When records produced by complex modern business machines are suspected of having been manipulated, document examiners may be among the first to be consulted.[40]

Many of these activities have explicit parallels in computer forensics as it is practiced today. Recovering erased data, authenticating digital documents, and identifying the source of an electronic object are all routine activities for the specialist. But while computer forensics may seem like a natural extension of the questioned document examiner's purview—Hilton's reference to "modern business machines" seems to point the way forward—in practice the two have remained separate domains. Questioned document examination's reference works, even very recent ones, tend to treat "computer documents" exclusively in terms of hard copy.

Both questioned document examination and computer forensics belong to a branch of forensic science known as "trace evidence," which owes its existence to the work of the French investigator Edmond Locard. Locard's famous Exchange Principle may be glossed as follows: "a cross-transfer of evidence takes place whenever a criminal comes into contact with a victim, an object, or a crime scene."[41] Locard, a professed admirer of Arthur Conan Doyle who worked out of a police laboratory in Lyons until his death in 1966, pioneered the study of hair, fibers, soil, glass, paint, and other small things forgotten,

---

their long letters, however illegibly they may write. There is vacillation in his *k*'s and self-esteem in his capitals'" (Sir Arthur Conan Doyle, *The Sign of Four*).

40.   Hilton, *Scientific Examination of Questioned Documents*, Revised Edition (New York: Elsevier, 1982), 4.

41.   Joe Nickell and John F. Fischer, *Crime Science: Methods of Forensic Detection* (Lexington: University Press of Kentucky, 1996), 10.

primarily through microscopic means. His life's work is the cornerstone of the stark dictum underlying contemporary forensic science: "Every contact leaves a trace." This is more, not less, true in the delicate reaches of computer systems. Much hacker and cracker lore is given over to the problem of covering one's "footsteps" when operating on a system uninvited; conversely, computer security often involves uncovering traces of suspicious activity inadvertently left behind in logs and system records. The 75-cent accounting error that kicks off Clifford Stoll's *The Cuckoo's Egg*, a hair-raising account of computer detective work that culminated in the seizure of several Eastern Bloc agents, is a classic example of Locard's Exchange Principle in a digital setting.[42]

Insights from computer forensics have the potential to overturn many of the chestnuts governing the critical conversation on new media and electronic textuality. Marcos Novak asserts the following, for example: "Everything that is written and transmitted via electronic media is erasable and ephemeral *unless* stored or reinscribed (emphasis added)."[43] My contention would be that the subordinating conjunction "unless" is called upon to do a great deal of unrealistic work. Practically speaking, most things that are written and transmitted via electronic media *are* stored and reinscribed. A simple e-mail message may leave a copy of itself on a half a dozen different servers and routers on the way to its destination, with the potential for further proliferation via mirrors and automated backup systems at each site. As storage costs continue to

42. See Clifford Stoll, *The Cuckoo's Egg* (New York: Pocket Books, 1989). For a more literary expression of the exchange principle, there is this passage from Hari Kunzru's novel *Transmission* (New York: Dutton, 2004): "Whenever he entered and left the secure area, his bag was checked for storage media. As numerous laminated signs in the corridor pointed out, if a disk went into the [anti-virus] lab it did not come out again" (51).

43. See Novak's passionate online essay "TransTerraForm" at http://www.krcf.org/krcfhome/ PRINT/nonlocated/nlonline/nonMarcos.html. The sentence I quote is in the context of a broader argument that sets up a contrast between the supposed ephemerality of digital inscription and the literal inscription of microchips, which Novak describes as "immensely compactified books, active yet permanent, carved enduringly in silicon." Novak's essay is a meditation on the coming liquidity of inscription in chip design (of the sort now being realized by the MRAM technology I briefly discuss in the introduction). It is therefore unfortunate that the silicon chip is put forward as the primary site of inscription in the computer's architecture; the notion of "erasable, liquid" hardware configurations is a tantalizing one, but Novak misses the fundamental sense in which inscription is the essence of computer storage media, which is presented in the essay only as the site of the absent trace.

plummet, the trend will no doubt be to save more and more data so that the variety of ephemera routinely written to disk becomes ever more granular. Likewise, even the popular myth that RAM is always absolutely volatile, gone forever at the flip of a switch, proves false; there are at least experimental techniques for recovering data from RAM semiconductor memory.[44] While it may be technically possible to create the conditions in which electronic writing can subsist without inscription and therefore vanish without a trace, those conditions are not the medium's norm but the special case, artificially induced by an expert with the resources, skill, and motive to defeat an expert investigator.[45] For the remainder of this section I want to focus on three specific sets of observations from computer forensics in order to challenge some of the common assumptions about electronic textuality that characterize what I have been calling the medial ideology. They are as follows: that electronic text is hopelessly ephemeral, that it is infinitely fungible or self-identical, and that it is fluid or infinitely malleable.

Ephemerality Lay users often know that when they delete a file from their trash or recycle bin it is not immediately expunged from their hard drive. What happens instead is that the file's entry in the disk's master index (on Windows machines called the File Allocation Table or FAT, which we will discuss in more detail in the next chapter) is flagged as space now available for reuse. The original information may yet persist for some time before the

44. See, for example, Peter Gutmann's discussion in "Data Remanence in Semiconductor Devices," http://www.cypherpunks.to/~peter/usenix01.pdf.

45. Some readers may immediately think of dev/null, the file on the UNIX operating system used as a "bit bucket" because it is not attached to a disk or any other physical hardware device. Writing to dev/null consigns data to virtual oblivion, but while the existence of dev/null is common knowledge piping data to it is not the same as performing a secure deletion of a previously saved file. A further case in point, demonstrating the extremes one must go to in order to avoid leaving trace evidence, is a net art project by Greg Sidal. His "Illicit Images" consists of a set of color ink jet renderings of commercial image files originally harvested from the Web using automated collection routines routed through anonymous redirection services (to avoid leaving traces in access logs). These images are then encrypted so as to destroy all semblance of their previous identity, the randomly generated encryption keys themselves are securely deleted, and the hard drives in the machines on which all of these operations took place eventually physically destroyed. See http://www.asci.org/digital2001/sidal/sidal.htm.

operating system gets around to overwriting it. Indeed, because a file's physical storage location will change each time it is opened and modified, its earlier incarnations will also persist until such time as that data may be overwritten. The easiest way to recover data, therefore, is by simply locating a "deleted" file on the storage media after its entry has been stripped from the FAT but before any new data has been written to the same location. This is typically the way commercial recovery utilities work, hence the standard instruction to allow as little time as possible to elapse before attempting to restore a lost file. As hard drive capacities continue to increase, information will persist for longer and longer amounts of time on the surface of the platter before it is overwritten even once, thus expanding the window in which stored data remains recoverable.

But that alone does not account for the uniquely indelible nature of magnetic storage, or the uncompromising pronouncements of computer privacy experts like Michael Calonyiddes: "Electronic mail and computer records are far more permanent than any piece of paper."[46] Creating a file and saving it to a hard drive does not yield a simple one-to-one correspondence between the document (or file of whatever type) and its record on the disk. First, word processors and other productivity software routinely include an auto-save function that writes a snapshot of an open file to the disk at set intervals. The presence of such files is not always obvious: often they have opaque or arbitrary-seeming names (a copy of this document, for example, currently exists in one of my temporary directories as ~WRL0005.tmp). Nor do they always appear in standard directory listings (this same file would be invisible to me if the directory was configured to only display files with common extensions).[47] This phenomenon is sometimes known as "ambient data", the term emphasizing the way in which records accumulate on a file system absent the intervention of any single, conscious (human) agency. Most computers also use a portion of their hard disk as an extension of their RAM, a type of storage known as virtual memory or swap space. Forensic investigators recover all manner of otherwise-ephemeral matter, including passwords and encryption keys, from the swap space. So-called slack space—not to be confused with swap space—presents yet another opportunity for extracting remnants of supposedly

46.   Michael Caloyannides, *Computer Forensics and Privacy* (Norwood, MA: Artech House, 2001), 4.

47.   Caloyannides, 25.

long-discarded files. Data on a magnetic hard drive is stored in clusters of a fixed length; 4096 bytes is typical. (This is what accounts for the discrepancy between the actual size of a file and its "size on disk," as revealed by Windows Properties; even a one byte file—a single ASCII character—will require the allocation of a full 4096-byte cluster to store.) If a file is smaller than that (or larger, but not equivalent in size to some precise multiple of 4096), then the extra space in the cluster is filled out by information in the computer's RAM memory at the moment the file is committed to disk. But since files themselves are rarely the exact same size (and hence occupy variable numbers of clusters), it is also frequently possible to find the partial remains of earlier files at the end of a so-called cluster chain, a phenomenon sometimes known as "disk slack" (as opposed to file slack). A skilled investigator develops an instinct for where slack of either kind is to be found. The problem is exacerbated still further by the fact that in addition to temporary copies and other multiples of the actual file, metadata—the name of the file, the file type, date and time stamps—proliferates even more aggressively through the operating system, so even if the *content* of a file is completely erased it is still possible to recover evidence testifying to its past presence.[48] The interactions of modern productivity software and mature physical storage media such as a hard drive may finally resemble something like a quantum pinball machine, with a single simple input from the user sending files careening n-dimensionally through the internal mechanisms of the operating system, these files leaving persistent versions of themselves behind at every point they touch—like after-images that only gradually fade—and the persistent versions themselves creating versions that multiply in like manner through the system. There is, in short, no simple way to know how many instances of a single file are residing in how many states, in how many different locations, at any given moment in the operating system. Thus, as one textbook has it, "Deleted file information

---

48. "[C]omputers," Caloyannides opines, "are a forensic investigator's dream because, in addition to the files themselves, they contain data about the data" (35). Caloyannides devotes particular attention to the "registry," which on Windows systems is actually a confederation of files that store basic, persistent information about the state of the user's system, including (potentially) indelible records of every piece of software installed (and removed), internet browsing histories, names and other personal identifying data, and so forth. A privacy activist as well as an author, Caloyannides makes it his business to describe in detail how to purge a registry of potentially incriminating content.

is like a fossil: a skeleton may be missing a bone here or there, but the fossil does not change until it is destroyed."[49] Nor is there any simple way to know how many metadata records of a file (or any of its ambient versions) exist. Given all this, it is not hard to see why one expert is left to conclude, "Secure file deletion on Windows platforms is a major exercise, and can only be part of a secure 'wipe' of one's entire hard disk. Anything less than that is likely to leave discoverable electronic evidence behind."[50]

Fungibility The preceding should make clear the extent to which a lay user's view of a file system—accessed only through standard directory structures or a Find function, or with the aid of menus, and manipulated using commands like Copy, Rename, and Remove—is optimized and impoverished, a partial and simplistic window onto the diverse electronic records that have accumulated on the surface of the magnetic disk. Because of this, when a hard disk is duplicated for forensic investigation it is not enough to simply copy the files in the usual manner (dragging and dropping the folders). Instead, an investigator will want to create a so-called bitstream image of the original file system. A bitstream is exactly that: every bit recorded on some original, physical instance of storage media is transferred in linear sequence to the copied image, whether it is part of a file currently allocated in the FAT or not. This means that all of the other ambient data on the original media is retained as part of the forensic object, including even (if the process is done right) data in "bad" or corrupted sectors no longer otherwise accessible. Since no forensic lab wants to work on the original source media and risk compromising its integrity, the proper execution of the imaging process is essential for creating legally admissible digital evidence. Legally, a bitstream copy of the original bits can usually stand in for the original digital object—what is known in courtroom parlance as documentary, rather than merely demonstrative, evidence.[51] While bitstream drive imaging and its legal status as documentary evidence would seem to reinforce the familiar postmodern argument about the digital simulacrum—copies without an original—it in fact underscores

49. Dan Farmer and Wietse Venema, *Forensic Discovery* (Upper Saddle River, NJ: Addison-Wesley, 2005), 159.

50. Caloyannides, 28.

51. See http://faculty.ncwc.edu/TOConnor/426/426lect06.htm for more on the distinction between documentary and demonstrative evidence in the context of applied computer forensics.

the heterogeneity of digital reproduction. The more mundane kinds of file reproduction we all perform in our daily interactions with a computer fall short of the forensic ideal.

Nor are these necessarily matters solely of relevance to legal investigation and standards of juridical evidence. In 2001, new media artist Joshua Davis (best known for praystation.com) released the Praystation Hardrive [*sic*], a limited edition CD-ROM consisting of "original source files, art, text, accidents, epiphanies, all as they appear in Davis' own hard drive ... 397 folders, 3637 files, 462 Meg of raw data: a snapshot of the studio of a major new media artist, frozen and time and delivered to you for exploration, study, inspiration, and for use in your own work."[52] Accompanied by liner notes pointing out highlights and packaged in a black plastic case vaguely reminiscent of a hard drive, the work is admirable in a number of ways: it manifests an open source ethos of creativity that feeds off of ever more capacious storage media, media that allows innumerable versions and layers and masters and derivatives to co-exist without the need to delete the extraneous matter to make room for more. It is also an invaluable historic document that captures a working set of software practices, the kind of artifact we need to learn to cultivate and appreciate. There is even a photo section featuring seemingly random personal photos of trips to San Diego and Paris. Rather than an executable launch platform, the only interface to the CD-ROM's content is the user's own desktop, where it is simply appended to the file system to be accessed via the normal directory navigation tools. Nonetheless, the data is not quite as raw as we are led to believe (figure 1.3). This is not a bitstream copy of the sort described above, and it is far indeed from a forensically sound copy of the hard drive itself, since none of the ambient data that would represent the systems-level workings of the files is present. Despite the conceit that we have been granted unmediated access to Davis's hard drive (or its digital surrogate), there is a greater artifactual distance between this copy and the original data objects than most users would commonly acknowledge. While I would not want to suggest that the failure to produce a bitstream simulacrum compromises Davis's project in any meaningful way, it does expose the merely rhetorical nature of some of its claims about the rawness of the data it provides. More importantly for my purposes, the example demonstrates the heterogeneity that I have asserted

52. Text quoted from the Eastgate Systems catalog entry, http://www.eastgate.com/catalog/Praystation.html.

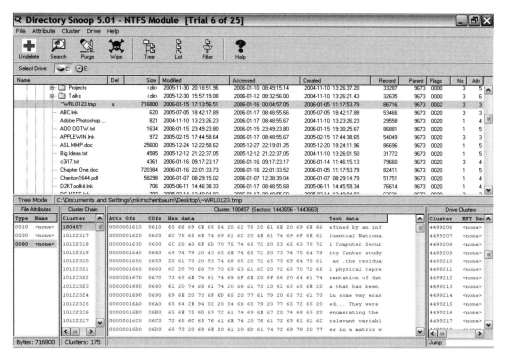

Figure 1.3 View of the author's own desktop through a hex editor, here featuring a "deleted" "temporary" copy of the current file for this chapter. This kind of ambient data is not available on the Praystation CD, though it would have been present on Davis's file system. Screenshot by the author.

attends different kinds of digital copies, and serves to defamiliarize the Copy command itself—a command so mundane that we find it under every Edit menu, but which in fact condenses complex behaviors related to storage media, file integrity, and the various states data can inhabit.

The integrity of a bitstream image can be verified using as technique known as hashing. As we will see in the next chapter, hashing is a long-established electronic textual operation that has a role in domains ranging from error checking to cryptography. A hash algorithm generates a numeric value that is the mathematical surrogate for a particular bitstream. If the bitstream is altered in any way, by even so much as a keystroke, its hash value will be compromised, providing evidence of the tampering. Here is how one forensics textbook explains a cryptographic hash such as MD5 (developed by

Ronald Rivest, the MIT cryptographer who also worked on the popular RSA public key encryption standard):

A cryptographic hash algorithm is a one-way form of encryption, taking a variable-length input and providing a fixed-length output. As long as the size of the original object is within the operational restraints of a particular implementation, it is statistically impossible for cryptographically secure hash algorithms to allow two different source files to have intersecting values, effectively making the hash value into the fingerprint of the original file. Such an algorithm is designed to be collision free, meaning that it is functionally impossible to create a document that has the same cryptographically secure hash value as another document. Because of this characteristic, a hash value can serve as a surrogate for the object it is derived from.[53]

Hashing thus demonstrates that electronic objects can be algorithmically individualized. If Locard's Exchange Principle is the first basic tenet of forensic science, the second is individualization—the core faith that no two objects in nature are ever exactly alike, and no two objects ever break or wear down in the same way. Individualization, which we will explore in more detail later, is the principle underlying standard identification techniques like fingerprinting and DNA. An MD5 hash, which yields 2^{160} different values, is in fact a more reliable index of individualization than DNA testing.[54]

Fixity and Fluidity   We tend to fixate on the fluidity of electronic text, its malleability and putative instability. Yet there is nothing essentially fluid about data in an electronic environment, and there are important areas in which the stability and verifiability of electronic documents is essential, ranging from secure e-commerce to security and defense. Anyone who has ever needed to edit a file in a directory to which they do not have access rights knows exactly how stubbornly resilient electronic text can suddenly become. On a more specialized level, Intelligent Computer Solutions has developed a product line popular in the forensics and law enforcement communities called Image MaSSter DriveLocks:

53.   Warren G. Kruse II and Jay G. Heiser, *Computer Forensics* (Boston: Addison-Wesley, 2002), 89; emphasis in original.

54.   Kruse and Heiser, 89.

Designed exclusively for Forensic applications, the DriveLock IDE device provides a secure hardware write protect solution for hard disk drives. Sensitive Forensic hard disk drive data can be previewed, acquired or analyzed without the possibility of altering the drive's contents. The device is designed to block write commands sent to hard disk drives connected through the computer's P-ATA interface. No special software is needed. The unit is compact and is easily portable.[55]

The existence of tools and technologies like DriveLocks and digital watermarking or signatures should remind us that the conditions governing electronic textuality are formal conditions—artificial arrays of possibility put into play by particular software systems. Just as the electronic textual field can be thrown open to revision by virtue of its susceptibility to formal manipulation, so too can this potential be—formally—foreclosed. (The ultimate arbitrariness of the situation is perhaps best brought home by the inevitable existence of the Image MaSSter's antiproduct, WipeMaSSter, marketed by the same parent company and "designed as a compact, standalone hardware solution for sanitizing and erasing drive data for up to nine drives simultaneously at speeds exceeding 3GB/min.")[56]

Secure digital document design—creating documents that can be electronically signed and sealed as guarantors of authenticity—is currently a thriving field. And questions of authenticity are directly related to an electronic object's ability to not only resist but also to expose tampering. Johanna Drucker, in an illustrated essay in the type design magazine *Émigré*, makes the point with characteristic acuity: "The authority of written documents . . . does not depend upon their pristine and unaltered condition. Quite the contrary—it is the capacity of the material documents to record change that makes them such believable witnesses."[57] Michael Hancher, in a perceptive essay that amply demonstrates the fruits of a textual scholar's encounter with electronic media, argues much the same point, by way of the eighteenth century legal theorist William Blackstone.[58] For Blackstone, the

---

55.   http://www.atp-p51.com/html/drivelock.htm.

56.   http://www.atp-p51.com/html/wipemasster.htm.

57.   Johanna Drucker, "The Future of Writing in Terms of its Past: The New Fungibility Factor." *Émigré* 35 (Summer 1995).

58.   Michael Hancher, *Littera Scripta Manet*: Blackstone and Electronic Text," *Studies in Bibliography* 54 (2001): 115–132.

most suitable surface for deeds, contracts, and other official documents was paper rather than stone, leather, wood, or other writing surfaces, which were not unknown in an era when linen rag paper was expensive and comparatively scarce. Paper, however, has the virtue of being both durable and secure— secure meaning precisely that it is fragile and vulnerable enough to readily reveal tampering. Stone, on the other hand, is inviolate—stains could be lifted or otherwise expunged without physically damaging the underlying surface, thus affording no guarantee that the writing has not been tampered with (122–123). Hancher then extends the argument to electronic text and suggests neither that it is not durable (he realizes that durability consists in multiplication as well as persistence), nor that it is not secure (he is aware of state-of-the-art technologies using electronic keys and signatures). Rather, his point is that authenticating electronic documents requires the services of an expert "postmodern technician" because "it deals with a disembodied reality inaccessible to and unassessable by the laity" (130). The fact that one can educate oneself in the particulars of electronic keys and signatures notwithstanding, most users will simply not have entrée to the mechanisms governing their individual interactions with supposedly secure and authentic electronic information. According to Hancher, one must ultimately take the security of electronic documents on "faith" (131).

Regardless, electronic document security—situated at the intersection of encryption, computer security, e-commerce, digital rights management, and digital archives and records management—can only underscore the limited and arbitrary nature of any medial ideology that celebrates only the fluidity and fungibility of electronic text. Powerful and well-financed constituencies are lobbying for a very different electronic textual condition, and the research and development is well under way.

None of what I have been describing yet accounts for the physical properties of magnetic media, or for the behavior of the drive's actual writing mechanism (which is responsible for a phenomenon known as shadow data, when bit representations turn out to be imperfectly overwritten). I will discuss these in the next section.

Inscription and Instrumentation

A document such as the Clearing and Sanitization Matrix is born of electronic data's eventual (and often immediate) status as inscribed trace; that is, an intervention in or modification of a physical substratum. We see this vividly in the phenomenon of data remanence, the physical remains of data deposited on computer storage media:

As early as 1960 the problem caused by the retentive properties of AIS [automated information systems, i.e., computers] storage media (i.e., data remanence) was recognized. It was known that without the application of data removal procedures, inadvertent disclosure of sensitive information was possible should the storage media be released into an uncontrolled environment. Degaussing, overwriting, data encryption, and media destruction are some of the methods that have been employed to safeguard against disclosure of sensitive information. Over a period of time, certain practices have been accepted for the clearing and purging of AIS storage media.[59]

This concern is not limited to national security and shadowy government agencies. Corporations and institutions of all kinds, not to mention private individuals, routinely discard computers, often with little or no attention to the risk of data remaining intact on the hard drive. One recent study examined a sampling of discarded hard drives and found that nearly all of them contained sensitive information that was recoverable to varying degrees.[60] Indeed, sometimes not even a token attempt had been made to delete files from the disk. In other cases the utilities used were insufficient to address the ambient data that had accumulated. Contrary to popular belief, initializing a disk does *not* erase or overwrite all of its data; it only erases the FAT and resets the basic formatting information. Actual data remains on the disk, and can be recovered using well-known techniques.[61]

59. National Computer Security Center, "A Guide to Understanding Data Remanence in Automated Information Systems," NCSC-TG-025, http://all.net/books/standards/remnants/index.html.

60. Simson L. Garfinkel and Abhi Shelat, "Remembrance of Data Passed: A Study of Disk Sanitization Practices," *IEEE Security and Privacy* (January–February 2003): 17–27. The authors conclude: "With several months of work and relatively little financial expenditure we were able to retrieve thousands of credit card numbers and extraordinarily personal information on many individuals. . . . If sanitization practices are not significantly improved, it's only a matter of time before the confidential information on repurposed hard drives is exploited by individuals and organizations that would do us harm" (27).

61. See Garfinkel and Shelat, 17–27.

The considerations in play here go a step beyond those discussed in the previous section, where the problem of deleting data was strictly a function of its proliferation under a swarm of system processes not directly controlled by the user. Data remanence is also a function of the physical properties of storage media and the difficulty of reversing or obscuring what are tangible interventions in a physical medium. "Virtually all erasures can be detected by a thorough examination," wrote Ordway Hilton in his *Scientific Examination of Questioned Documents* (96). But he may as well have been talking about computer storage media. "You can't really erase a hard drive," unequivocally state the authors of one computer forensics textbook, likening it to the way a child's Etch A Sketch retains the images of previous drawings.[62] In fact you *can* erase a hard drive, but it is a deliberate and painstaking process, best attempted with the proper tools by an expert who understands the full extent of the issues involved. (Better still, perhaps, to simply run it over with a tank, as the NSA originally suggested, though modern data recovery abounds with seemingly miraculous stories of data extracted from hard drives subjected to near-Biblical levels of fire, flood, and blunt force trauma.[63] The recoveries performed on the World Trade Center hard drives are one such example.)

The paper that made much of this common knowledge within computer security and privacy circles was published in 1996 by Peter Gutmann, a researcher at the University of Auckland. Titled "Secure Deletion of Data from Magnetic and Solid-State Memory," Guttman's paper begins by making

62. Kruse and Heiser, 77.

63. Some of the best tales of data recovery I know come from the Web site of a company called DriveSavers, which includes testimonials from the likes of Keith Richards, Sean Connery, Sarah Jessica Parker, Sting, Industrial Light and Magic, and Isaac Hayes. Yet one client in particular stands out. As the Web site tells it, a technician was working on the hard drive of someone he assumed must be a hardcore *Simpsons* aficionado: the disk was full of character stills, icons, animations, renderings, etc. Then the technician came across a folder labeled "Scripts." It turned out that the drive belonged to a writer for the show, and the damaged disk contained the only copies of the scripts for twelve then unproduced episodes. The scripts, which included the famous season finale "Who Shot Mr. Burns," were all recovered successfully. Thus at least one signature artifact of pop culture owes its existence to the art of forensic data recovery. Other entries on the site tell of recovering data from laptops submerged in the Amazon river, scorched in house fires, and overrun by an 18-wheel truck. See http://www.drivesavers.com/fame/index.html.

the point that while most of what we know about data remanence comes from intelligence agencies, it is not in these sources' best interests to disclose everything they actually know.[64] Therefore he cautions against underestimating official capabilities. His point of departure is an esoteric technology known as magnetic force microscopy, or MFM. Pioneered in the late 1980s, magnetic force microscopy was and is the method of choice for imaging data representations recorded on magnetic media. Its primary application is not forensic recovery but industrial research and development: MFM studies are an integral part of evaluating laboratory advances in magnetic recording. MFM is actually an umbrella term for several closely related procedures and technologies, all based on the scanning tunneling microscope (STM; a variety of electron microscope), and it in turn offers only one of several known methods for imaging magnetic phenomena. A magnetic force microscope, as the name implies, is essentially a feedback device. A flexible probe, made of iron, is positioned just above the surface of a magnetic media. Figure 1.4 is an example of the kind of output generated.

What we see here are not simply bits, but patterns of magnetic flux reversals, a number of which may be necessary to constitute a single bit (which I discuss in more detail in chapter 2). Thus while bits are the smallest symbolic units of computation, they are not the smallest inscribed unit, a disjunction that underscores the need to distinguish between the forensic and the formal in discussions of computational materiality.

In order to generate these images, the tip of the microscope is moved above the surface of the platter, typically at a distance of only a few nanometers. Electrons "tunnel" from the surface of the platter to the tip of the probe, repelling or attracting it; the microscope, meanwhile, exerts greater or lesser force to keep the tip at a constant distance from the surface. Thus, the energy

64. Peter Gutmann, "Secure Deletion of Data from Magnetic and Solid-State Memory," first published in the *Sixth USENIX Security Symposium Proceedings*, San Jose, California, July 22–25, 1996. Online at http://www.cs.auckland.ac.nz/~pgut001/pubs/secure_del.html. Gutmann's paper has not gone without challenge and critique. Daniel Feenberg, a researcher at the National Bureau of Economic Research, contends that it is "overwrought," pointing out that there has never been a known, actual instance of MFM technology being employed for forensic data recovery by an intelligence agency or other government entity. See http://www.nber.org/sys-admin/overwritten-data-guttman.html. Nonetheless, MFM serves to demonstrate the irreducibly physical basis of digital inscription.

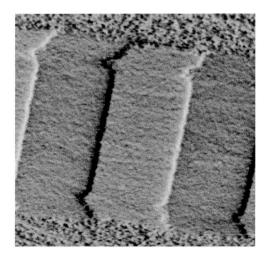

Figure 1.4 Magnetic force microscopy (MFM) image of bits on the surface of a hard disk. 15 × 15 microns (μm). http://web.archive.org/web/*http://www.boulder.nist.gov/magtech/mfm .htm, Mar 06 2005.

the probe expends is the basis for measuring the magnetic force. The raw images are then subjected to layers of higher-level image processing to generate the kind of image depicted here. As a visual rendition of the magnetic fields active on the surface of the source media, an MFM image is ultimately more akin to a physician's ultrasound than the detective's magnifying glass. The bits themselves prove strikingly autographic, all of them similar but no two exactly alike, each displaying idiosyncrasies and imperfections—in much the same way that conventional letterforms, both typed and handwritten, assume their own individual personality under extreme magnification. It seems counterintuitive to think of bits as revealed artifacts—rectangular, with an aspect ration of 8:1, measuring here about $4 \times .5$ microns—yet this is where Hayles's "flexible chain of markers bound together by the arbitrary relations specified by the relevant codes" comes to its end, as an actual inscribed trace. (The smallest possible bits we can write are probably about 10 nanometers, 400 times smaller than what is the norm today. At this level bits will approach what scientists called the superparamagnetic limit—the point at which a physical surface area is no longer capable of retaining a magnetic charge.)

While MFM sounds like an exotic technology, Gutmann suggests barriers to its use are less than one might imagine:

Even for a relatively inexperienced user the time to start getting images of the data on a drive platter is about 5 minutes. To start getting useful images of a particular track requires more than a passing knowledge of disk formats, but these are well-documented, and once the correct location on the platter is found a single image would take approximately 2–10 minutes... (2)

Guttman concludes that "Faced with technologies such as MFM, truly deleting data from magnetic media is very difficult" (2). Data remanence of the sort that MFM exploits is ultimately a function of the physical properties of the magnetic substrate and the material limitations of the drive's write technology—the "inability of the writing device to write in exactly the same location each time"—as well as variations in sensitivity and the strength of magnetic fields on the source media (2). This effect satisfies the forensic principle of individualization, which insists upon the absolute uniqueness of all physical objects. The core precepts of individualization construct a hard materiality of the kind that ought to resonate with textual scholars and others in the traditional humanities: "No two things that happen by chance ever happen in exactly the same way; No two things are ever constructed or manufactured in exactly the same way; No two things ever wear in exactly the same way; No two things ever break in exactly the same way."[65] That the scale here is measured in mere microns does not change the fact that data recording in magnetic media is finally and fundamentally a forensically individualized process.[66]

65. Harold Tuthill *Individualization: Principles and Procedures in Criminalistics* (Salem, OR: Lightning Powder Co., 1994), 20.

66. On November 14, 2003, I visited Professor Romel Gomez at the Universiy of Maryland's Laboratory for Applied Physics. Professor Gomez heads the Lab's nanomagnetics group. I observed a Digital Instruments (now Veeco) magnetic force microscope in action. The device was recognizable as a microscope, with familiar elements such as a stage and ocular tubes. Three monitors provide views: one shows an optical magnification of the surface of the media sample, the second displays feedback from the instrumentation and settings, and the third displays reconstructed images of the magnetic data, both AFM and MFM. The process is time- and labor-intensive, more so than Guttman seems to suggest: acquisition rates hover around 1 bit (not byte) per second, and the surface area of a sample is small—perhaps five square millimeters.

The phenomenon that speaks most directly to electronic data's status as an individualized inscription is well-documented in the MFM literature: tracking misregistration. It occurs in two different forms. Large misregistrations leave the remnants of earlier data representations plainly visible along the edges of the track, exposed to forensic detection and recovery—a classic palimpsest effect, sometimes known as shadow data. "Given intrinsic limitations in the positioning of the head, this effect might be more ubiquitous than previously realized."[67] Thus when Bruce Clarke, a sophisticated theorist, writes "material . . . if deleted and overwritten, leaves no scratch on any surface" (31) he is correct only in the narrow, literal sense that electronic data does not impinge on the surface of its substrate in the form of a scratch.[68] In addition to the presence of shadow data, when new bits are recorded the positioning of the write head may also be off just enough that the magnetic field is strong enough to erase the old data, but not strong enough to successfully record the new data. This creates what is known as an erase band along the edges of the data track, a magnetic anomaly that has a characteristic signature when viewed with MFM imaging (see figure 1.5). The erase band is the blurred area near the top of each image where there is no definite magnetization of

---

If we do the math—eight bits in a byte—we can see that we might, assuming optimal conditions, be able to image seven or eight bytes per minute. A single 512 byte sector would require well over an hour to image completely. A relatively modest ten kilobyte text file would require 24 hours of continuous imaging under optimal conditions. A 1 MB media file would take months. Though recoveries of complete files are theoretically possible (through what is known in the trade as "heroic efforts"), the process would be extraordinarily painstaking and take weeks or months. For a good general introduction to MFM, see Gomez et al., "Magnetic Force Scanning Tunneling Microscopy: Theory and Experiment," *IEEE Transactions on Magnetics* 29 (November 1993): 2494–2499. A new technology, known as spin-stand imaging and capable of attaining much higher acquisition rates, is in development. See I. D. Mayergoyz et al., "Spin-Stand Imaging of Overwritten Data and its Comparison with Magnetic Force Microscopy," *Journal of Applied Physics* 89 (June 2001): 6772–6774.

67.   Gomez et al. (1993), 2499.

68.   Bruce Clarke, "Thermodynamics to Virtual Reality" in Bruce Clarke and Linda Dalrymple Henderson, eds., *From Energy to Information: Representation in Science and Technology, Art, and Literature*, (Stanford: Stanford University Press, 2002): 17–33.

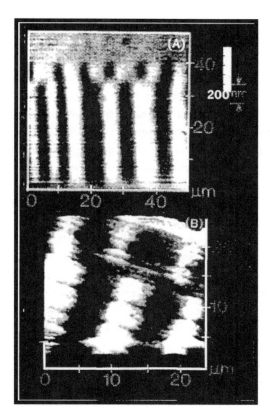

Figure 1.5 MFM erase band study. Taken from R. D. Gomez, E. R. Burke, A. A. Adly, and I. D. Mayergoyz. "Magnetic Force Scanning Tunneling Microscope Imaging of Overwritten Data," *IEEE Transactions on Magnetics* 28 (September 1992): 3141.

the source media. Also visible here are data imperfectly overwritten due to larger (relatively speaking) alterations in the positioning of the head as it makes successive passes over the same data track.

The conclusion researchers have reached describes a condition serving to distinguish magnetic recording from other kinds of inscription, such as ink staining a fibrous sheet of paper or the grooves incised on a wax cylinder:

For small tracking misregistrations, localized remnants of overwritten data may no longer be distinctly detectable but continue to perturb the system by its influence on the characteristic trackwidth variations of the newly created data. Thus, it is quite

"Every Contact Leaves a Trace"

possible that even with direct overwrite...complete elimination of the effects of previous data may not be achieved.[69]

Gutmann puts it this way: "Each track contains an image of everything ever written to it, but the contribution from each 'layer' gets progressively smaller the further back it was made" (3). In other words, magnetic inscription is a temporal as well as a planographic intervention, whereby even data that has been overwritten continues to resonate as a result of the ongoing oscillation of the magnetic field. This basic property of magnetic media is known as hysteresis. Gutmann's solution involves not erasing, but writing and rewriting— thus repressing the lingering effects of earlier data. The bulk of his paper develops a set of 35 patterns designed to ensure that ones are overwritten with zeros overwritten with ones, while zeros are overwritten with ones overwritten with zeros. This goes on through so many layers of recursion that eventually the ability of a scanning device (like MFM) to detect significant enough fluctuations in field strength to recuperate earlier data patterns is negated. Gutmann's patterns have since become canonical, so much so that disk sanitizing utilities encode them as an explicit option, as is visible in figure 1.6.

In many respects, MFM represents the continuation of a scientific imaging tradition dating back to Faraday's drawings of lines of magnetic force in the 1830s. Digital inscription is itself inseparable from practices of instrumentation, and the history of science and technology is marked by continuous attempts to visualize and render such insubstantial phenomena as the ether, electricity, and electromagnetism. Indeed, the ether into which digital objects are often said to vanish is a historically constructed and contested site, with a rich tradition of visualization and imaging/imagining that erupted in the late nineteenth century.[70] One outcome of an encounter with a technology like MFM is that "the virtual" turns out to be a more heterogeneous category than we may have first thought, since at least some of what is usually subsumed in that category is in fact not virtual, but only very small, so

69. Gomez et al. "Microscopic Investigations of Overwritten Data," *Journal of Applied Physics* 73.10 (May 1993): 6001–6003.

70. See, for example, Bruce J. Hunt, "Lines of Force, Swirls of Ether" in Bruce Clarke and Linda Dalrymple Henderson, eds., *From Energy to Information: Representation in Science and Technology, Art, and Literature*, (Stanford: Stanford University Press, 2002): 99–113.

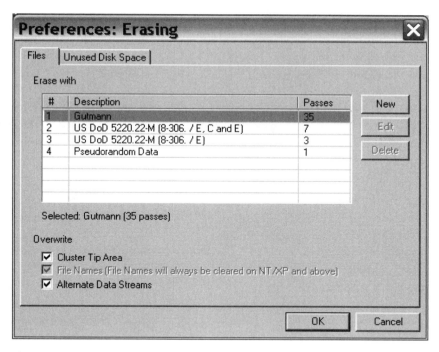

Figure 1.6 Preferences window of a popular utility for secure deletion called Eraser. The options for the 35 Gutmann patterns are available, as are various DoD-sanctioned patterns. Note too the option to erase unused disk space ("slack") alongside of actual files, something that is impossible with Windows systems commands alone. Screenshot by the author.

small as to be invisible to wave length optics even under the most extreme magnification.[71]

71. The history of microscopy in the forensic field of questioned document examination is instructive here. Recent textbooks treat the microscope briefly and unremarkably, assuming the investigator's knowledge of and readiness to employ the instrument. For example, David Ellen's *The Scientific Examination of Questioned Documents: Methods and Techniques* (New York: Wiley and Sons, 1989) matter-of-factly states: "Magnification is an important part of document examination. Some enlargement can be produced by the use of photography and video methods, and also by a magnifying glass, but the optical microscope is the most used tool of the examiner" (163). Hilton, meanwhile, devotes none of his pages to the microscope as such, but simply furnishes examples of its application throughout the text. This was not always the case, however. Albert S. Osborn's *Questioned Documents*, whose first edition was published in 1910, gives over an entire chapter to the role of the microscope, misconceptions about it, and the dangers of its potential

Yet magnetic force microscopy is also unabashedly an instrument in Bruno Latour's sense of the word: "I will call an instrument (or inscription device) any set-up, no matter what its size, nature and cost, that provides a visual display of any sort in a scientific text."[72] For Latour, it is essential that the instrument assumes a rhetorical disposition as evidence marshaled in the service of scientific discourse. This is the forensic function of the MFM images, not only in courts of law, but in science and engineering circles, where they contribute to insights related to the low-level physical properties of magnetic recording. Entire articles in the literature are given over to improving the computer-mediated image processing techniques used to render the images resulting from the MFM process, which it must be remembered are not optical magnifications but force-feedback renderings.[73] Ultimately, as Nathan Brown presciently argues, the scanning tunneling microscope (of which MFM is a subclass) "constitutes an event in the history of writing machines insofar as it makes marks on a scale *beyond* optics, at which visual (re)presentations are predicated on the radical priority of a haptic interface" (175; emphasis in original).[74] Our most persuasive evidence for the autographic individualization of

---

abuse. The following prose is characteristic: "The objections to the use of the instrument usually are based upon the somewhat natural but erroneous idea that if a thing exists that is really significant it can be seen by unaided vision. It seems to be overlooked by those who object to the microscope that ordinary spectacles are simply lenses placed between the eye and the object looked at . . . and that the most elaborate and complicated microscope is nothing more than an extension of this same principle. To be consistent one who objects to the use of the microscope should also insist that the judge and jury should be compelled to remove spectacles before examining a document that is questioned in a court of law" (74). Thus Osborn wants to buttress the spectrum of the "physical" so that the evidence refracted through the compound lenses of the microscope is finally no less persuasive than what might be seen with the naked eye, or the quotidian intervention of spectacles.

72. Latour, *Science in Action*, 68.

73. For example, I. D. Mayergoyz, A. A. Adley, and R. D. Gomez, "Magnetization Image Reconstruction from Magnetic Force Scanning Tunneling Microscopy Images," *Journal of Applied Physics* 73, no. 10 (May 1993): 5799–5801.

74. Nathan Brown, "Needle on the Real: Technoscience and Poetry at the Limits of Fabrication." *Nanoculture*, ed. N. Katherine Hayles (Bristol, UK: Intellect Books, 2004): 173–190.

bit-level digital inscription comes not from sight, but from the instrumental touch of the mechanism.

Coda: CTRL-D, CTRL-Z

The Consumer Electronics Show, Las Vegas, Nevada, 1978. The most popular personal computers on the market are Radio Shack's TRS-80, the Commodore PET, and the Apple II. All use off-the-rack television sets for their displays and a standard cassette recorder for data storage. After driving all day, Apple's Steve Wozniak and Randy Wigginton arrive at the convention hall. The centerpiece of their booth is the Disk II, the first floppy disk drive for the home computer market. In time, the Disk II would become as important and iconic a part of the Apple II's identity as the computer itself. Woz and Wigginton, working straight through the previous week, have written some wildly inventive routines that dramatically improve the response times of the high-end corporate disk systems the drive is modeled on, notably replacing hard sectoring—which keyed data storage geometries to a hole physically punched into the disk—with so-called "soft sectoring," which allowed DOS to arrange the physical media however it saw fit. Apple historian Steven Weyrich chronicles what happened next:

When they got to Las Vegas they helped to set up the booth, and then returned to working on the disk drive. They stayed up all night, and by six in the morning they had a functioning demonstration disk. Randy suggested making a copy of the disk, so they would have a backup if something went wrong. They copied the disk, track by track. When they were done, they found that they had copied the blank disk on top of their working demo! By 7:30 am they had recovered the lost information and went on to display the new disk drive at the show.[75]

Thus the disk handling routines that took the nascent personal computer industry by storm were accidentally overwritten on the very morning of their public debut—but recovered and restored again almost as quickly by those who had intimate knowledge of the disk's low-level formatting and geometry. Nowadays we toggle the CTRL-D and CTRL-Z shortcuts, deleting content and undoing the act at a whim. Gone and then back again, the keyboard-chorded Fort and Da of contemporary knowledge work.

75.   http://apple2history.org/history/ah05.html.

The perceived volatility of electronically recorded data is one of the signature affordances of new media, from casual users who "lose" files when hard drives crash or network accounts expire, to librarians, archivists, and others charged with the preservation of cultural heritage. Computer forensics counteracts this anxiety, teaching investigators to evaluate the relative stability or vulnerability of data in memory states and storage locales throughout an operating system. This tension between erasable and indefinitely retainable data storage was explicitly anticipated as a key element of designing usable digital computing machinery by pioneers like Norbert Wiener.[76] As we will see in the next chapter, the hard disk drive was a landmark achievement in computer engineering precisely because it offered a solution for erasable but nonvolatile random access storage. Computing is thus situated within a millennia-long tradition of reusable writing technologies, a tradition which also includes wax writing tables, graphite pencils, and correctible typewriter ribbons. We see this in the names of popular file removal utilities: Wiper, FileWiper, BCWipe, CyberScrub, Eraser, Shredder, Shred-It, Shred-X, Burn. Peter Gutmann's patterns for overwriting magnetic media are not so different in their way from the recipe for the ink and varnish used to create erasable surfaces for Renaissance writing tablets.[77]

For our purposes, contrasting experiences revolving around the erasure and the restoration of digital data can be usefully parsed as differences of forensic and formal materiality. Whereas formal materiality depends upon the use of the machine's symbolic regimen to model particular properties or behaviors of documents or other electronic objects (CTRL-Z thereby allowing one to "undo" a deletion by recapturing an earlier, still-saved state of file), forensic materiality rests upon the instrumental mark or trace, the inscription that is as fundamental to new media as it is to other impositions and interventions in the long technological history of writing. The Clearing and Sanitization Matrix with which we began the chapter clearly establishes the heterogeneity of

76. Wiener's exact prescription from *Cybernetics* (1964) was as follows: "That the machine contain an apparatus for the storage of data which should record them quickly, hold them firmly until erasure, read them quickly, erase them quickly, and then be available immediately for the storage of new material" (4).

77. For the key study of erasable writing tablets, see Peter Stallybrass, Rogier Chartier, John Mowery, and Heather Wolfe, "Hamlet's Tables and the Technologies of Writing in Renaissance England," *Shakespeare Quarterly* 55, no. 4 (Winter 2004): 379–419.

digital inscription—not just in the range of potential source media, but in the variety of procedures used to create, destroy, and recover data. Overwriting information is not the same as degaussing it. Degaussing methods employ two basic kinds of magnetic fields, alternating (AC) and unidirectional (DC); the strength of the field required to reset the magnetic media to its unrecorded state is known as the media's coercivity, measured in oersteds (Oe). A weak degausser cannot securely erase media rated at a coercivity above 750 Oe, as most hard disks are. Likewise, overwriting may use a variety of different patterns and schemas to ensure that every bit is superimposed by its symbolic inverse. The debate over the effectiveness of these different patterns, and the effort to develop new, even more effective ones, is ongoing. The point is one that will be familiar to any student of writing technologies: writing practices engender an eruption of tools and techniques to fix, expunge, and recover their meaning-bearing marks and traces.

Formally then, electronic data is pernicious by virtue of its susceptibility to symbolic propagation in an environment explicitly built and engineered to model ideal conditions of immateriality (the essence of digital computing, as we will discuss in chapter 3). Forensically, electronic data is survivable by virtue of both dramatically expanding storage volumes (which make it trivial to retain redundant copies of an electronic object) and the limits of the material mechanism, as revealed in the spectral erase bands visible in the MFM images. Here, at tolerances measured in microns, is where we begin to locate the forensic imagination.

2

Extreme Inscription: A Grammatology of the Hard Drive

Had however this friction really existed, in the many centuries that these heavens have revolved they would have been consumed by their own immense speed of every day . . . we arrive therefore at the conclusion that the friction would have rubbed away the boundaries of each heaven, and in proportion as its movement is swifter towards the center than toward the poles it would be more consumed in the center than at the poles, and then there would not be friction anymore, and the sound would cease, and the dancers would stop . . .

—LEONARDO DA VINCI, *THE NOTEBOOKS*, F 56 V

One Monday morning, one of my customers had their WIN NT 3.51 server hard drive crash. It was a head crash, you could hear the heads riding the platter. An awful noise . . . I spent 16 hours pulling data from that hard drive, and once I was done (I had pulled as much data as I could) we opened up the drive to discover that the head on the bottom platter had fallen down, and had been riding there over the weekend. It had etched away at the platter for so long that the platter had actually fallen down and was sitting in a pile of . . . shavings at the bottom of the drive.

—POSTED TO SLASHDOT.ORG BY JRHELGESON, MONDAY OCTOBER 06, 2003 @12:58PM

As a written trace, digital inscription is invisible to the naked eye but it is not instrumentally undetectable or physically immaterial. Saying so is not a theoretical proposition but a discernible fact, proven by the observable behavior of some 8.5 million terabytes of storage capacity brought to market in one recent year alone.[1]

I am referring to the devices we call hard drives. The hard drive, and magnetic media more generally, are mechanisms of *extreme* inscription—that is, they offer a limit case for how the inscriptive act can be imagined and executed. To examine the hard drive at this level is to enter a looking glass world where the Kantian manifold of space and time is measured in millionths of a meter (called microns) and thousandths of a second (milliseconds), a world of leading-edge engineering rooted in the ancient science of tribology, the study of interacting surfaces in relative motion.

Some may object that the attention I will be giving to the hard drive is arbitrary. Tape, not the more expensive disks, was the dominant industry choice for decades, and is still widely used. The late 1970s personal computer boom likewise got under way without the hard drive. They are, of course, by no means the only storage media in common use today, and many believe they will be supplanted, if not by solid state or laser optical devices then by more advanced techniques such as holography. Nonetheless, hard disk drives have been the primary storage media for personal computers since the mid-1980s, as well as for countless Internet and intranet servers. Though their speed, capacity, and reliability have all increased dramatically—increases in disk capacity have in fact outstripped the famous Moore's Law for processor speeds— basic drive technology remains remarkably unchanged since it was first introduced by IBM in the 1950s. The hard drive is therefore central to any narrative of computing and inscription in the second half of the twentieth century, yet it has received scant attention from critical observers of the new media.[2]

1. Simson L. Garfinkel and Abhi Shelat, "Remembrance of Data Past: A Study of Disk Sanitization Practices." *IEEE Security and Privacy* (January–February 2003): 17–27. Also available online at http://www.computer.org/security/garfinkel.pdf.

2. One recent exception appears to be an issue of the journal *Mediamatic* on "Storage Mania" edited by Geert Lovink, under the sign of Kittler: http://www.mediamatic.net/article-200.5944.html. Lev Manovich also makes passing mention of a "database complex," an "irrational desire to preserve and store everything" (274) but for him storage seems to collapse into the data structures of the database rather than actual storage devices themselves. The history of com-

Despite being (or really because it is) the most overtly mechanical component of the computer, a hard drive is physically sequestered from any direct observation. The drive resides within the machine's external case and is further isolated inside a sealed chamber to keep out dust, hair, and other contaminants. When a drive is opened for repair or data recovery the work is done in a clean room, similar to those used to print microprocessors. *Most users will never see their hard drive during the life of their computer.* As a writing instrument it thus remains an abstraction—presented as a pie chart to show disk space remaining—or else apprehended through aural rather than visual cues (the drive is audible as it spins up or down).[3] That the physical seclusion of the hard drive renders it an almost literal black box should not be underestimated as a reason it has gone unremarked upon in discussions of electronic textuality to date. As Lisa Gitelman has observed of early typewriters, which only brought a line of text into view after the next line had been typed, "The machine's upstrike design seemed to refute the possibility of error, however unrealistically, and in removing the act of inscription from the human eye seemed to underscore its character as a newly technological and automatic

---

puter storage media has also been well chronicled in corporate histories of the computer industry. See Charles J. Bashe, Lyle R. Johnson, John H. Palmer, and Emerson W. Pugh, *IBM's Early Computers* (Cambridge: MIT Press, 1986), and Edmund W. Pugh, Lyle R. Johnson, and John H. Palmer, *IBM's 360 and Early 370 Systems* (Cambridge: MIT Press, 1991).

3. The aural dimension of our experience of hard drives is not to be underestimated. Hard drive manufacturers routinely make recordings of sounds made by failing drives available online, so users can learn to recognize them in time to back up their data. In at least one instance, these have been remixed as techno compositions, with titles like "Crizzash" and "Drive Time (Jane's Book of Computer Disaster's Mix)." See http://gizmodo.com/gadgets/announcements/hard-drive-dying-dance-track-winner-151666.php. At my local Apple Store not long ago, I observed a technician diagnose an ailing hard drive by taking a laptop into the back room (where it was quiet) and listening to it for a minute or two. Nor should this be an unfamiliar phenomenon. Jay Clayton, in a critique of Friedrich Kittler's idiosyncratic historiography (that it gives short shift to communications over storage technologies), points to the profound importance of the sound of the machine among early telegraph operators: "Every nineteenth century book on the telegraph contains sections on the wonders of reading by sound" (65). See Clayton's *Charles Dickens in Cyberspace: The Afterlife of the Nineteenth Century in Postmodern Culture* (Oxford: Oxford University Press, 2003), 64–70.

event."[4] The hard drive occupies a similar position, I would argue, only one that is subject to vastly more complex forms of instrumentation and mediation. Since hard disks in most users' experience either work flawlessly or crash spectacularly, the notion of the device as a binary black box with no capacity for error short of global failure is perhaps inevitable. These functional extremes are precisely what reinforce the dominant perception of immateriality.[5]

A Book That Can Be Read Without Being Opened and A Day of Solid Achievement

Among the attractions at the 1958 World's Fair in Brussels, Belgium, visitors could behold Professor RAMAC, a four-ton IBM machine capable of offering up responses to users' queries on a two-thousand-year historical span ranging from "... the birth of Christ to the launching of Sputnik 1."[6] Described as an "electronic 'genius'" with "almost total historical recall and the ability to speak 10 languages" the Professor offered the general public its first encounter with the magnetic disk storage technology today called the hard drive. Technically known as the RAMAC 305, the machine had been developed at IBM a few years earlier and was then in use by a handful of corporate clients, notably United Airlines.[7] It was typically paired with an IBM 650, a general purpose business computer. The RAMAC was capable of storing five million 7-bit characters on 50 vertically stacked disks, each two feet wide and rotating at 1200 RPM. In contemporary parlance this means that the first hard drive

4. Gitelman, *Scripts, Grooves, and Writing Machines*, 206.

5. Yet error or global failure is often what brings the drive's quotidian materiality into brute force focus. A student offers this story of a friend who revived her dying hard drive long enough to get vital data off of it: "Here is what he did: took out the hard drive, put it in a ziploc, and *stuck it in the freezer overnight*. The metal contracts, and when you take it back out, it expands at different rates (for the different types of metal), allowing stuck bearings to come unstuck and non-spinning heads to spin up one last time." Personal e-mail to the author from Jess Henig, August 20, 2004, 12:28 PM.

6. My account of Professor RAMAC is heavily indebted to Mitchell E. Morris's historical article on the subject, "Professor RAMAC's Tenure," published in the industry magazine *Datamation* (April 1981): 195–198. I would like to acknowledge Paul E. Ceruzzi's *A History of Modern Computing* (Cambridge: MIT Press, 1998) as my source for the initial citation to Morris.

7. IBM's first corporate client took delivery on a RAMAC in June, 1956—perhaps ironically, it went to the Zellerbach Paper Company in San Francisco.

had a capacity of about 5 megabytes. The machine leased for $3200 a month, ran on vacuum tubes, and was taken off the market by 1961; some 1500 were manufactured in all.

When the RAMAC was first announced in 1956, Thomas J. Watson, Jr., president of IBM, opined that it was "the greatest product day in the history of IBM."[8] The remark was arguably not an overstatement. The RAMAC, which stood for Random Access Memory And Control, was, as its name implies, a random access storage device. This was fundamentally different from the punched paper or magnetic tape that then dominated the storage industry. As Paul E. Ceruzzi notes, "In time, the interactive style of computing made possible by random access disk memory would force IBM, as well as the rest of the computer industry, to redefine itself."[9] This is a powerful insight, and not often grasped by students of new media, who tend to ascribe "interactivity" to the advent of the screen display, the graphical user interface (GUI), and the mouse in a genealogy that runs from the SAGE air defense network through Ivan Sutherland's Sketchpad to Douglas Englebart's 1968 "mother of all demos." Yet the advent of random access disk storage goes to the heart of contemporary critical assumptions about new media. For Lev Manovich, for example, new media is characterized by a "database paradigm," manifested in the modular nature of a digital production's constituent objects and the lack of an essential narrative or sequential structure for how those objects are accessed and manipulated: "In general, creating a work in new media can be understood as the construction of an interface to a database."[10] While Manovich is reluctant to associate database and narrative with specific storage technologies in any deterministic sense—the codex book, he notes, is the random access device par excellence, yet it is a haven for some of our most powerful narrative forms (233)—computers could not have expanded from

---

8.   http://www-03.ibm.com/ibm/history/exhibits/650/650_pr2.html.

9.   Ceruzzi, *A History of Modern Computing*, 70. This was prefigured by earlier advances in storage. In the case of the UNIVAC, its revolutionary character was manifest to the end user less in its implementation of the stored program concept or the speed of its processor than, as Ceruzzi notes, in its magnetic tape storage system: "To the extent that its customers perceived the UNIVAC as an 'electronic brain' it was because it 'knew' where to find the desired data on a tape, could wind or rewind the tape to that place, and could extract (or record) data automatically" (30).

10.   Manovich, *The Language of New Media* (Cambridge: MIT Press, 2001), 226.

their role as wartime calculators to new media databases without the introduction of a nonvolatile, large-volume, inexpensive technology affording operators near-instantaneous and simultaneous access to all stored records. Magnetic disk media—more specifically the hard disk drive—was to become that technology and, as much as bitmapped-GUIs and the mouse, usher in a new era of interactive, real-time computing.[11]

In Brussels, the RAMAC's press kit promised the following:

Visitors to the fair will be able to ask the machine what were the most important historical events in any year from 4 B.C. to the present and RAMAC will print out the answers on an electronic typewriter in a matter of seconds. . . . A query to the professor on what events took place in the year 30 A.D., for example, would yield answers like this: "Salome obtained the head of Saint John the Baptist." In 1480? "Leonardo da Vinci invented the parachute." In 1776? "Mozart composed his first opera at the age of 11."[12]

There are several observations to make here, starting with the Professor's title and vocation. In 1950 Edmund C. Berkeley published a book entitled *Giant*

11.   Paul N. Edwards, in chapter 3 of his important *The Closed World: Computers and the Politics of Discourse in Cold War America* (Cambridge: MIT Press, 1996) argues that the Air Force's billion-dollar SAGE air defense network (developed and deployed from 1954–1961) was the first real-time computer system, hence the birth of interactive computing. SAGE was certainly the first real-time *distributed* computer system and, not coincidently, was instrumental in refining the performance of magnetic core memories, then the primary alternative to magnetic disk for random access storage. Moreover, SAGE operators used light pens to plot aircraft movements on the cathode ray tubes that were the first implementation of a real-time screen display. SAGE's significance to the history of both hardware and software cannot be overstated; as Edwards documents in detail, the demands of a real-time command and control network definitively tipped the balance of government funding in favor of digital over analog computation. See also Paul E. Ceruzzi, *A History of Modern Computing* (Cambridge: MIT Press, 1998), 49–53, and for a discussion of the importance of SAGE to the history of software, see Martin Campbell-Kelly, *From Airline Reservations to Sonic the Hedgehog: A History of the Software Industry* (Cambridge: MIT Press, 2003), 36–41. I would argue, however, that Edwards overlooks the simultaneous importance of the demand for inventory and production control solutions in both the military and commercial sectors as a catalyst for real-time computing, expressed in particular through IBM's development and marketing of the RAMAC.

12.   Morris, "Professor RAMAC's Tenure," 198.

Brains: or Machines That Think, the first work to introduce computers to a general audience.[13] The shift from Berkeley's anthropomorphism to the RAMAC's personification as a "professor" or "genius" hints at the kinds of synthetic identities that would culminate with Arthur C. Clarke's HAL 9000 only a decade later. Second, we should note that while the Professor's "almost total historical recall" was strictly hardwired—it could only respond to questions for which it had already been fed the answer—the notion of a computer endowed with an encyclopedic capacity (something we today take for granted in this era of world wide webs and electronic archives) would have then seemed quite novel. Much of the American public had first encountered computers during the 1952 presidential campaign, when the UNIVAC 5 (correctly) forecast Eisenhower's victory over Adlai Stevenson a month ahead of time on live TV. Computers were thus understood as instruments of prediction and prognostication, not retrospection. The RAMAC, by contrast, represented what was perhaps the first digital library. Its multilingual capability, a brute force flourish clearly meant to impress, is also worth a comment: in the context of the World's Fair it no doubt served to establish the machine's credentials as a global citizen with an omniscient and impartial command of the human record—at least until one realized that with the exception of Interlingua, an artificial language, the languages in question were those of the major European nations and the two postwar superpowers.[14] As perhaps the earliest computational personality on record (almost a decade before Weizenbaum's ELIZA), the Professor thus occupied a very specific geopolitical demographic, an archetypal denizen of what Paul N. Edwards has called the "closed world" of the Cold War.[15]

The problem that led to random access disk storage had been succinctly delineated a few years earlier by a government scientist at the National Bureau of Standards named Jacob Rabinow, in a 1952 article for the journal *Electrical Engineering*:

13. Edmund C. Berkeley, *Giant Brains: or Machines That Think* (New York: Wiley, 1950).

14. RAMAC knew English, French, Italian, Dutch, Spanish, Swedish, Portuguese, German, and Russian.

15. The Professor is probably even more aptly described as an ancestor to systems like BASEBALL, an "automatic question answerer" from the early 1960s that was capable of offering up vast stores of baseball trivia. See Nick Montfort, *Twisty Little Passages: An Approach to Interactive Fiction* (Cambridge: MIT Press, 2004), 81.

As the operations of government and private business become more varied in nature and larger in scope, the problem of adequate record keeping is continually becoming more acute. Not only is the volume of records rising to unprecedented magnitude, but also the time required to store and later reach this information is becoming continually of greater importance. (745)[16]

The prose here recalls Vannevar Bush, who in the far more famous essay "As We May Think" had seven years earlier used much the same language to describe the impetus behind his Memex, a microfilm-based document management system long celebrated as a prescient anticipation of electronic hypertext. Unlike the Memex, however, which was never actually built, magnetic disk storage became an industry reality in just a few short years. Rabinow, for his part, was sensitive to the precedents for his work within the history of writing technologies, noting that the "3-dimensional storage of information, as in a book, utilizes space most efficiently" (745). His idea was for a structure he described as a "doughnut," consisting of an array of disks suspended in vertical profile to a central spindle on which one or more read/write heads would be mounted; each disk would have a large notch that would allow the heads to pass through as the disks rotated about the spindle. Both sides of a disk would be available for data storage. One early model featured 147 20-inch aluminum disks (with the design expandable to 588 disks), and 128 heads; total storage capacity was to be about a quarter of a billion bits. It sounds like a bizarre and eccentric contraption, yet the codex book was an explicit touchstone:

The notched-disk memory "doughnut" can be thought of as a kind of book in which round pages are slotted in such a way that each line on each page can be read by merely spinning the page for one revolution; the notches in the pages provide the "windows" through which the selected page can be read. In other words, the book can be read without being opened. (746)

This is a rich passage, which gives us one of the very first glimpses of an electronic book. The comparison of disks to pages and of the concentric recording tracks (still a basic feature of magnetic disks today) to the lines on the page is also striking, an acknowledgement of the extent to which efficient inscription

16. Jacob Rabinow, "The Notched-Disk Memory," *Electrical Engineering* (August 1952): 745–749.

demands the rationalization of the writing space, regardless of medium. Perhaps most noteworthy, however, is the final line, the "book [that] can be read without being opened."[17] This image, a throwaway, seems to anticipate much in our own contemporary response to electronic storage media: the book has become a black box, and whatever is inscribed within its pages is destined for other than human eyes. Like the telegraph's automatic writing or the "call" of the telephone, the book that can be read without being opened offers up a whiff of the uncanny, a hint of haunted media.[18]

Rabinow's notched-disk doughnut was never brought to market. The solution for nonvolatile random access storage belonged instead to IBM, which had recently opened a West Coast lab in San Jose under the direction of Reynold B. Johnson, a seasoned inventor who had been given an Edison-like mandate to develop new projects.[19] New storage technologies were high on the priority list. As two IBM executives admitted in 1946, "The problem of electronic storage of numbers during the calculation is of fundamental importance, and we have no adequate solution of the problem."[20] Before the technology stabilized with magnetic tape and disk in the late 1950s, all manner of media and materials would be pressed into service to capture and record computer-generated data: paper cards and tape, but also cathode ray tubes, quartz crystals, glass filament, acoustic pulses in tubes of mercury, coils and

17. Terry Belanger of the University of Virginia Rare Book School informs me of the following: "In the RBS collections is a 'book,' which consists of a 1/4″ stack of 2″ paper disks, with a spiral binding around the entire circumference (with the result that the book cannot be opened). Its 'titlepage' (the top disk) has a single word on it: 'unbound.'" Personal e-mail to the author Wed, 10 Sep 2003 14:07:07.

18. I'm thinking here of Jeffrey Sconce's *Haunted Media: Electronic Presence from Telegraphy to Television* (Duke University Press, 2000) and Avital Ronell's *The Telephone Book: Technology—Schizophrenia—Electric Speech* (University of Nebraska Press, 1989). See also Gitelman (1999) and Kittler (1999) for discussions of automatic writing.

19. Johnson would later remark: ". . . I would be free to choose projects to work on. One half of my projects were to be new products and one half were to be devices in support of customers' special engineering needs. No projects were to be duplicates of work in progress at other IBM laboratories. The laboratory was to be dedicated to innovation." Quoted in Eric D. Daniel, C. Denis Mee, and Mark H. Clark, *Magnetic Recording: The First One Hundred Years* (New York: IEEE Press, 1999), 273.

20. Quoted in Bashe, Johnson, Palmer, and Pugh, *IBM's Early Computers*, 231.

loops of wire, magnetic ringlets, drums, doughnuts, plates, and finally disks. This diverse and exotic assortment of materials was prepared and treated with equally exotic layers of lubricants, coatings, and sealants. (Eventually the engineers at San Jose would borrow the same iron oxide paint that gives the Golden Gate Bridge its distinctive hue to magnetically coat their first disk platters.)[21]

The immediate impetus at San Jose for the research that led to the hard drive was the prospect of a contract with the U.S. Air Force, who wanted to automate inventory control for supply stocks. To appreciate the technical challenge posed by such a quotidian demand it is necessary to understand something about commercial and government data processing during the period. "Computing" consisted primarily of the batch processing of data stored on paper or magnetic tape. This worked well for tasks that could be performed in a regular and predictable manner—payroll accounts every Friday, for example—but was not practical for applications like inventory control that demanded ongoing and irregular access patterns.[22] Shipping clerks constantly needed to look up and modify records in no predictable order. Sequential access storage media such as paper or magnetic tape were of little use: conceivably the operator might need to go through an entire reel before arriving at the record in question. The medium of choice for random access data storage was punched paper cards, which clerks would keep in units resembling library catalog drawers, rifling through these so-called "tub files" manually to select a record, deliver it to a machine called a card reader, and then (manually) return it to the file. Obviously such cards, at least different portions of them, had to be legible to both the machines and the operators. Human- and machine-readable inscriptions thus coexisted and were codependent in the feedback loops of a rationalized workplace where cybernetic precepts, coupled with the new ideal of "automation," governed human-computer interaction.[23] (Such

21. Brian Hayes, "Terabyte Territory," *American Scientist* 90 (May–June 2002): 212–216. Hayes adds that the paint was first filtered through a silk stocking and then "poured onto the spinning disk from a Dixie cup" (212).

22. See Bashe et al., *IBM's Early Computers* 277–279.

23. According to Ceruzzi, "automation," as articulated by John Diebold, consisted in the application of cybernetic feedback mechanisms to business and the industrial workplace (32). Its proponents quickly embraced the UNIVAC and the new generation of general purpose digital computers.

scenes offer a glimpse of what digital textuality "looked like" before we could see it on a screen.)[24]

The language of cybernetics and automation was also conspicuous in IBM's press announcement for the RAMAC:

[B]usiness transactions will be completely processed right after they occur. There will be no delays while data is grouped for batch processing. People running a business will be able to get the fresh facts they need, at once. Random access memory equipment will not only revolutionize punched card accounting but also magnetic tape accounting. Automatic production recording [APR] will provide the much-needed link between the production floor and the data processing department. APR closes an important segment of the "loop" needed for full automation.[25]

This represented a significant realignment of workplace practices. It also foreshadows a massive realignment in textual practice. Statistically, electronic textuality is almost always automated textuality—which is to say that most of the textual events in a modern operating system, or network, occur without the impetus of a human agency. The kind of intentional writing we routinely do with a word processor or a text editor is actually responsible for only a small fraction of the electronic textual output of modern computing systems.

24. Indeed, there is much productive work to be done by scholars at the interface between paper and electronic systems during this early era of data processing. In the same 1956 press release as the RAMAC, for example, Watson announced a programmable electric typewriter, a reading and writing machine described in the following terms: "An electronic 'reading' device has been added to the IBM electric typewriter so that typists will no longer have to set tabulating stops while filling in the hundreds of different varieties of forms that are used every day in a business office. Business forms will be printed with vertical lines of electrically-conductive ink associated with each blank fill-in area for which the typist would normally set the tab. These lines, in effect, program the typewriter. No matter what variety of form the typist rolls into the machine, the tabs will be automatically set. All the typist need do is operate the tab key, and the machine, 'reading' the lines on the form, will position the carriage before the next fill-in area. The new typewriter will sell for $520." Henry W. Reis, Jr., sales manager of IBM's Electric Typewriter Division, added "Our endowing the typewriter with an 'electronic intelligence' is just one of the many strides we will make as we continue to incorporate scientific developments into the typewriter of the future." See http://www-03.ibm.com/ibm/history/exhibits/650/650_pr2.html.

25. http://www-1.ibm.com/ibm/history/exhibits/650/650_pr2.html.

Throughout the 1950s and on into the 1960s, the American populace was swept up in a wave of anxiety about automation, the most potent and immediate manifestation of which was workers' fears of losing their jobs to computers.[26] Indeed, the coming of even a literal Professor RAMAC did not seem too far-fetched in an era when "leading scientific journals will [soon] accept papers written by giant brains of the non-human kind."[27] While this most overt manifestation of automated electronic textuality was not to be, that automated textual processes were taking their place in the feedback loops governing increasingly intensive cycles of human-computer interactions could not be denied. A little over two decades later, DOS, the Disk Operating System, would arise precisely because of the need to displace the process of reading and writing data to and from the floppy or other magnetic media. The essential function of the operating system that thus paved the way for personal computing was to remove the inscriptive act from the direct oversight of the human user, screening it first by the command line and then by a graphical user interface. Read and Write (or later Save) became words to be typed or menu items to be selected rather than actions to be manually performed. The basic DOS repertoire (Copy, Rename, Remove) in fact constituted a robust inscriptive regimen.

Magnetic disk storage was thus borne of a deliberate strategy to exploit a segment of the market and make its workflow more efficient.[28] And automation was to again and again prove a critical locus for the development of electronic textual practice. For example, since data would be added to and removed from the disk in no predictable pattern, the drive's seeker head also needed to be able to find and access information that had been written or addressed to the disk in arbitrary arrangements. How does a mechanical device reliably identify and retrieve information once it is written to the disk in an unpredictable location? The "addressing problem," as it came to be known, proved to be one of the most formidable issues in the development

---

26. For a succinct overview of this phenomenon, see Sharon Gumari-Tabrizi, *The Worlds of Herman Kahn* (Cambridge: Harvard University Press, 2005), 31–35.

27. Gumari-Tabrizi, *The Worlds of Herman Kahn*, 33.

28. Specifically, the impetus came from an invitation to bid on a U.S. Air Force contract to automate its inventory control systems, a task requiring a random access solution for some 50,000 card records see Bashe et al., *IBM's Early Computers*, 279.

of disk storage, and the method by which it was resolved offers a unique window onto the textuality (and numeracy) of low-level data storage.[29]

The major figure here is Hans Peter Luhn, who was based at IBM's Poughkeepsie lab. Luhn is well known for his contributions to modern information retrieval, not least for his pioneering work on keyword-in-context indexing (KWIC). But in the early 1950s, he carried out the research on randomization and probability that became the basis for a solution to the RAMAC's addressing problem. Luhn began by rejecting the standard binary search model, which, interestingly, can be conveniently analogized by way of the codex book. An example of a binary search would be opening a telephone directory to the approximate middle, and depending on whether the individual being sought was listed prior to or antecedent to this opening, flipping the pages to the approximate middle of the first or second half of the book (thereby quartering the volume), and so on, each iteration of the search halving the area left to be examined until the phone number is located. While easily applied to computation, the accompanying mechanical process would have been slow in comparison to the actions of a human clerk.[30] The details of Luhn's approach involve a set of formal transformations to convert alphanumeric file names ("keys") into arbitrary (but deterministic) numeric strings of a predetermined length (called an "index"). Rather than seeking to exploit any latent structure in record names (for example, a tendency to assign each sequential record a numeric identifier one digit higher than its predecessor), he opted for an absolutely arbitrary solution. To quote Bashe et al.: "His fundamental insight was to see merit in deliberately abusing keys, thereby attempting to destroy every vestige of structure" (291). The values thus created were used to leverage the problem of access; structure—and with it predictable access routines for the drive's mechanical read head—emerged from normal patterns of statistical distribution among the numeric indices rather than from any kind of semantic correlation between index and key. Yet Luhn's method was precisely not random; a given key would always yield the same unique index. This technique is now known as "hashing" and it plays a major role in cryptographic authentication, error detection and correction, forensic computing, and numerous other domains besides data storage, many of them covered in this book. Here

29. My description of the addressing problem in this and the next paragraph is heavily indebted to Bashe et al., *IBM's Early Computers* 288–293.

30. Bashe et al., IBM's Early Computers, 289–290.

is an electronic notation removed from human eyes that is capable of the exact same kinds of transformations dramatized at the screen level, when binary ASCII code is refigured as Roman letterforms. In other words, the low-level textuality of hashing accords with Hayles's conception of a "flexible chain of markers bound together by the arbitrary relations specified by the relevant codes." The process is also reminiscent of Bruno Latour's familiar account of inscriptions, which function as a "cascade of successive representatives" (235).[31] The development of the hard disk required not only prodigious feats of mechanical engineering, but also important innovations in low-level electronic textual practice.

A number of other problems needed to be solved in San Jose, not least of them the air bearing technology that would allow the magnetic read/write heads to "float" at a stable distance just above the surface of the spinning platter (more on this in the next section). Nevertheless, on February 10, 1954, researchers successfully transferred a simple English sentence from a punched paper card to a hard disk drive and back again, a sentence that probably deserves to take its place alongside of "What hath God wrought," "Mary had a little lamb," and "Mr. Watson—come here—I want to see you." It is a sentence that is more understated than any of these, appropriate to Big Blue's corporate pedigree: "This has been a day of solid achievement."[32]

The Grammatology of the Hard Drive: A Machine Reading

Digital inscription is a form of displacement. Its fundamental characteristic is to remove digital objects from the channels of direct human intervention. This is reflected in even the most casual language we use to relate the inscription

31. Bruno Latour, *Science in Action* (Cambridge: Harvard University Press, 1987). See especially chapter 6.

32. These are, of course, what are generally accepted as the first messages or recordings for the telegraph, the phonograph, and the telephone, respectively. The first email message was sent by Ray Tomlinson in 1971; it bears the distinctive markings of yet another writing technology: "QWERTYUIOP." The hard drive's "This has been a day of solid achievement" is documented in Reynold B. Johnson's talk to the DataStorage '89 Conference, September 19, 1989, San Jose, California, http://www.mdhc.scu.edu/100th/reyjohnson.htm. Bashe et al. corroborate this as the date for the first successful read/write operation, but do not provide the text of the message (287).

process. The commonplace is to speak about writing a file *to* a disk; to say writing "on" a disk sounds vaguely wrong, the speech of someone who has not yet assimilated the relevant vocabulary or concepts. We write *on* paper, but we write *to* a magnetic disk (or tape). Part of what the preposition contributes here is a sense of interiority; because we cannot see anything on its surface, the disk is semantically refigured as a volumetric receptacle, a black box with a closed lid. If we were writing *on* the disk we would be able to see the text visibly, like a label.[33] The preposition is also a legacy of the von Neumann model, where storage is a physically as well as logically distinct portion of the computer. Writing data "to" the storage element thus entails a literal as well as a logical displacement.

Not knowing exactly what happens to our data or how to properly articulate our relationship to it once it scrolls off the edge of the screen is a minor but perceptible trope in writing on new media. Recall Michael Heim's notion of system opacity, as discussed in the previous chapter. Lisa Gitelman finds occasion to mention her "own kooky ideas of where the data go 'into' this beige box and 'onto' my hard drive."[34] The scare quotes around the prepositions testify to the disorientation of the disembodied stance we adopt with regard to our storage media. "We might know how to launch Microsoft Word and type up an essay with graphics, tables, and elaborate fonts, but, with each stroke of the keyboard or click of the mouse, do we realize what's happening in the discourse networks of the purring, putty-colored box?" asks Marcel O'Gorman.[35] William Gibson remarks: "It wasn't until I could finally afford a computer of my own that I found out there's a drive mechanism inside— this little thing that spins around. I'd been expecting an exotic crystalline

---

33. We do often speak of *putting* a file on a disk. Likewise, "saving to" and "saving on" a disk appear to be used with about equal frequency. Since it is clear that we can thereby conceive of disks or other storage media as a form of material support for data, it becomes all the more conspicuous that we only seldom speak of *writing* a file on a disk. The OED helps chart this lexical unease: in the 1940s, one could comfortably say either write "on" or write "to" tape or disk (or indeed, more commonly, write "into"). Since the 1950s, however, the preferred locution has been simply "to."

34. Gitelman, *Scripts, Grooves, and Writing Machines*, 229.

35. See paragraph 41 in "Friedrich Kittler's Media Scenes—An Instruction Manual." *Postmodern Culture* (September 1999), http://www3.iath.virginia.edu/pmc/text-only/issue.999/ 10.1.r_ogorman.txt.

thing, a cyberspace deck or something, and what I got was a little piece of a Victorian engine that made noises like a scratchy old record player. That noise took away some of the mystique for me; it made computers less sexy."[36] Even Jacques Derrida mines this vein:

With pens and typewriters you think you know *how* it works, how "it responds." Whereas with computers, even if people know how to use them up to a point, they rarely know, intuitively and without thinking—at any rate, *I* don't know—*how* the internal demon of the apparatus operates. What rules it obeys. This secret with no mystery frequently marks our dependence in relation to many instruments of modern technology. We know how to use them and what they are for, without knowing what goes on with them, in them, on their side (23).[37]

The hard drive, though indispensable to the scene of textuality in which these very keystrokes are being recorded, remains a dim totem, lodged within the remote recesses of its beige (or black) box.

I take Derrida's "secret with no mystery" to mean that while knowledge of a computer's physical systems is esoteric, it is not controversial or contested once one goes to the trouble of seeking it out. This is one (direct, literal) route to awareness of the mechanism, a plunge into techné. Here I propose a close reading, a reading both close to and of a piece with the machine—a *machine reading* whose object is not text but a mechanism or device.[38] What then are its essential characteristics—its grammatology—as an inscription technology?

36. See Larry McCaffery, *Storming the Reality Studio* (Durham: Duke University Press, 1991), 270. Likewise, in the afterword to the Voyager Press electronic edition of his first three novels: "I bought [an Apple] IIc in an end-of-line sale at a department store, took it home, and learned, to my considerable disappointment, that personal computers stored their data on little circular bits of electromagnetic tape, which were whirled around to the accompaniment of assorted coarse sounds. I suppose I'd assumed the data was just sort of, well, held. In a glittering mesh of silicon. Or something. But silently." Available online at http://163.152.22.77/shim/monalisa.htm.

37. The quotation is from "The Word Processor," an interview with Derrida conducted by Béatrice and Louis Seguin for *La Quinzaine Littéraire* in August 1996. Reprinted in Derrida's *Paper Machine*, trans. Rachel Bowlby (Stanford: Stanford University Press, 2005): 19–32.

38. Kittler's essay "Protected Mode," which essentially amounts to a close reading of a series of Intel microchips, is one strong precedent for what I have in mind here. See *Literature, Media, Information Systems* (G+B Arts, 1997), 156–168.

Here is my list: it is *random access*; it is a *signal processor*; it is *differential* (and *chronographic*); it is *volumetric*; it is *rationalized* (and *atomized*); it is *motion-dependent*; it is *planographic*; and it is *nonvolatile* (but also *variable*). I cover each of these items in further detail in the following paragraphs, while also addressing certain operational aspects of the device.[39]

It is random access. Like the codex and vertical file cabinets and vinyl records, and unlike the scroll or magnetic tape or a filmstrip, hard drives permit (essentially) instantaneous access to any portion of the physical media without the need to fast-forward or rewind a sequence.[40] Lest there be any doubt about the affinity between these random access technologies, at least one company now markets designer hard drives whose exterior case has the appearance of a handsome clothbound book.[41]

It is a signal processor. The conventional wisdom is that what gets written to a hard disk is a simple magnetic expression of a bit: a one or a zero, aligned as a north or south polarity. In fact, the process is a highly condensed and complex set of symbolic transformations by which a "bit," as a binary value in the computer's memory, is converted to a voltage that is passed through the drive's read/write head where the current creates an electromagnetic field reversing the polarity of not one but several individual magnetic dipoles—a whole pattern of flux reversals—embedded in the material substrate of the disk. Likewise, to read data from the surface of the platter, these patterns of magnetic fields (actually patterns of magnetic resistance), which are received

39. I want to make explicit my debt to one resource in particular in the section that follows, the online *PC Guide*, written and maintained by Charles M. Kozierok, which offers by far the most detailed nonspecialist's discussion I know of the components and operation of a hard disk drive: http://www.pcguide.com/ref/hdd/.

40. But it is not necessarily the case that the random access paradigm will endure indefinitely: at least one leading practitioner, Jim Gray, head of Microsoft's Bay Area Research Center, foresees a return to sequential access as drives scale up past the terabyte threshold: "Certainly we have to convert from random disk access to sequential access patterns. Disks will give you 200 accesses per second, so if you read a few kilobytes in each access, you're in the megabyte-per-second realm, and it will take a year to read a 20-terabyte disk. If you go to sequential access of larger chunks of the disk, you will get 500 times more bandwidth—you can read or write the disk in a day. So programmers have to start thinking of the disk as a sequential device rather than a random access device." See Patterson and Gray, "A Conversation with Jim Gray," http://www.acmqueue.org/modules.php?name=Content&pa=showpage&pid=43.

41. See http://www.boingboing.net/2005/03/08/bookshaped_hard_driv.html.

as analog signals, are interpreted by the head's detection circuitry as a voltage spike, which is then converted into a binary digital representation (a one or a zero) by the drive's firmware.[42] The relevant points are that writing and reading to and from the disk are ultimately a form of digital to analog or analog to digital signal processing—not unlike the function of a modem—and that the data contained on the disk is a second-order representation of the actual digital values the data assumes for computation.

It is differential. The read/write head measures reversals between magnetic fields rather than the actual charge of an individual magnetic dipole. In other words, it is a differential device—signification depends upon a change in the value of the signal being received rather than the substance of the signal itself. (Readers may recognize similarities to the classic Saussurian model of differential relations in linguistics.) As noted above, the magnetic patterns on the surface of the disk are not a direct representation of bit values but an abstraction of those values, filtered through a range of encoding schemes that have evolved from basic frequency modulation (FM) to the current state of the art, which is known as Run Length Limited (RLL). There are several reasons for this, but the most important concerns the drive head's need to separate one bit representation from another: if the disk were to store a long, undifferentiated string of ones or zeros, the head would have no good way to determine precisely where in that long string it was located—was it at the forty-fifth zero or the fifty-fourth zero? Frequency modulation, which was the first encoding scheme to address the issue, began each bit representation with a flux reversal, and then added another reversal for a one while omitting a second reversal to represent a zero. RLL uses a more sophisticated model to determine how the dipoles are magnetized, such that a variable and always minimum number of reversals are used to encode a given bit value. The net result is that even a long string of absolute ones or zeros will consist of frequent flux reversals that the head uses to ascertain its physical position; representations of ones and zeros in turn depend on whether or not the head registers a transition within a certain length of time. (Thus we can say that the hard drive is also a *chronographic* in-

---

42. In point of fact, read and write heads are no longer the same entity. The development of first magnetoresistive heads and then giant magnetoresistive heads—in 1991 and 1997 respectively—forced the creation of a separate read head, based on substances whose electrical resistance changes in the presence of a magnetic field. The introduction of magnetoresitive heads led to dramatic increases in aerial density (Hayes 214–215).

scription device, in that its operation bears an irreducible temporal dimension. See also *motion-dependent* later on in this section.) Success in developing more efficient encoding schemes is one important factor in the rapidly escalating storage capacity of hard disk drives. Partial Response Maximum Likelihood (PRML), which is used for read but not write operations, is especially interesting in this regard because, as its name implies, it is predictive rather than iterative in nature: rather than detecting the voltage spikes associated with each and every flux reversal, the firmware makes guesses as to the value of the bit representation using a sample of the overall pattern. In practice this sampling, coupled with sophisticated error detection and correction routines built into the signal processing circuitry, works extremely well—users don't notice that there is any guesswork involved in reading their data—but the performance does not change the essential characteristics of the process, which at this very low level are interpolative and stochastic.

It is volumetric. A hard disk drive is a three-dimensional writing space. The circular platters, sometimes as many as ten, are stacked one atop another, and data is written to both sides (like a vinyl record but unlike a CD-ROM). The read/write heads sit on the end of an actuator arm known as a slider, and are inserted over and under each of the individual platters. The slider arms themselves all extend from a common axis. Thus, a drive with four platters will have a total of eight separate read/write heads. That the hard disk offers a volumetric space for data storage is reflected in its common parlance, such as when we say a drive is "empty" or "full."

The physical capacity of the platter to record bit representations is known as its aerial density (sometimes also bit density or data density), and innovations in drive technology have frequently been driven by the desire to squeeze more and more flux reversals onto ever-decreasing surface space (for example, IBM now markets a hard disk device called a Microdrive, a single platter one inch in diameter). Typical aerial densities are now at around 10 billion bits (not bytes) per square inch. Technologies or techniques that heighten the sensitivity of the drive head's detection circuitry are critical to increasing aerial density. As bits are placed closer and closer together their magnetic fields must be weakened so that they don't interfere with one another; indeed, some researchers speculate that we are about to hit the physical limit of how weak a magnetic field can be and still remain detectable, even using new generations of magnetoresistive drive heads and stochastic decoding techniques like PRML. It is important to recognize that bit representations have actual physical dimensions at this level, however tiny: measured in units called microns (a millionth of a meter, abbreviated μm), an individual bit representation is currently a rectangular area about 4.0 μm high and .5 μm wide. In contrast, a red blood cell is about 8 μm in diameter and an anthrax spore is about 6 μm. Individual bit representations are visible as traceable inscriptions using laboratory instrumentation like magnetic force microscopy (see chapter 1). While all storage media, including printed books, are volumetric—that is, the surface area and structural dimensions of the media impose physical limitations on its capacity to record data—the history of magnetic media in particular has been marked by continuous attempts to increase aerial densities.[43]

It is rationalized. There is no portion of the volumetric space of the drive that is left unmapped by an intricate planar geometry comprised of tracks (sometimes called cylinders) and sectors. Put another way, the spatial tolerances within which data is written onto the drive (and read back from it) are exquisitely rationalized, much more akin to a Cartesian matrix than a blank canvas. Tracks may be visualized as concentric rings around the central spindle of each platter, tens of thousands of them on a typical disk. Sectors, meanwhile, are the radial divisions extending from the spindle to the platter's edge. The standard size for a sector is 512 bytes or 4096 bits; if we remember that aerial densities of 10 billion bits per square inch are common, we can get some idea of just how many sectors there are in each of the disk's many thousands of tracks. (A technique called zoned bit recording allows the outermost tracks, which occupy the greatest linear space, to accommodate proportion-

43. Some readers may suggest that a book is only incidentally volumetric, since more pages can always be added to accommodate additional content. This is true in a very generic sense, but students of printing history and bibliography will know that counterexamples are everywhere once one arrives on the shop floor: in the handpress period, for example, compositors were known to have changed the spelling of words to make them conform to the length of a line. Nearly all mass-produced books are printed in signatures, very large pages that are then cut and folded into individual leaves. Authors are often asked to add or remove content so as to bring their raw page counts into alignment with the multiples of a signature. Word processing and desktop publishing software, meanwhile, typically offers a "Make It Fit" feature that will take a few stray words alone at the end of a document and format them on the preceding page. These quick examples, from early modern to contemporary desktop publishing, indicate that the codex is volumetric in all three of its dimensions (length, breadth, and depth).

ately more sectors than the inner tracks.) Formatting a disk, an exercise that many will have performed with floppies, is the process by which the track and sector divisions—which are themselves simply flux reversals—are first written onto the media. There is thus no such thing as writing to the disk anterior to the overtly rationalized gesture of formatting. There is in addition a very low-level type of formatting, always done at the factory, called servo writing. This entails writing a unique identifier (called a servo code) for each separate track so that the head can orient itself on the surface of the platter. Formatting a disk in the way that most of us have does not alter the servo codes, which the drive's firmware prevents a user from even accessing. This information is permanently embedded in the platter for the life of the drive. Thus digital inscription, even on the scale of flux reversals embedded in magnetic media, is never a homogenous act.

Every formatted hard disk stores its own self-representation, a table of file names and addresses known (on Windows systems) as the File Allocation Table (FAT).[44] The FAT, which dates back to DOS, is the skeleton key to the drive's content. It lists every file on the disk together with its address. (The ubiquitous eight character/three character file naming convention of DOS and early Windows systems was an artifact of the FAT.) The basic unit for file storage is not the sector but rather the cluster, a larger grouping of typically 32 or 64 contiguous sectors in a track. Clusters are not necessarily contiguous; larger files may be broken up into clusters scattered over the volumetric interior of the drive. Thus a file ceases to have much meaning at the level of the platter; instead the links of its cluster chain are recorded in the FAT, where files exist only as strings of relative associations. (In a very basic way then, all electronic data is "hypermedia" to the FAT.) Defragmenting a disk, another maintenance task with which readers may be familiar, is the process of moving far-flung clusters physically closer to one another in order to improve the performance of the drive (since the only active mechanical motion the slider arm performs is moving the heads from one track to another, the more this motion can be kept to a minimum the faster the disk array's access times). The FAT, and the data structures it maps, are arguably the apotheosis

44. This is a simplification. FAT is actually a family of technologies, and the actual implementations include FAT12, FAT16, FAT32, and VFAT. On more recent systems such as Windows 2000 and XP, FAT is replaced by a technology known as NTFS. And neither UNIX nor Macintosh computers use FAT all; they have their own file system technologies.

of a rationalization and an atomization of writing space that began with another random access device, the codex.[45]

As we have seen in chapter 1, deleting a file does not actually remove it from the disk, even after emptying the so-called Recycle Bin. Instead, in keeping with the volumetric nature of disk storage, the delete command simply tells the FAT to make a given file's clusters available again for future use—a special hex character (E5h) is affixed to the beginning of the file name, but the data itself stays intact on the platter. File recovery utilities work by removing the special character and restoring files to the FAT as allocated clusters; more advanced forensics techniques are sometimes capable of deeper recoveries, even after the clusters have been rewritten. The key point here is the master role played by the FAT, itself a purely grammatological construct, in legislating the writing space of the drive.

It is motion-dependent. Computing is a culture of speed, and hard drives are no exception. Motion and raw speed are integral aspects of their operation as inscription technologies. Once the computer is turned on, the hard disk is in near-constant motion.[46] The spindle motor rotates the platters at up to 10,000 revolutions per minute.[47] This motion is essential to the functioning of the drive for two reasons. First, while the read/write head is moved laterally across the platter by the actuator arm when seeking a particular track, the head depends upon passive motion to access individual sectors: that is, once the head is in position at the appropriate track it simply waits for the target sector to rotate past. (Platters spin counterclockwise, meaning that the head actually reads and writes right to left.) The rotation of the disk is what allows the head to detect reversals in the magnetic fluctuations on the surface of the

45. For a good discussion of the codex as a random access device (by way of comparison to the linear scroll), see Jeffrey Masten, Peter Stallybrass, and Nancy J. Vickers in their editors' introduction to *Language Machines: Technologies of Literary and Cultural Production* (New York: Routledge 1997).

46. However, there are experimental hard drives with no moving parts. IRAM, for example: http://techreport.com/reviews/2006q1/gigabyte-iram/index.x?pg=1. (My thanks to Will Killeen for this reference.)

47. The speed at which the disk rotates around the spindle remains one of the critical bottlenecks in hard drive development. At least one British firm, Dataslide, is experimenting with instead using vibration generate the movement necessary for read/write heads to detect magnetic fluctuation changes. See http://www.dataslide.com/, particularly the articles listed in the "News" section.

platter. In the past, heads were not sensitive enough to read sectors as they spun by, which lead to elaborate encoding schemes that "interleaved" or staggered the sectors such that sequential pieces of the file were accessed over the course of multiple rotations. Due to a number of factors, heads are now sensitive enough to read each sector in passing, and interleaving is no longer necessary.

Motion is also fundamental to the operation of the drive in a second and even more basic sense. Unlike other forms of magnetic media such as video or audio tape, or even floppy disks, where the read/write heads physically touch the surface of the recording medium, the head of a hard disk drive "flies" above the platter at a distance that is a tiny fraction of the width of a human hair. (The actual distances are measured in units called nanometers. Earlier we encountered microns; one micron equals 1000 nanometers. Thus even the length and breadth of bit representations vastly exceed the flying height of the drive head.) The rapid motion of the disk creates an air cushion that floats the head of the drive. Just as a shark must swim to breathe, a hard drive must be in motion to receive or return data. This air-bearing technology, as it is called (pioneered by IBM at San Jose), explains why dust and other contaminants must be kept out of the drive casing at all costs. If the heads touch the surface of the drive while it is in motion the result is a head crash: the head, which we must remember is moving at speeds upward of one hundred miles per hour, will plow a furrow across the platter, and data is then often almost impossible to recover. Thus, a key aspect of the hard drive's materiality as a functioning agent of digital inscription is quite literally created out of thin air.

It is planographic. Methods of writing and inscription can be broadly classified in one of three ways, depending on the altitudinal relationship of the meaning-bearing marks and traces to the media that supports them. Relief processes, like woodcuts and letterpress type, rely on raised height to transfer marks from one surface to another. Intaglio processes, like etching and engraving, rely on indentation, holding ink in grooves where it is transferred by the downward force of a press. Planographic surfaces are a relative latecomer, and are exemplified by lithography, which uses a mixture of grease and water to separate ink on the smooth surface of a printing stone. Hard drives are planographic in that the surface of the disk, in order to fly scant nanometers beneath the air bearings, must be absolutely smooth. The platter supporting the magnetic layer where read/write operations take place has traditionally been made

Extreme Inscription

of aluminum; now production is shifting to glass (more silicon). Nothing in nature is perfect, of course, and the surface of a hard drive will always reveal topographic imperfections when examined at high resolution with a scanning electron microscope. Nevertheless, the hard drive is by far the most exquisitely realized planograpic surface in the history of writing and inscription, with tolerances measured at the nanoscale.[48]

It is nonvolatile (but variable). As we have seen, the refinement of erasable but nonvolatile random access storage was a landmark in both computer engineering and in what computers were marketed as being able to do. The development of magnetic tape storage was roughly contemporaneous with disk technology, but magnetic tape (and paper tape, which was used earlier) is of course a serial medium. Magnetic core memories, which were bulky mechanical precursors to disk storage, were random access but with much lower storage capacities, and permanent data had to be rewritten with each successive access. Paradoxically, just as important as magnetic disk storage's non-volatility was the fact that its same volumetric area could be overwritten and used again. Holographic storage, which some think will eventually replace magnetic media—data is stored in a solid array of crystals—is not generally reusable.[49] (The speculation is that holographic storage will be so cheap and capacious that it will not be functionally or economically necessary to ever erase *anything*.) Such a technology would reimagine human-computer interaction as fundamentally as random-access non-volatile (but variable) storage media did in the 1950s. However, there are indications that magnetic storage media is itself approaching this same vanishing point.

"You Are Your C": Discourse Network 2007

John Guillory observes that "information" (undoubtedly the transcendental signifier of our age) is functionally defined by its capacity for both storage and transmission, and that these two qualities are codependent precisely and paradoxically because they are mutually exclusive: "Information demands to be transmitted because it has a shelf life, a momentary value that drives the

48. I am grateful to Kari Kraus for suggesting "planographic" as one of the hard drive's grammatological primitives.

49. For an overview of the current state of the art, see Margaret Quan, "Holographic Storage Nears Debut," *EE Times*, April 26, 2001, http://www.eetimes.com/story/OEG20010423S0113.

development of our information technologies in their quest to speed up, economize, and maximize the effectiveness of transmission. Missing the right moment of transmission, information must be stored to await its next opportunity" (110).[50] Storage, then, is a kind of suspended animation, a coma or waking death, oddly inert yet irreducibly physically present; hence its association with the uncanny, the unconscious, the dead. (Perhaps the most iconic rendition of this in popular culture is the final scene from the original *Raiders of the Lost Ark* film [1981], where a wooden crate presumably bearing the Ark of the Covenant is wheeled into the vast recesses of the Smithsonian's acres of storage beneath the National Mall, identical-looking anonymous containers piled floor to ceiling receding in a classic display of linear perspective.) Guillory, writing specifically of the common office memo—by his argument the "purest" of information genres by virtue of its being so very ordinary—stares the cultural logic of storage down to the same vanishing point: "[I]t might be read once, or never. But however vanishingly ephemeral its interest it must nevertheless be preserved, that is, *filed*. It must stand forever at the ready in its stored form to be consulted if desired by some hypothetical future reader" (113). From this idea comes the policy, implemented by many office managers, of printing (and filing) all e-mail correspondence, creating printed surrogates of born-digital documents.[51]

Obsessive-compulsive printing and filing of e-mail and other electronic ephemera is a phenomenon born of easy access to affordable desktop printing services (the networked laser as a ubiquitous feature of the corporate IT environment), coupled with deep-seated suspicion and unease about the reliability of long-term electronic data storage. The issue is manifestly *not* the physical capacity of hard drives and other storage devices. By the time this book goes to press we will likely have both feet in "terabyte territory" (a terabyte is a thousand gigabytes).[52] If, as Lisa Gitelman claims, new inscription technologies "signal new subjectivities," then we would do well to begin asking what

50. John Guillory, "The Memo and Modernity," *Critical Inquiry* 31 (Autumn 2004): 108–132.

51. This phenomenon is more than mere anecdote. In *The Myth of the Paperless Office*, Sellen and Harper point to statistics that capture a worldwide shift in the installed base of copy machines between 1988 and 1993 at only 5 percent, while the installed base of printers increased by 600 percent (14).

52. Hayes, "Terabyte Territory," *American Scientist* 90 (May–June 2002): 212–216.

new kinds of subjectivities are embodied and inscribed by the hard drive and its ever-expanding volumetrics.[53] Here are some data points:

- Mark Bernstein, hypertext designer and software developer, muses in his blog: "From time to time, I tidy up my hard disk. I delete useless old files and excess Tinderbox notes. I weed out the worst snapshots, the redundant images and the blurred pictures and the pictures I accidentally took of someone's feet. *This is probably a mistake.* It often costs more to decide to throw something away than to save it forever" (emphasis in original).[54] Bernstein runs the numbers, and based on the plummeting price of disk space and the concomitant increase in storage capacity, concludes that it will cost him less than a penny to store a one megabyte file for at least the next three years. By contrast, storage costs for IBM's original RAMAC apparently ran to about $10,000 per megabyte; if the cost today is less than a dollar per *gigabyte* then, as Brian Hayes notes, it is considerably less than the cost of paper.[55]

- Google launches its Gmail service, having apparently arrived at much the same conclusions. All new users receive the following advice: "Archive, don't delete: With 1000 megabytes of free storage, you'll never need to delete another email. Just archive everything and use Gmail's search to find what you need." 1000 megabytes is one billion ASCII characters, or (at least) the equivalent of 1000 book-length works of prose. While Google's claim that this represents a lifetime quota may be exaggerated, 1000 megabytes (as of this writing Google actually offers about 2.8 gigabytes) makes not deleting one's e-mail a viable long-term solution.[56] Similarly, Flickr, the popular Web-based photo-sharing service, imposes no restraints on the number of images users can store, only limits on the bandwidth consumed in order to upload them (at least for the free "Basic" account). The business model obviously relies on storage costs that are so negligible that the company can afford to give disk space away, while simultaneously capitalizing on an increasingly outmoded consumer perception of storage itself as commodity.[57]

53. Gitelman, *Scripts, Grooves, and Writing Machines*, 11.

54. http://markbernstein.org/Apr0401/ThrowingStuffOutisObsolete.html.

55. Hayes, "Terabyte Territory," 214.

56. This state of affairs is drolly satirized here: http://www.jacobgrier.com/humor/Gmail.html. "Man becomes first to fill Gmail account quota. 'Almost entirely porn' says Google."

57. http://www.flickr.com/help.gne#34.

- Seagate, the manufacturer that makes about one-third of all the hard drives on the market, has announced plans to offer the Lindows [sic] operating system pre-installed on all its new hard drives. The hard drive, in other words, comes with a complete operating system—like putting fluoride in the water, as the Lindows press release has it.[58] This underscores the fact that as storage capacities continue to expand, the operating system and associated applications will occupy only a small corner of the disk (a rising tide of bloatware notwithstanding). Whereas computer users of a decade ago had to maintain a delicate balance between disk space devoted to data and disk space devoted to their applications, this kind of resource management is now largely a thing of the past.

- Information scientist Michael Lesk, known for his regular "How Much Information is There in the World" reports, concludes that the total annual media output of the planet now amounts to "1.5 exabytes of storable content. . . . This is 1.5 billion gigabytes, and is equivalent to 250 megabytes for every man, woman, and child on earth."[59] Lesk arrives at his figures by quantifying media such as books, photographs, film, and music. He notes that shipped hard drive capacity doubles every year, and that "magnetic storage is rapidly becoming the universal medium for information storage." Meanwhile, industry experts such as Hayes point out that at current levels of production 120-terabyte drives will be on the market by 2012, even though others, such as Seagate's Mark Kryder, suggest that the super-paramagnetic limit—the smallest physical space that can retain a magnetic charge, measured at the nanoscale—will be reached by around 20 terabytes.[60]

- A glimpse of this future is perhaps to be found in Microsoft researcher Gorden Bell's MyLifeBits project, described as "a lifetime store of *everything*. . . . Gordon Bell has captured a lifetime's worth of articles, books, cards, CDs, letters, memos, papers, photos, pictures, presentations, home movies,

58. http://www.linspire.com/lindows_michaelsminutes_archives.php?id=82.

59. Lesk, "How Much Storage is Enough?" *Storage* 1, no. 4 (June 2003), http://www .acmqueue.org/modules.php?name=Content&pa=showpage&pid=45.

60. See Hayes, "Terrabyte Territory," 215, and "A Conversation with Jim Gray," *Storage* 1, no. 4 (June 2003), http://www.acmqueue.org/modules.php?name=Content&pa=printer _friendly&pid=43&page=1.

videotaped lectures, and voice recordings and stored them digitally. He is now paperless, and is beginning to capture phone calls, television, and radio."[61] Bell's research group understands that storage is not defined by capacity alone. The challenge also lies in access, making it much the same problem that occupied the developers of the RAMAC and that was resolved by Luhn. In print archives, so-called hidden collections denote materials that are not documented and cataloged in a finding aid, and are thus invisible to a user. Tellingly, Bell's MyLifeBits is ultimately framed as a database project, with a research agenda defined by the problem of indexing, accessing, and annotating the massive volume of information collected. Data mining—technologies that use machine-learning algorithms to search vast reserves of archival data for unexpected patterns and associations—is a direct outgrowth of the massive quantities of random access storage available from magnetic disks.

· A recent article in the *New York Times* reports that all 90,000 volumes in the University of Texas at Austin undergraduate library are about to be removed to an off-site location where they will be available for recall and retrieval.[62] Other colleges and universities are following suit. This is the von Neumann architecture concretized at the macro level. The discourse network assumes fractal formations as the bricks and mortar of the library building—the storage unit—are reconfigured to house a state-of-the-art media and information center packed with computers, which are themselves packed with state-of-the-art server arrays and hard drive assemblies. The books, meanwhile—the random access devices of old—are being placed (recursively, it would seem) in *storage*, shunted away to a remote locale where they will be available upon request, after a modest wait. They have become informationalized, and now share the fate of Guillory's memo, filed away in the closed stacks (one day soon to be served only by robotic retrieval devices) until such time when—*if*—they are needed.

Gmail's mantra, "archive, don't delete;" the capacity for infinite Undo, terabyte-scale drives retaining every state of every file for the lifetime of their user; Bell's omnivorous MyLifeBits, explicitly conceived as a "fulfillment" of

61. See http://research.microsoft.com/barc/mediapresence/MyLifeBits.aspx.

62. Ralph Blumenthal, "College Libraries Set Aside Books in a Digital Age." *New York Times*, May 14, 2005.

the idea of the Memex[63]—this is a sea change in the production and management of human knowledge records, one whose implications go far beyond the hard disk drive alone as a technology of writing and inscription. As Derrida notes in *Archive Fever*, "what is no longer archived in the same way is no longer lived in the same way."[64] Consumer electronics devices such as the iPod and the TiVo, both based on hard drive technology, are already demonstrating this—these products have transformed the storage of digital music and digital video with appropriately far-reaching effects for the music and television industries, as well as on individual users' listening and viewing habits. For example, the personalized jukebox-style playlists of MP3s have supplanted the artist's sequencing of tracks on a record album or CD, while TiVo confers the ability to screen out commercials, mix shows together, and sustain an idiosyncratic viewing schedule. The iPod, with its trademark white headphones and back-to-the-future curves, is probably the first magnetic storage device to become a fashion accessory. Podcasting—the practice of downloading news, commentary, poetry, lectures, rants, or whatever else, typically by means of autosynching the iPod to a computer—now feeds back into the production of all areas of digital content. TiVo executives, meanwhile, can track a user's every play, fast forward, and rewind command; the company insists this is for ratings purposes only.[65]

John Schwartz, a columnist for the *New York Times*, writes about buying a used iPod from a colleague and discovering the thousands of tracks left behind on the hard drive. "What if I hated Ken's taste? Would I lose respect for him? I'm not talking about the Paula Abdul songs; we're all entitled to our guilty pleasures. But what if it was all bubblegum, or deeply dull? It would be like opening his closet and finding Star Trek uniforms."[66] By relegating a music collection in toto to a portable, migratory device, magnetic disk storage makes

63. See, for example, Jim Gemmell, Gordon Bell, Roger Lueder, Steven Drucker, and Curtis Wong, "MyLifeBits: Fulfilling the Memex Vision," available online at http://research.microsoft.com/barc/mediapresence/MyLifeBits.aspx.

64. Jacques Derrida, *Archive Fever: A Freudian Impression*, trans. Eric Prenowitz (Chicago: University of Chicago Press, 1995), 18.

65. See http://www.thewbalchannel.com/technology/7333617/detail.html for documentation on TiVo data collection.

66. John Schwartz, "To Know Me, Know my iPod." *New York Times*, November 28, 2004 Late Edition—Final, Section 4, Page 6, Column 1.

available the kind of intimacy perhaps only previously achieved by visiting someone's home, browsing their bookshelves and poking into their closet (the same article makes reference to "podjacking," plugging into a friend or stranger's iPod).[67]

This impulse toward equating subjective identity with personal data stores is emerging as one of the most dramatic features of contemporary discourse networks. "You are your C," proclaims the title of a net art project by Carlo Zanni dedicated to "electronic soul mirroring." When the project is accessed online, the contents of the viewer's hard drive are displayed on the screen as the standard Windows file tree, as though they were simply another component of the World Wide Web. "Eyes are no more the soul mirror of a person; on the contrary the computer or the hard disk are."[68] (The "C" refers to the conventional mapping for a hard drive mounted on a Windows file system— the hard drive is the "C" drive, or, interestingly, the "see" drive; note also Zanni's play on soul/sole.) The project is straightforward enough, but the dialectic between screen and storage, reflections and reservoirs, is instructive; as Zanni notes, the fear of having one's private information exposed, made *visible* on the Web, is an explicit dimension of the work: "It is an old hacker trick ... usually people were thinking that the visualization was available for all the web audience, in truth it was only available in local for your machine."[69] Clearly for Zanni, life on the screen manifests a sometimes uneasy relationship to the life on the disk.

Indeed, there are indications that hard drive-specific net art projects are becoming their own minor genre. Mary Flanagan's forensically inflected {Phage} (2000) uses fragments of old media files residing on the user's hard disk to construct a 3-D representation of the computer's supposed unconscious. Executed in Virtual Reality Modeling Language (VRML), images are texture

67. Adam Porter, a Philadelphia DJ, now makes his living by renting out iPods he fills with customized playlists for restaurants and other clients http://citypaper.net/articles/2003-06-12/music.shtml. For many, however, the iPod has come to function more as a generic storage device than a music player; so much so that the United Kingdom Ministry of Defense (and an increasing number of private corporations) has deemed them a security risk for their ability to facilitate the rapid transfer of very large volumes of data. See http://www.consolationchamps.com/archives/001142.html. Cases of identity theft in which iPods figure prominently are also on the rise.

68. Artist's statement online at Rhizome.org's Artbase, http://rhizome.org/art/.

69. Personal email from Zanni to author, 8 Jan 2005 19:47:53 +0100.

mapped onto geometric solids, creating startling visual extrusions that drift like Dalían phantasmagoria. She calls the basic process a virus.[70] Likewise, Cory Arcangel's net art *Data Diaries* (2002) uses Quicktime video to stream ambient data files obtained by a core dumping of his hard drive's various buffers and memory caches, yielding abstract atonal video compositions keyed to specific calendar days: "If ever computers had a subconscious, this is it," writes Alex Galloway. "They look like digital dreams—the pure shapes and tones of real computer memory. Each video documents a new day, and each day the computer offers us a new set of memories."[71] But in fact, the conceit of a window onto a computer's anthropomorphized unconscious or subconscious is as much of an idealized fiction as the notion that the databases of MyLifeBits yield entrée to the totality of Gordon Bell's life experiences. VRML and Quicktime are both high-end production environments, and the visual and aural experiences that each can generate are, as much as anything else, an artifact of their own formal particulars. Taken together, *{Phage}* and *Data Diaries* embody some very different behaviors and conceits: the former is interactive and to some extent immersive and open-ended, the latter is simply a clip that one watches to completion. *Data Diaries* adopts a very deliberate authorial persona, though we might ask what role we, the viewer, are cast in. Flanagan's *{Phage}*, for its part, asks us to accept the conceit of a virus, an artificial life form, and plays off of common fears about destructive intrusions into our data sanctuaries. This virus, however, is generative, delivering pleasures by recycling our digital detritus. What is conspicuous in both projects is that storage—to the exclusion of the CPU or any other portion of the computer's architecture—is the locus of identity and the soul of the new machine.

This convergence of life, memory, and data storage was explored even earlier in fiction—William Gibson's "Johnny Mnemonic" is an obvious example, as its protagonists wrestle with the problem of unlocking the data consigned to the neuromantic mule's wetware drive: "I had hundreds of megabytes stashed in my head on an idiot/savant basis, information I had no conscious access to.... I'm not cheap to begin with, but my overtime on storage is

70. *{Phage}* can be found at http://www.maryflanagan.com/virus.htm.

71. See http://www.turbulence.org/Works/arcangel/. Alex Galloway's remarks are available in his introduction to the piece, http://www.turbulence.org/Works/arcangel/alex.php.

astronomical."[72] The theme appears in more quotidian form in Douglas Coupland's *Microserfs*, which also offers a counterpoint to Gmail, Flickr, and Bernstein's calculus of storage costs above (consumer hard drives weighed in at around 1 GB when the novel appeared):

Susan was doing her biannual hard-drive cleanup, which is half chore/half fun—going on a deleting frenzy, removing all those letters that once seemed so urgent, that now seem pointless, the shareware that infected your files with mystery viruses and those applications that seemed groovy at the time.

Susan's own efforts did get me to do a brief cleanup of my own hard drive. I thought of Karla's equation of the body with the computer and memory storage and all of that, and I realized that human beings are loaded with germs and viruses, just like a highly packed Quadra . . . I posted a question on the Net, asking bioheads out there what lurks inside the human hard drive.[73]

This passage already functions as a documentary account of computing practices driven by a set of storage affordances that are no longer meaningful or relevant. Or to take one final instance: "[Y]ou are the sum total of your data. No man escapes that," says Don Delillo in the voice of a government technocrat in *White Noise*.[74]

These literary examples all complicate the ambitions of MyLifeBits, whose rhetoric at times is disarmingly literal. A PowerPoint presentation available on the project's Web site, for example, shows Gordon Bell dissolving into a pixilated representation of himself, with the caption "*I am data*" (emphasis in original).[75] It is tempting to continue in this posthuman vein: the double helix as the ultimate data structure. Yet there is also something that seems almost willfully naive about Bell's claims and ambitions—are we really to accept we are simply the sum total of all of the media we produce and consume? ("But where does the outside commence?" asks Derrida in *Archive Fever*; "This

72. In Gibson's collection *Burning Chrome* (New York: Ace, 1986, 2).

73. *Microserfs* (New York: HarperCollins, 1995), 178. See also the following, spoken by Karla: "Bodies are like diskettes with tags. You click on them and you can see the size and type of file immediately. On people, this labeling occurs on the face" (205).

74. *White Noise*, Viking Critical Library, ed. Mark Osteen (New York: Penguin, 1998, 141).

75. See "Jim Gemmell's MyLifeBits talk," February 2004, available online at http://research .microsoft.com/barc/mediapresence/MyLifeBits.aspx, Slide 5.

question is the question of the archive. There are undoubtedly no others."[76])
The question, in other words, is not whether we will have the storage capacity
to accumulate copies of every book, film, song, conversation, e-mail, etc. that
we amass in a lifetime (yes, eventually) but how do these accumulations, these
massive drifts of data, interact with irreducible levels of lived experience? A
project such as Zanni's achieves part of its effect, I would argue, through its
shock value: not only by putatively displaying one's private information to the
world—it doesn't, really—but in holding up the mirror and allowing the
user to see, objectively and defamiliarized, the entirety of what he or she has
amassed on their hard drive. The work depends *not* on the simple equation of
life with data, but on the proposition that *if* you were equated with your data,
this is what (and who) you would be. In other words, for the work to have its
real impact the user must retain some sense of self apart from their data, some
subjective reserve that says in effect, "No, there must be more to me than
this." Delillo is making this very same point by way of his postmodern irony;
Jack Gladney's tribulations in the second half of Delillo's novel come about
through the friction of his escape velocity from the gravitational bands of his
data fields. Such awareness is lacking in MyLifeBits, where the algebraic equation of life and data is treated as simple and self-evident.

Part of what enables the myth (or the meme) of MyLifeBits is the slippage
between media convergence and total recall. The opening of the PowerPoint
mentioned above, for example, features a short animation depicting a messy
array of media forms—papers, telephone, file cabinets, music CDs, computer
software—all collapsing into a single blip on a hard drive.[77] Skyrocketing
storage capacities are complemented, even motivated, by the putative flattening out of all media into homogeneous ones and zeros. Nicholas Negroponte
supplies the classic formulation: "[B]its commingle effortlessly. They start to
get mixed up and can be used or reused together or separately. The mixing of
audio, video, and data is called *multimedia*; it sounds complicated but is nothing more than commingled bits."[78] Friedrich Kittler is even more succinct:
"The general digitization of channels and informations erases the differences

76.   Jacques Derrida, *Archive Fever*, trans. Eric Prenowitz (Chicago: University of Chicago Press,
1995), 8.

77.   "Jim Gemmell's MyLifeBits talk," http://research.microsoft.com/barc/mediapresence/
MyLifeBits.aspx, Slide 1.

78.   Nicholas Negroponte, *Being Digital* (Cambridge: MIT Press, 1995), 18.

among individual media."[79] But in this book I have been working to discover the heterogeneity of digital inscription to the furthest extent possible—indeed to the nanoscale, where, with the aid of a magnetic force microscope, individual bits take on their own weight and heft (like snowflakes, no two are quite alike). Even without the aid of such exotic instrumentation, however, the nonvirtual realities of our contemporary media ecology should lead us to question the homogenizing myth of convergence. All media are bound to the materialities of their particular forms, materialities that materialize in the shape of intellectual property, incompatible standards (ask anyone who has ever tried to navigate the treacherous shoals of region-specific DVD codes), obsolescence, IPOs, sell-outs, buy-outs, and so on.[80] Nonproprietary data standards deflect one brand of materiality, that of corporate influence, but all media remain part of a social, political, and economic landscape whose shifting contours resist any attempts at erosion through the mere rhetorical invocation of homogenous ones and zeroes. What happens when the titanic ambition of my desire to save a copy of every song I've ever listened to collides with the iceberg of digital rights management?[81] The lesson here is that the same channels of optical fiber networks that flatten media down to a universal symbolic regimen can also be employed to leverage that same regimen to write out or write-protect any data stream encoded to operate within it. Formally, there is no essential state of the discourse network.

In March 2006, Samsung debuted a laptop with 32 MB of flash memory storage—but no hard drive.[82] At almost the same time, Google placed a

79. See *Gramophone, Film, Typewriter*, trans. Geoffrey Winthrop-Young and Michael Wutz (Stanford: Stanford University Press, 1999), 1.

80. For some related work on this theme, see my "The Word as Image in an Age of Digital Reproduction" in *Eloquent Images: Word and Image in the Age of New Media*, eds. Mary E. Hocks and Michelle R. Kendrick (Cambridge: MIT Press, 2003): 137–156 and "Virtuality and VRML: Software Studies After Manovich": http://www.electronicbookreview.com/thread/technocapitalism/morememory.

81. In conversation with me, MyLifeBits' Jim Gemmell suggested that the solution might ultimately be to record metadata about a particular song, and then rely on digital services to retrieve an appropriately licensed copy of the actual music if the user really desired to listen to it. Such a solution only underscores the point about the social and economic materiality of data, and the ways it will resist universal storage.

82. See http://hardware.slashdot.org/article.pl?sid=06/03/21/200234&from=rss. It would be a mistake to assume that flash drives demonstrate the possibility of storage without materiality:

PowerPoint presentation online that included outlines of the company's future plans. In the notes field for one of the slides, which was inadvertently left in the public copy of the presentation, there was a description of an "infinite storage" service whereby people entrust all of their data to a network repository. Accessible from any computer, this repository becomes the "golden copy."[83] Taking these two occurrences together, we see that the hard drive is not so much confronted with obsolescence as it is with further displacement, no longer even residing in the same physical machine the user lays hands on. At a glance this appears little different from the network computers being touted in the late 1990s by Sun Microsystems and others—stripped down processor boxes that were only intended as gateways to the Web. The difference, however, is that not only will Google eventually have the raw storage capacity, but they will be able to integrate the service (apparently to be called GDrive) with their other technologies. Google Desktop, for example, currently brings the Google search engine to an individual user's isolated hard drive; with GDrive, it is not difficult to imagine scenarios whereby users might create public share folders whose contents were exposed to Google's search algorithms. Searching "the Web" thus becomes a function not only of the data available on Web servers, but also of the files and content that make up any individual user's personal information stores, at least insofar as those users are willing to allow it. The effect resembles that of peer-to-peer applications, except the distinction between desktop and Web, local and remote, generally dissolves. Couple all this with GooglePrint, which promises to make the world's bibliographical record increasingly available online, thus

---

"Because they are written by forcing electrons through an layer of electrical insulation onto a floating transistor gate, re-writeable ROMs will only withstand a limited number of write cycles before the insulation is permanently damaged. In very old EAROMs, this damage could occur in as few as 1,000 write cycles. In modern flash EEPROMs, the life may be in excess of 10,000 or even 100,000 cycles, but it is by no means infinite. It is partially for this reason (as well as their limited, more-expensive capacity) that Flash ROMs are unlikely to completely supplant magnetic disk drives in the near future." See http://en.wikipedia.org/wiki/Read_only_memory (accessed November 14, 2004).

83. The PowerPoint presentation and slide notes, which were circulated widely around the Web, first appeared on Greg Linden's blog: http://glinden.blogspot.com/2006/03/in-world-with-infinite-storage.html.

dissolving the distinction between the Web and the library; couple it with version control and document management systems, so that not only are the end products of contemporary knowledge work exposed for search and retrieval, but also the process of creating them; couple it with folksonomy and other bottom-up social networking practices, not to mention wilder stuff like Bruce Sterling's "spimes," information-rich objects searchable in space and time (the "internet of things").[84] Take limitless storage reserves, the vast reservoirs of the Web's global data pool as it floats atop the millions of magnetic platters making up servers; take durable, plastic consumer electronics devices, off the rack and vacuum sealed, which can nestle in the folds of the ear or tumble in a coat pocket; take Google; take ubiquitous WiFi hotspots; take Bluetooth technology, auto-synch schedulers, peer-to-peer, and desktop data mining—these are the essentials of the new discourse network. Screens are secondary—still vital, of course, but somehow almost . . . vestigial.

Early RAMAC disk arrays were often proudly displayed: at the United Airlines terminal at Denver's Stapleton Field, visitors were allowed to observe the machine in its dedicated glass-walled room as it recorded and retrieved their reservations (the actress Eva Gabor was reportedly mesmerized).[85] By the time they became a standard part of personal computer systems, hard drives had already retreated inside the case, and they are now further dematerializing as a consequence of their soaring capacities. At the same time, storage is more visible than it's been in quite some time, accentuated by the sleek white contours of the iPod or the Day-Glo colors of flash memory sticks.[86] Indeed, the suddenly ubiquitous memory sticks are perhaps the first storage media capable of coordinating with a user's apparel. Just as cell phones and MP3 players now have their holsters, memory sticks are made with pocket clips (hearkening back to the pocket protectors of old), while others come with nylon sports bands so the stick can be slung around the neck, often as not to ride there alongside a photo ID (access and storage becoming tangled and intertwined during a brisk stride around the downtown at the lunch hour). Today being wired means being well-outfitted, whether it's with a cellular earpiece (to stay

84. See http://www.viridiandesign.org/ or Sterling's design tract *Shaping Things* (Cambridge: MIT Press, 2006).

85. Morris, "Professor RAMAC's Tenure," 196.

86. As of this writing, Apple has released its first flash memory-based iPods; as flash memory devices continue to proliferate and improve they will compete for the portable market and perhaps force hard drives back inside the protective environs of the case.

in touch) or iPod ear buds (to stay well-informed with a PodCast, or else to just rock out with the latest MP3 to hit the music blogs). More novel storage accessories are also available: flash memory bundled in a pair of earrings, for example, or Day-Glo plastic wrist bracelets, or an executive fountain pen.[87] If a decade ago storage was confined to the desktop and a handful of immediately ancillary devices (Jazz and Zip, the CD-ROM, even the odd floppy) nowadays it's more distributed, more intimate, and more mobile—in a word, more fashionable. Storage now has a generation gap, as is perhaps captured in a Web page that instructs readers in how to turn their old hard drives into wind chimes suitable for porch-hanging.[88]

Coda: "My Computer"

I remember my own first encounter with a computer hard drive. I had grown up using an Apple IIe and was accustomed to swapping $5\frac{1}{4}$-inch disks in and out of my system's two external Disk II floppy drives whenever I wanted to use a new application or save some data. The first time I saved a file to a hard drive (on a PC at school) was a very different kind of experience: there was no diskette to label and pocket, nothing for me to take back home after class. My work was suddenly somehow part of the computer itself, not shunted back out to peripheral media. The computer was no longer just a processing engine sandwiched between input and output devices, but something more like an individualized entity, with its own unique internal memory. In a roomful of otherwise identical-looking terminals I could point to one in particular and say, "that's *my* computer" (the very phrase Microsoft would eventually use to label the desktop icon that allows users to browse their file systems). Of course from an architectural standpoint nothing had really changed and personal computers still conformed very much to the classic von Neumann model. The storage device had simply retreated inside the case. But the psychological impact of saving data inside the machine, rather than to some external locale, cannot be overlooked. I believe that it is, in its own way, as significant as the advent of the GUI, the more commonly celebrated revolution of that era.

87. http://www.theinquirer.net/?article=30384 and http://www2.pny.com/256MB-EXECUTIVE-ATTACHE-USB-FLASH-DRIVE-PENCOMBO-P16670.aspx, respectively. My thanks to Will Killeen for these links.

88. http://halogen.note.amherst.edu/~wing/wingie/tech/hdchime/hdchime.php.

3

"An Old House with Many Rooms": The Textual Forensics of Mystery_House.dsk

"People" who never existed did things that never took place, upon a stage of fragmented software that currently sits on a hundred thousand disks in dusty boxes, chroniding [sic] events that happened only by mutual wish-fulfillment.
—PATRICK K. KROUPA, AKA "LORD DIGITAL," ON 1980S BBS CULTURE

Like old bones to the forensic scientist, prints give up their secrets if you know where and how to look.
—ROBERT N. ESSICK AND JOSEPH VISCOMI, "AN INQUIRY INTO BLAKE'S METHOD OF COLOR PRINTING"

The bibliographer must always start with the postulate of normality.
—FREDSON BOWERS, *BIBLIOGRAPHY AND TEXTUAL CRITICISM*

To begin, a parable:

Once upon a time there was a scholar, learned and wise in the ways of texts. One day, as was his wont, this scholar found himself in a library, among its many books and papers. Before him lay a volume of poetry by an important and influential figure. Certain details of the typesetting caught his eye. He noticed that of the six initial capital Ts to be found printed in this book's pages, five were conspicuously ornate, a throwback, it seemed, to an earlier time. One was of a plainer italic style. Now why had the book been printed that way? This was the kind of question the scholar loved, so he set about the task of discovering an answer. Eventually, in the printer's proofs for this particular edition (for such things were also to be had in libraries and archives), he read a note in the poet's own hand indicating that the supply of ornamental Ts had "run out" and instructing his printer to substitute a plainer version of that letter, for, as the poet said, "the old printers did this when fancy capitals ran out." Yet, based on various other evidences and conjectures, the specifics of which are not relevant to recount here, the scholar was led to put aside this explanation, preferring instead to see the decision to print a plain, unadorned T as the "old printers" might have done as a deft and deliberate choice, a "factive synecdoche" for the "larger memorial acts" performed by the text as a whole.[1] "The italic T on page 16 is not merely Pound's allusion to the 'old printers,' it is the index of a massive act of reverential recollection which is being executed in Hugh Selwyn Mauberley," *was what the scholar set down in his own papers (160).*

Before very long another scholar, indisputably learned and wise in the ways of texts himself, examined the volume and attendant evidence. He arrived at a much different explanation for why that one particular T had been printed in the plain style, an explanation all about practical measures and expediencies. Again, the details are not relevant to recount here, except insofar as to say they were born of a deep vocational understanding of the mechanical processes by which the text had been made and reproduced. This explanation was so complete and unassailable as to immediately collapse the other scholar's conclusions. Grand notions about factive synecdoche and massive acts of reverential recollection became the mere shavings of Occam's razor, to be replaced by the minute particulars of how type was set forth in formes, and sheets folded into pages, and how and in what format the leaves of the book were printed. In the end the facts were very much as they had been given in the poet's own note in the printer's proofs: there simply had not been enough Ts.[2]

1.   Some readers may have already recognized that the basis for my "parable" is Jerome McGann's discussion of the typesetting in the Ovid Press edition of Ezra Pound's *Hugh Selwyn Mauberley* in chapter 7 of *The Textual Condition* (Princeton: Princeton University Press, 1991), 153–176, 172.

2.   The refutation of McGann is Shef Rogers, "How Many Ts Had Ezra Pound's Printer," *Studies in Bibliography* 49 (1996): 277–283. Rogers concludes: "Ironically, it was McGann's own dictum that critics must consider the production process as an inseparable part of a text's meaning that first drew my attention to these questions and, in this instance, to his errors. McGann's concepts of textual materialism and bibliographic codes provide intriguing new per-

It would be tempting, but wrong, to view this as a cautionary tale about bibliographical hubris and the limits of archival knowledge. While one scholar got it wrong in this one particular instance, there are numerous other examples of more durable factive synecdoches in bibliography, textual criticism, and allied pursuits. Recently, for example, Robert N. Essick and Joseph Viscomi have marshaled detailed arguments about certain technical aspects of Blake's color printing process—whether he "pulled" the press once or twice—that have direct bearing on our high-level critical conceits about the poet and printer's work. An essay featuring an exhaustive discussion of pinholes in one particular impression of one particular copy of one particular book printed by Blake ends with observations about the artist's psychology, cosmology, and aesthetic program.[3] Such an approach typifies recent

---

spectives on authorial intent and reader interpretation, but these concepts must themselves consistently acknowledge, not just exploit, the historical practices they seek to reinstate within the critical horizon" (283). It should be noted, however, that Rogers fails to observe that the episode as a whole is presented as part of a dialogue bibliographically coded to separate the speaker from McGann himself.

3.   See Robert N. Essick and Joseph Viscomi, "An Inquiry into Blake's Method of Color Printing," *Blake: An Illustrated Quarterly* 35, no. 3 (Winter 2001/2002): 74–103. The essay is occasioned by arguments put forward by Michael Phillips in his *William Blake: The Creation of the Songs: From Manuscript to Illuminated Printing* (London: The British Library, 2000). In their essay, Essick and Viscomi write: "Let us assume that Blake did use two pulls to produce each of his color prints. What sort of Blake, as an artist and as a writer on the arts, would this assumption lead us toward? We would encounter a man who favored precision over variation, for two-pull printing relies heavily on the former and bars the printer from the latter. He would base his activities on the arts of memory rather than imagination, for no printing technique provides a better externalization of returning to a prior activity (first pull) and repeating it (second pull). He would emphasize the mechanical over the autographic. He would be much concerned with the division of images and labor into discrete segments at the expense of any notions of a seamless unity between invention and execution. Fitting plate to the bed of the press and paper to plate would be among his major endeavors. In that pursuit, freedom would have to be restrained, as it must be in all crafts that emphasize imitating/repeating over creating. As readers of Blake's comments on art and epistemology will recognize, the foregoing characterization of his activities and their implications reverses every one of Blake's own values when he considers the same

scholarship in textual studies, where ideally, as McGann puts it, "[t]he archival materials and bibliographical analysis fund a larger critical and interpretive program" (160). The point addressed by the Ts is that *both* the interpretative implications of the undecorated type *and* the counterevidence against them were to be found amongst the archival materials and bibliographic evidence. That is, the material text of the book and associated documents such as the printer's proofs sustained a complete hermeneutic cycle of inquiry, proposition, and (as eventually happened in this instance) refutation. Printed books and manuscripts routinely support such propositions about the codependency of medium and message, and these propositions lend literary criticism executed within their realm a satisfying epistemological crunch. Yet where is this hermeneutic cycle—this capacity for "archival materials and bibliographical analysis to fund a larger critical and interpretative program"—to be found in the new digital media? Can theory or criticism of born-digital objects benefit from attention to the minute particulars of archival data, and if so, in what do those details consist?

Mystery_House.dsk: A Forensic Walk-through

My starting point in addressing these questions is a walk-through of a 140-kilobyte electronic file comprising a disk image (.dsk) of the 1980 Sierra On-Line game *Mystery House*, written by Roberta and Ken Williams for the Apple II, notable as the first piece of interactive fiction to feature inline graphics (in the form of 70 vector line drawings). The disk image in question was obtained from a public FTP server that warehouses games and other vintage Apple II software.[4] A walk-through is a set of guided instructions, presented either in narrative form or as a simple list of commands, revealing how to navigate a work of interactive fiction's locales, manipulate its constituent objects, and

---

choices" (101). Subsequent issues of *Blake: An Illustrated Quarterly* carried responses to Essick and Viscomi from Phillips and other scholars, as well as subsequent responses by Essick and Viscomi themselves. I know of no better example of the import of bibliographic knowledge than this high-level exchange conducted in the pages of a scholarly journal by some of the world's most notable Blake experts, all revolving around the question of one pull or two.

4.   ftp://ftp.apple.asimov.net/pub/apple_II/images/games/adventure/.

solve its puzzles in an optimal or effective sequence. Here I want to conduct a walk-through of my own, but with forensic rather than purely ludic intent.

It is important at the outset to be very clear about what is meant by a "disk image." A disk image is not a picture of a floppy disk, nor is it a duplication of a disk's electronic content in the usual sense. As we saw in chapter 1, a disk image is a literal representation of every *bit* of information on some original instance of source media, in this case some actual, physical, specific $5\frac{1}{4}$-inch floppy disk long lost or consigned to a shoebox under a bed or some similar oblivion. It is not simply a copy of all of the files that were once on that original diskette; rather the disk image, like the facsimile or photograph suggested by the term, preserves all of the *information* that was recorded on the disk in its original storage geometry. My objective in what follows is to read through this one particular disk image, cultivating a thick textuality as a potential model of critical practice; a model encompassing both screen-level text and machine-level instructions, embracing both normal interaction with the game and activities closer to hacking or cracking, and ultimately demonstrating a distinction between what I will term forensic and formal materiality. This distinction is where, I believe, McGann's bibliotextual interpretive program can be most effectively located in new media.

Some of what follows is unabashedly technical. The detail is necessary in order for the presentation to be faithful to conditions of electronic textuality that we are no longer used to encountering because they are executed outside of normative software practices. Pedagogy is also among my motives; it is my hope that from this example others may be led to undertake similar walk-throughs or forensically replete readings of new media objects, and thereby perhaps add to the repertoire of activities we are able to perform as scholars of electronic literature and digital culture.

To begin: Figure 3.1 is a view of a small portion of the disk image using FishWings, a freeware utility for inspecting and manipulating Apple II disk images in a Windows environment.[5] FishWings is not capable of actually running any of the programs contained on the disk image; for this one employs an emulator, such as APPLEWIN.

The left-hand window presents the contents of the disk in a conventional tree view. In addition to various text files (HELLO, MYSTERY.HELLO, MESSAGES), there are numerous "BLOCKS" of binary data, a block being

5.   FishWings is available at: http://mysite.verizon.net/charlie.d/fishwings.htm.

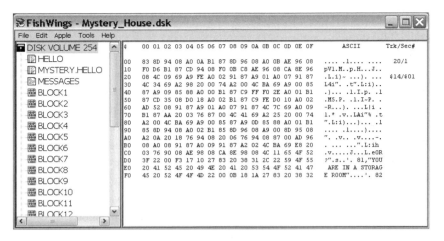

Figure 3.1 The FishWings viewer, showing a typical disk sector. Screenshot by the author.

equivalent to two sectors (more about sectors later). The tree view is useful for a quick high-level look at the image, but there is more interesting information to be had in the right-hand window.

There we find, in hexadecimal notation, a record of every byte on the disk, whether program or data, preserved according to its actual storage geometry. Each disk is laid out in 35 concentric tracks (numbered 0–34, with the highest number closest to the center); each track contains 16 radial divisions called sectors, numbered, counterclockwise, 0–15. There are 560 sectors per disk. The view here is of a single sector, specifically track 20, sector 1 (see top right-hand corner; immediately below we find the same information about track and sector in hexadecimal notation). There are 256 bytes in a sector for a total of 4,096 per track and 143,360 per disk, assuming the disk is not double-sided. Each individual byte is represented by a hexadecimal pair—for example 83, 8D, 94, reading from the top left—with 16 bytes per row in this display. Each of the two digits in a pair resolves to a 4-bit binary number; two such 4-bit binary numbers side by side therefore yields a single 8-bit byte. 8D, for example, is the hexadecimal notation for the binary number 10001101, which is also the decimal number 141. Hex itself is nothing more than a shorthand convenience, a concession to the human visual system as a way of notating binary numbers (which are themselves symbolic or shorthand conveniences for voltage differentials in the computer's circuitry). The individual bytes are either opcodes (direct requests to the processor), operands (data associated with a given opcode, such as a memory address), or strings of program data (this last category including legible text). With a little practice one can use a hex editor to roam freely about the disk image, inspecting the exact bytes recorded at any location on its virtual surface. Of course what we see here remains very much in the realm of abstraction, for (as with a contemporary hard drive) even binary machine language is a symbolic interpretation of the actual magnetic encoding on the original disk itself (in the case of the Apple II performed using an encoding scheme called Group Code Recording [GCR]).

Over toward the far right-hand side of the display we find an alternative presentation of the very same bytes. Here, however, wherever the byte matches a particular value in the ASCII character set, that ASCII character is displayed. A period indicates that the binary value falls outside the range of standard ASCII (0–127 decimal). In the first row, three separate ASCII characters appear: a space at offset 5, a 1 at offset 7, and another space at offset 12. It would be a mistake to associate these characters with intentional text, however.[6]

6.   But how do we know what is and is not intentional text? In a 1982 essay entitled "Against Theory," Steven Knapp and Walter Benn Michaels construct an elaborate thought experiment that posits the existence of a "wave poem." It goes like this: suppose you're walking along the beach and come upon some squiggles in the sand you recognize as the first verse of Wordsworth's "A Slumber Did My Spirit Seal." The text seems unambiguously the product of *someone's* intentions, and you may, consciously or unconsciously, decide it was written by a fellow human being, perhaps with a stick. Just then a wave washes ashore, and, in its wake, immediately below the first stanza of the poem, the second stanza now appears. What has changed? Chiefly the question of intentionality, which suddenly seems more urgent. Is this writing the product of some intentional agent, such as the sea itself or the ghost of Wordsworth (however fantastic those explanations might be)? Or is the writing an accident, some unlikely but absolutely arbitrary by-product of the water's ebb and flow over the sand? As Knapp and Benn Michaels point out, the moment you decide the latter the writing ceases to be language; instead it merely resembles language and therefore is stripped of any intentionality. If, on the other hand, you decide in favor of one of the former explanations, then you realize that in order to accept the marks in the sand as language you must ascribe to them someone or something's intentions, however fantastical. Thus, there is no language without intention. The authors add a further development to the example: you notice a submarine surfacing offshore. Figures appear on the deck, and one can be seen to observe the sand in front of you with binoculars and is distantly heard to shout, "It worked!" You now have, as Knapp and Benn Michaels point out, new and empirical evidence for authorship, which immediately restores the squiggles to the realm of intentional language. Their point is that intention is always empirically rather than theoretically

They are machine language instructions whose binary value happens to correspond with one of the values in the human-readable ASCII set. Since an eight-bit string can have one of 256 possible values and since the ASCII character set encompasses exactly half of those, such an outcome will not be uncommon. It is important to understand too that a byte is merely a string of binary numbers that can be interpreted by different programs in different ways—there's nothing *essential* about 01000001 that makes it an "A." It could just as easily be interpreted as a 6502 opcode (specifically EOR indirect, X) or the decimal number 65, depending on the programmer's instructions. Further down, however, we do find what appears to be some intentional text: bytes 221 through 247 of this sector encode a 27-character message that is one of the screen-level texts of the game, what Espen Aarseth has taught us to call a "scripton": "YOU ARE IN A STORAGE ROOM."[7]

Indeed.

Yet because this is *not* a storage room, not really, it is worth pausing for a moment to reflect on exactly what kind of textual conditions a tool like Fish-

---

determined, and that no mere theory can adjudicate questions of intentionality. See Knapp and Benn Michaels, "Against Theory," in *Against Theory: Literary Studies and the New Pragmatism*, ed. W. J. T. Mitchell (Chicago: University of Chicago Press, 1985), 11–30.

We can easily map the terms of this improbable example onto the example of electronic text sitting before us. It is worth noting that semantic meaning seems of secondary importance in this example: a wave text composed of random or nonsensical, but nonetheless obviously alphabetical, characters would really seem only slightly less remarkable than a wave writing Wordsworth. The notion that writing may be procedurally or algorithmically determined is captured in the final stage of their example, where some unspecified (that is, black boxed) but overtly "scientific" (that is, the product of human agency) process is apparently held responsible for the appearance of the squiggles on the sand. Knapp and Benn Michaels themselves proffer the question, "Can a computer speak?" as an example of a real-world application of their arguments. They note that the relevant issue is not "Can there be such a thing as intentionless speech?" (no, there cannot be) but rather "Can a computer have intentions?" This in turn is ground well trodden in debates on artificial intelligence and the philosophy of mind. Daniel C. Dennett is the leading proponent of what he terms "intentional systems," a line of argument that couples intentionality with reliable and predictable patterns of behavior.

7. See Aarseth, *Cybertext: Perspectives on Ergodic Literature* (Baltimore: Johns Hopkins University Press, 1997).

wings promotes. Matthew Fuller observes the variable interpretations of the written act that are made manifest in such disparate tools as BBEdit, vi, Word, and LaTeX, claiming "each piece of software constructs ways of seeing, knowing, and doing in the world that at once contain a model of that part of the world it ostensibly pertains to and that also shape it every time it is used."[8] If this is true, then the model of the world (or word) on display here will seem strange even to many who are acclimated to contemporary new media. Working with a hex viewer is, first and foremost, a slow and deliberate process, more oriented toward inspection and observation than intervention and productivity. Files are no longer the focus of attention; rather, one learns to think in terms of tracks, sectors, even individual bytes. The visual layout is tabular, bearing some resemblance to a spreadsheet. This layout follows from the fact that it is data's physical addressability that is being foregrounded, a very literal expression of what Jay David Bolter once called topographic writing. Even a "blank" disk fills the screen with ordered rows of unassigned bytes—FF FF 00 00—a stark contrast to the barren void of a new file opened in a text editor or word processor. The finite, volumetric nature of storage is reinforced by this presentation, as opposed to the fiction of unlimited space propagated within textual environments framed by scrollbars. The relentless geometry of 16 bytes per line, indiscriminately enjambing human-legible text whenever it does appear, further reinforces how far from conventional reading (and writing) the hex editor takes us. The display area is dominated by numeric rather than alphabetic characters, or more precisely by their juxtaposition (in the conventions for hex notation and the ASCII rendition of binary values). Yet the display also acknowledges the symbolic transformations of code, the arbitrary repetition—what Lev Manovich calls variability—that is a fundamental property of new media, since the hexadecimal notation is mirrored by its corresponding ASCII presentation. Neither the hex notation nor its corresponding ASCII rendition is machine readable in any actionable sense, however foreboding they might appear to those unaccustomed to their conventions. Rather, the hex editor assumes a user (and a reader) for whom the byte-level layout of the disk is meaningful information.

Hexadecimal notation and machine language were not always the sole purview of hackers, crackers, geeks, and gurus. The authoritative technical

8. Fuller, *Behind the Blip: Essays on the Culture of Software* (Brooklyn, NY: Automedia, 2003), 19–20.

publication from this era, *Beneath Apple DOS*, by Don Worth and Pieter Lechner (1985), spent over 100 weeks on the best-seller list, a feat testifying to the allure of such matters for a surprisingly catholic audience. Indeed, the book addresses itself to "the advanced programmer or the novice Apple user who wants to know more about the structure of diskettes."[9] The appeal to both "advanced programmers" and "novice Apple users"—mutually exclusive constituencies—captures something important about this moment of electronic textuality. I first learned about tracks, sectors, bytes, and nibbles as a teenager by using disk utilities to copy software with my Apple II. I was by no means an "advanced programmer," nor had I aspirations to become one; I just wanted to be able to swap programs around with my friends.[10] But this helps demonstrate why it is important to historicize our encounters with new media; Katherine Hayles, for example, in the course of an essay that does a lot of good work, glosses some of Espen Aarseth's terminology with a reference to "the textons of underlying code, which normally remain invisible to the casual user."[11] She is not talking about any particular software package or moment in digital culture. Yet, as *Beneath Apple DOS*'s performance on the 1980s best-seller lists shows, there was clearly a time when casual users were strongly motivated to PEEK and POKE at their textons; indeed, when they took such actions for granted.[12]

9.   Don Worth and Pieter Lechner, *Beneath Apple DOS*, (Quality Software, 1985), 1–1.

10.   The Help documentation in the APPLEWIN emulator, written by Michael O'Brien and Oliver Schmidt, testifies to the importance of these matters: "Unlike the PC, the Apple II had to perform much of its disk encoding in software. If programmers wanted to get tricky, they could bypass the operating system and do their own encoding, possibly changing the size of the sectors on the disk or the way in which the sectors were identified or stored. This prevented standard operating systems like DOS, along with their standard copying utilities, from accessing the disk. However, programs which were copy protected in this manner could still be copied with more sophisticated 'nibble copiers,' which copied each track on the disk bit for bit, rather than copying a sector at a time."

11.   See Hayles, "Flickering Connectivies in Shelley Jackson's *Patchwork Girl*: The Importance of Media-Specific Analysis," *Postmodern Culture* 10, no. 2 (2000), paragraph 9, online at http://www.iath.virginia.edu/pmc/text-only/issue.100/10.2hayles.txt.

12.   Mid-1990s Web design is another example of a moment when casual users were encouraged to examine code or "textons." Neophytes were routinely informed that the best way to learn HTML was by using the browser's View Source function (readily accessible from its top-

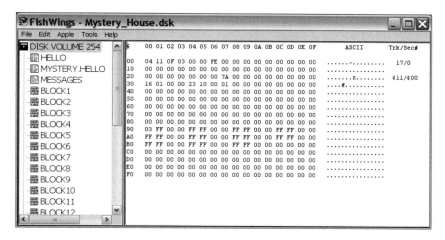

Figure 3.2 The Volume Table of Contents, track 17, sector 0. Screenshot by the author.

Track 17, sector 0: at first glance, this sector appears mostly barren. It is, however, the skeleton key to all of the disk's contents, including a map of where sectors are allocated in each and every track. Every DOS 3.3-formatted disk image will reveal this same information stored at track 17, sector 0, known as the Volume Table of Contents (VTOC) (figure 3.2). The location might appear arbitrary—presumably track 0 would be a more intuitive choice. However, track 17 lies at the radial midpoint of a 35-track disk. It therefore requires the least movement on the part of the mechanical drive head, desirable because the information in this track will be accessed over and over again in the course of a session. (This is a good example of a

---

level menus) to see how a given page was laid out. This was both practical and effective in an era before complex embedded objects, applets, scripting, stylesheets, database calls, and above all the automated, often noncompliant code generated by on-the-fly export functions in productivity software. Nowadays one typically "learns" HTML by manipulating a default template that comes from a desktop design application or an ISP. (Lisa Gitelman has written about the phenomenon of so-called Scaal pages, the name of a make-believe coffee shop featured in a Dream-Weaver tutorial whose identity persists in the Title field of numerous HTML documents because the software's users neglect to change them from the template's default. See *Always Already New: Media, History and the Data of Culture* [Cambridge: MIT Press, 2006], 141–143.)

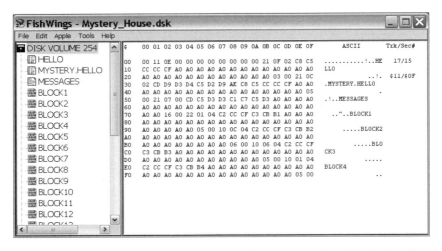

Figure 3.3 The disk Catalog. Note the entry for the file MESSAGES. Screenshot by the author.

seemingly arbitrary detail of the disk's formal geometry rendered transparent by an understanding of how the hardware works.) As one learns more about machine language, DOS, and low-level programming, the internal logic of the disk's topography begins to reveal itself, data clustering in consistent patterns and locales. DOS allocates those tracks that are adjacent to track 17 first, thereby continuing to minimize the physical distance the head must travel. Sectors 18–34 are allocated, working in toward the center of the disk, then tracks 16–0, moving out toward the edge. If I have a new disk without too much data I can predict the tracks where that data will be stored; as with many black boxes, the inner workings of DOS reveal themselves as mundane once the lid is lifted.

The second and third bytes in the VTOC (11, 0F in figure 3.2) point toward the beginning of the disk's Catalog entries, which are more granular records of the individual files stored on the disk. In this case the beginning of the Catalog is found in its traditional location, the last sector of track 17 (the same track as the VTOC); individual sectors of Catalog entries work their way back down toward the VTOC itself at sector 0 of the track. A typical Catalog entry appears in figure 3.3. For each file we discern the track and sector where it begins, its length, its name, and its type (Binary, Integer, Text, Applesoft). For example, MESSAGES begins at track 33, sector 6 (21h, 07h). It is a Text file (the 00 at byte 53) that extends for 22 sectors (16h at byte offset 72).[13] This file contains the predominant literary events in *Mystery House*, the simple screen-level texts that Espen Aarseth would call the game's scriptons and Nick Montfort its replies. Figure 3.4 shows how one of these

13. Before we take a closer look at MESSAGES, I want to discuss an anomaly that, in my earlier work with the disk image, I was not able to explain based on what I knew then about the functions of the electronic systems in question. "The bibliographer," writes Fredson Bowers in *Bibliography and Textual Criticism* (Oxford: Clarendon Press, 1964), his most deliberate meditation on the nature of material evidence, "must always start with the postulate of normality" (71). By this Bowers meant that printing and like activities were based on routine processes that are ultimately knowable and recoverable, and one should not assume that some unique bibliographical feature is an aberration—the result of error, ineptitude, stupidity, inebriation, etc.—unless there is "overwhelming evidence" (Bowers' phrase) that the phenomenon is exactly that. Such a stance is important because it creates the conditions for bibliographical knowledge; without it, "no laws of bibliographical evidence could exist, for the unknown human equation could successfully 'explain' any abnormality observed" (65). With electronic evidence, which is always at some level the result of formal, systematized, and automated functions and behaviors, the case for applying Bowers's postulate of normality is even stronger. While the appropriate explanation for some particular feature of an electronic object may or may not be known to an investigator, we can be sure that a normative process exists since any computational evidence is by definition the residue of some state of a formal system.

The value of Hex 16, Decimal 22 at the thirtieth byte in the VTOC means that no part of the program should have been found past track 22, the last track with sectors allocated to it. Yet the MESSAGES file, as we have seen, lies at tracks 33 and 34. Thus there is a contradiction. While it is possible for Apple II disks to contain files that operate outside of DOS—in fact a fairly common trick, which could increase the speed and efficiency of the program under the right circumstances—MESSAGES, as we have seen, has a perfectly normal DOS Catalog entry. How then to reconcile the evidence in the VTOC with what we find in the Catalog? The answer is of no practical consequence I can conceive, yet I still found the situation troubling because it suggested there was something about the function of the system in question (DOS) that eluded me, and I was reluctant to allow that state of affairs to persist. So I did more research, and I learned that many Apple II-era programs did not trouble themselves with updating the VTOC as they moved files around on the disk. For example, the popular Copy II program, one of the many utilities that might have been used to copy *Mystery House* onto the original diskette, is known to have not updated the VTOC. Presumably then it was Copy II or another such program that was used to overwrite earlier content on the disk with *Mystery House*. Although this conclusion is merely "probable" rather than "demonstrable" in Bowers' terms, I have succeeded in producing a reasonable explanation that can account for the state of the disk image. The alternative, to suggest that DOS, like a careless compositor setting type, had simply made a mistake in the VTOC, is not consistent with the behavior of formal systems as agents of textuality.

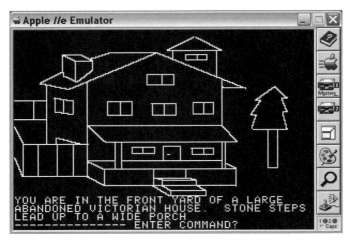

Figure 3.4 Mystery_House.dsk as it appears in the AppleWin emulator. Screenshot by the author.

texts appears on the opening screen of the game, in the APPLEWIN emulator environment.

This same text is available to us in the FishWings environment. There we can access all of the game's textons (which, continuing Aarseth's terminology, the program promotes to scriptons by way of its traversal function) in one continuous, linear sequence by opening the file named MESSAGES (visible earlier in the disk image's tree view). They appear to be in no particular order, and the experience of reading them in one long scrolling window feels unnatural, a violation of the fundamental ergodic features of interactive fiction, the rhythm of keyboard input and textual reward (see figure 3.5). Thus the game's replies, delivered to the screen as discrete utterances—a word, a phrase, a sentence or two at most—are visible here stored as a single file. The text appears unnatural because of both its linearity and the apparent arbitrary arrangement of its strings, which form no meaningful narrative if read strictly in sequence. This view, however, is still more conventionalized than the actual byte representations for this data in the hexadecimal environment (figure 3.6). Sectors of tracks are allocated in descending order, so the fragment "EHIND YOU WITH A BANG" visible at the top left of the ASCII column actually continues the reply "THE WALL CLOSES B," which occupies the last bytes in track 33, sector 1. Here we find that the physical geometry of the media is

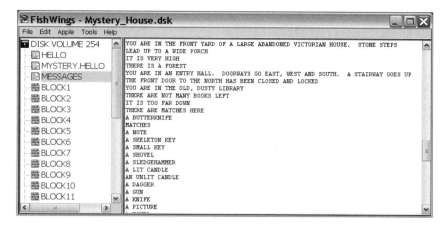

Figure 3.5   The MESSAGES file accessed in its entirety. Screenshot by the author.

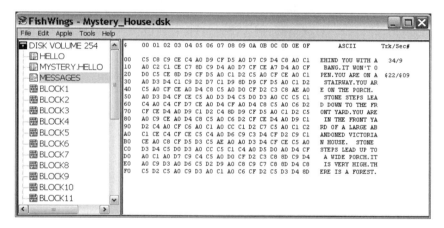

Figure 3.6   A disk sector containing a portion of MESSAGES, track 34, sector 9. Screenshot by the author.

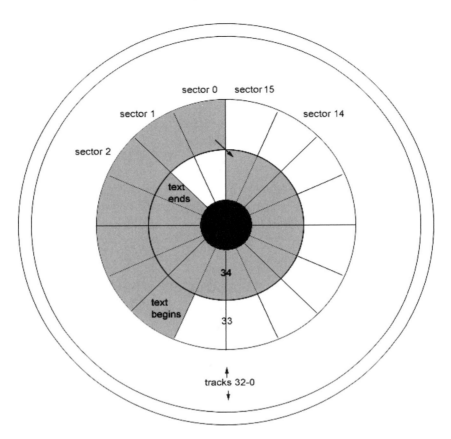

Figure 3.7 Diagram of MESSAGES' distribution across the Mystery_House.dsk disk image, showing the file beginning at track 33, sector 6 and spiraling clockwise and inward to completion at track 34, sector 2. Figure by the author.

primary, underscoring the ultimate binary self-identity of data at the level of the magnetic fluxes on platter—any linguistic unit above the level of a single character is vulnerable to the disruptions and interruptions of the relentlessly volumetric storage logic. My mapping of the distribution of the MESSAGES file across the 22 sectors of the disk image is shown in figure 3.7.

Track 24, sector 1: here, amid the ASCII noise of opcodes and operands, the sensational but somehow clipped and monotonic prose of the game replies ("IT IS SAM, THE MECHANIC. HE HAS BEEN HIT IN THE HEAD WITH A BLUNT OBJECT"), a joyful eruption (figure 3.8). This data—

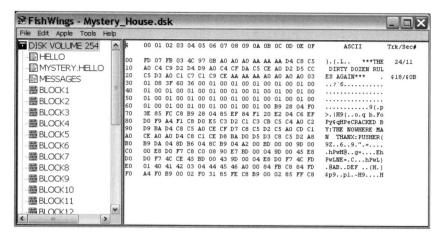

Figure 3.8 Remnants of previous data from the disk image reveal evidence of a pirated ("cracked") program. Screenshot by the author.

like four-color comic book ink splattered amidst the phosphorescent green pixels of an old monochrome monitor—does not belong to *Mystery House*.[14] Between tracks 23 and 33 we find evidence that at one time this disk had at least two other games stored on it: *Dung Beetles*, a 1982 *Pac-Man*-like maze/chase game created by Bob Bishop (published by Datasoft), and *Blitzkrieg*, a simple ground-to-air shooter by Mark Cross for Programma in 1979, with roots hearkening back to *Space Invaders* (figure 3.9). Like a palimpsest, or so-called dirty books laced with marginalia and marks from the readers who have previously owned them, beloved by some collectors (notably Henry Folger of the Folger Shakespeare Library) and pored over by historians of reading and writing, a floppy disk image can also reveal the hand of the reader or user. We do not know who this person was (though we might have, had there been personal documents or records present on the disk), but we can learn something about digital culture at this moment, and perhaps even more about electronic textual transmission in general.

14. The text we read here would have displayed on so-called crack screens, banners and marquees placed on or before the manufacturer's screens in the pirated versions of these games so that the crackers could claim credit. A collection of typical crack screens is available here: http://www.textfiles.com/artscene/intros/APPLEII/.

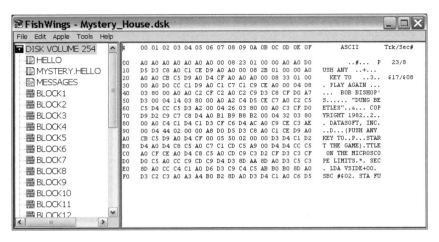

Figure 3.9 Remnants of a copy of Bob Bishop's *Dung Beetles* (Datasoft, 1982) on Mystery_ House.dsk. Screenshot by the author.

The space of the disk is volumetric and finite, precisely the qualities brought out by the hex editor. When a file is deleted, DOS adjusts its Catalog entry so that the sectors no longer appear to be occupied. But the actual bits remain intact until they are overwritten with new data. We have then bits that were recorded on some original source media, transferred to the electronic representation of that media that is the disk image as part of a bit-level copy, and revealed only in the specific environment of the hex editor. The closest analogy might be to a photographic facsimile image of a printed page containing invisible writing—such as the kind exposed under a blacklight—where that secret writing somehow transfers with the facsimile image (that was created only out of the wavelengths of the visible spectrum). At the very least this should complicate our sense of what it means to reproduce, or "copy," electronic content.

Here is what we know: *Mystery House* was released into the public domain in 1987, so the disk image must be later than that (for it includes the public domain announcement). That would make *Dung Beetles* and *Blitzkrieg* ancient by any gamer's standards, the state of the art having progressed dramatically since the first half of the decade. Of course *Mystery House* itself was also ancient, but it had a nostalgic resonance and historical interest that these other games, as derivatives of arcade archetypes, probably did not. So we can conjecture that at some point the user pulled out a well-worn floppy containing old games no longer much played and overwrote it with a copy of the now-public domain *Mystery House*. The user would have probably owned lots of games, many of them perhaps pirated, and might have been in the habit of writing over the older and less-played ones after a time. He or she would also have most likely had more than a casual appreciation for Apple II games or for interactive fiction, since it is doubtful *Mystery House* would have seemed very compelling on its own terms in 1987.

As the game's instructions remind us, "HI-RES ADVENTURE #1 ('MYS-TERY HOUSE') TAKES PLACE IN AN OLD HOUSE WITH MANY ROOMS." Game play revolves around a series of murders, with hidden treasure as the apparent motive. For its original players, Sierra On-Line's *Mystery House* would have been a mildly diverting piece of interactive fiction, with interest driven chiefly by the novelty of the embedded graphics. Solving the murder is not hard, and the game offers no replay value; once the mysteries of the house have been revealed there is no conceivable motivation to walk back up the steps and open up the front door again. As an electronic textual artifact then, normative play is perhaps the least interesting level on which to engage it. For a software pirate or cracker prior to the game's public domain release in 1987, *Mystery House* would have been a trophy, one of many, a small commodity in the underground economy of warez, tags, and reps—"THANX PUSHER, THE DIRTY DOZEN RIDES AGAIN." For the contemporary scholar and theorist of electronic literature, however, *Mystery House*—or more properly Mystery_House.dsk—becomes a multivalent forensic environment, one where all of these different levels of engagement—player, pirate/cracker, postmortem investigator—find their correspondences in the multiple layers of textual events that both drive the game as code and are explicitly thematized within its forensically charged spaces. By walking through Mystery_House .dsk, by reading the disk image forensically, we thus have the makings of what Katherine Hayles would call a media-specific analysis: a close reading of the text that is also sensitive to the minute particulars of its medium and the idiosyncratic production and reception histories of the work.[15]

15. Hayles first discusses media-specific analysis (MSA) in "Flickering Connectivities in Shelley Jackson's *Patchwork Girl*: The Importance of Media-Specific Analysis," *Postmodern Culture* 10, no. 2 (January 2000): http://www3.iath.virginia.edu/pmc/text-only/issue.100/10.2hayles.txt. "Useful as poststructuralist approaches have been in enabling textuality to expand beyond the printed page, they have also had the effect of eliding differences in media, treating everything

A postscript: importantly, the texts contained in the MESSAGES file are not the only form of writing in the game; "messages" also appear on several cryptic notes and other surfaces scattered around the house (like the Welcome mat at the front door), and these are rendered graphically, as part of the game's inline drawings. Their "text" is actually comprised by vector coordinates, which are stored elsewhere on the disk.[16] One consequence of this is that we can't hack the game and discover the text of the notes in advance by using a hex editor. (On the other hand, we *can* hack the game to discover the identity of the murderer!) There are four notes in all, presented here in the order they are discovered:

VALUABLE JEWELS ARE HIDDEN IN THIS HOUSE. FINDERS-KEEPERS.

$7 - 6 = 1$. THEN I AM DONE!

YOU WILL NEVER FIND IT! IT'S ALL MINE!

IT'S IN THE BASEMENT!

---

from fashion to fascism as a semiotic system. Perhaps now, after the linguistic turn has yielded so many important insights, it is time to turn again to a careful consideration of what difference the medium makes" (2). An alternative, or perhaps complement, to media-specific analysis and the kind of forensic reading I have done here is to be found in the realm of remix culture. Taking advantage of the fact that *Mystery House* is now in the public domain, in 2005, funded by an award from Turbulence.org, Nick Montfort, Dan Shiovitz, and Emily Short "re-implemented" the original game program as a "modern, free language for interactive fiction development . . . mak[ing] a kit freely available to the public so that others may modify *Mystery House Taken Over* as they see fit." See http://turbulence.org/Works/mystery/. They then commissioned ten contemporary interactive fiction authors and artists to re-imagine the original game. Montfort's contribution is entitled "Mystery House Kracked by the Flippy Disk" (flippy disk refers to the trick of double-siding a disk with a hole-puncher); it uses the hacker argot of skillz and warez to turn the house's internal spaces into an architectural mirror of the hacking and cracking cultures that once surrounded it, an instance of the forensic imagination wherein the inscriptive and computational particulars of certain specific software practices are aestheticized and presented as a new interpretation of the work.

16.   This computational divide between text as character data and text as image is commonplace in electronic environments, and it is telling to find it here in a game expressly conceived to unite word and image. Once again then, we discover the heterogeneity of digital inscription.

These simple texts provide no essential information (not even the last one) and they do not vary from one game to the next; as such there is no practical incentive to read them more than once. That the "author" of the notes is one of the nonplayer characters in the game becomes obvious only in the second and third texts, and the player never discovers any credible motivation for why they might have been written and deposited around the house in the first place. Still, they seem to consume an inordinate amount of the player's attention by operating differently from any other object in the game. The player can only have one note in hand at any given time. The game's instructions are explicit (and punning) on this point: "A NOTE OF CAUTION: CARRYING MORE THAN ONE NOTE MAY BE CONFUSING AS THE COMPUTER WILL ARBITRARILY DECIDE WHICH ONE TO READ OR DROP." We are therefore confronted with a programmatic instance of textual instability: if a player picks up more than one note at the same time he or she will not have any control over which one remains in hand; likewise, dropping one note in the presence of another will result in a random choice as to which one gets picked up. In fact, what we are witnessing is an artifact of the program's two-word parser, which prohibits the use of adjectival qualifiers like "First Note," "Second Note," and so on.[17] As electronic documents, or rather as programmed representations of printed documents, the notes are read-only—you can take hold of them, view them, and drop them, but not erase them, change them, or hang on to more than one of them.[18] (In that sense, they seem to function more like volatile RAM memory than long-term disk storage.)

So why were the notes included in the game? Perhaps they are a plot device of another kind. The graphics for *Mystery House* were created with a Versa-Writer, a primitive CAD tablet that worked by tracing a stylus (mounted on a mechanical armature) over a line drawing.[19] The software then plotted a

17. The player can also manipulate the various notes by using the terms MEMO, PAPER, LETTER—an interesting collapse of document types characteristic of interactive fiction, where the program is encouraged to respond to "synonyms."

18. A side effect of these conditions is that an earnest player may be led to transcribe the notes onto paper—thereby adding another layer of textuality to the play of the game and introducing all of the usual errors that accompany scribal transcription, even for these simple strings (there are several small errors, what textual critics would call accidentals, in the notes as they are reproduced in various walk-throughs around the Web).

19. See http://web.mit.edu/invent/iow/williams.html.

vector image that corresponded to the drawn art. It did best with perspectival renderings, such as a hallway or a room; hence its suitability for *Mystery House*'s architectural space. Given the ergonomics of the device—the way one worked it with one's hands—it was probably inevitable to experiment and see what it would do with handwriting. Perhaps Roberta Williams felt the allure of the machine "reading" her writing as she made its mechanical arm retrace her letterforms. So the notes, which became a major feature of the game, may have had their origin in the human hand's interaction with a very specific piece of hardware. Or not: while we know she worked with the VersaWriter, the rest of my scenario is conjecture. But it captures something of the instinct to write, to fill space with inscriptions, to leave an autographic mark on a computer screen—a surface which, even though only an arm's length away, must have seemed far more remote since it was heretofore accessible only through the inexorable mediations of code.[20] The allographic shapes of the letterforms would also have proven a very faithful subject for representation, much higher in fidelity than the crude stick figures and other objects depicted in the rest of the drawings. Ironically, the written notes yielded the most realistic images in the game.

Formal Materiality I: Being Digital

The varied forms of textuality made manifest in Mystery_House.dsk are indicative of a wider phenomenon. The kind of document modeling undertaken by Roberta and Ken Williams in the course of programming the notes' behaviors into the game is a fundamental characteristic of all digital media, where the interactive environment is a formal projection that replicates or models specific behaviors and affordances. Programming the notes in *Mystery House*, and programming the behaviors, features, and functionality of the word processor I am using to write this text, were both acts in which documents were formally modeled to behave in certain ways in certain environments: in other words, both the notes in *Mystery House* as well as my word processing document each manifest a distinctive *formal materiality*. The complement to forensic materiality as I have been defining it, formal materiality is the term I use to capture the multiple behaviors and states of digital objects and the relational

20. Not that the VersaWriter was exempt from such mediations. Quite the contrary, in fact: Ken Williams had to write the code himself to interface the device with their Apple II. See note 19.

attitudes by which some are naturalized as a result of the procedural friction, or torque (as I called it in the introduction), imposed by different software environments. My word processor presents me with a certain document model, and while its formal behaviors ultimately come to rest in the forensic materiality of chips, memory, and other aspects of the hardware configuration, much of what we tend to essentialize about new media is in fact merely the effect of a particular set of social choices implemented and instantiated in the formal modeling of the digital environments in question. Boot Mystery _House.dsk in the emulator and you will look under every floorboard, behind every picture frame, and still find no trace of the earlier games and cracker tags. Exposing this particular facet of the digital object that is the disk image in the hex editor creates the illusion of dramatic discovery only because we assume the emulator is the normative environment for Mystery_House.dsk. These assumptions and suppositions are wrong, I believe, and speak to a misapprehension about what being digital really means. Both the emulator *and* the hex editor are programmatic computational environments applying some particular logic—a certain formal materiality—to the string of bits in question. Both are modeling the digital object that is Mystery_House.dsk, imposing upon it a formal regimen that assigns certain behaviors and affordances and denies others.

What, then, is formal materiality? Danny Hillis's comments about digital computers are indispensable as a starting place: "[T]he implementation technology must produce perfect outputs from imperfect inputs, nipping small errors in the bud. This is the essence of digital technology, which restores signals to near perfection at every stage" (18).[21] This is the most effective and important formulation of the nature of the digital that I know. Crucially, the word *digital* in this sense does not necessarily mean electronic—Hillis's remarks are in fact based on a computer built out of Tinkertoys. The digital/ analog distinction has instead everything to do with Nelson Goodman's semiotic categories of the allographic versus the autographic. In Goodman's terms, allographic objects, such as written texts, *fulfill* their ontology in reproduction, while autographic objects, such as a painting, *betray* their ontology in reproduction.[22] A copy of the *Mona Lisa* is just that—a *copy* of an acknowledged

21.   W. Daniel Hillis, *The Pattern on the Stone: The Simple Ideas That Make Computers Work* (New York: Basic Books, 1998).

22.   See Goodman's influential *Languages of Art: An Approach to a Theory of Symbols* (Indianapolis: Hackett, 1976), especially chapters 3 and 4.

original—while a copy of Mary Shelley's novel *Frankenstein* is a perfectly valid way of experiencing the work (you don't have to go to the Bodleian Library in Oxford and sit down with the holograph manuscript to legitimately claim to have read *Frankenstein*). "Sameness of spelling" emerges as Goodman's chief criterion for allographic identification: so long as two texts have the same spelling—in other words, if every sentence in the novel or line in the poem were laid end to end as a single continuous character string—then they are allographically indistinguishable.[23] Sameness of spelling is, in turn, predicated on an allographic object's elementary *digital* composition. As Morris Eaves argues, digitization is the process by which complex units are made simpler by breaking them down into smaller units. It is not merely a phenomenon of the current age, but an active force throughout technological history. "As a rule of thumb, the more deeply digitization penetrates the more efficient the process becomes."[24] This has immediate and tangible repercussions in our technologies for reproducing texts and images. As Eaves goes on to say:

Alphabetic technology, the division of all words into a small set of uniform letters—twenty-six in the Latin alphabet, plus 10 numerals and a few "accidentals"—made efficient letterpress printing possible. Typesetters set their type in letters, not words or sentences, and a handful of little metal blocks could print every sentence. (186)

23. *Languages of Art*, 115. Goodman elaborates: "[T]he fact that a literary work is in a definite notation, consisting of certain signs or characters that are to be combined by concatenation, provides the means for distinguishing the properties constitutive of the work from all contingent properties—that is, for fixing the required features and the limits of permissible variation in each. Merely by determining that the copy before us is spelled correctly we can determine that it meets all requirements for the work in question" (116). Many readers will no doubt object that "sameness of spelling" elides all manner of practical editorial considerations—instances where it might be reasonable and intellectually defensible to emend the text—as well as the undeniably *autographic* dimension of a two-hundred-year-old literary manuscript (or indeed any material artifact). To be sure. My aim is not to suggest that Goodman's position is unimpeachable, but rather to convey the semiotic basis for his distinction between allographic and autographic objects. In digital media the allographic functions in an ideal state it could never really attain in other media—not because digital media are inherently immaterial, but because more than any media before them they have been endowed with the mechanisms to sustain that elusive state as a functional reality.

24. Morris Eaves, *The Counter-Arts Conspiracy: Art and Industry in the Age of Blake* (Ithaca: Cornell University Press, 1992), 186.

Replace Goodman's strings of characters or the letterpress typesetters' little metal blocks with a computer's strings of one and zeros, and add state-of-the-art error detection and correction to continually restore signals to their optimal state, and we can begin to understand why digital computers support and sustain an ideal allographic environment.

My argument, then, is this: computers are unique in the history of writing technologies in that they present a premeditated material environment built and engineered to propagate an illusion of immateriality; the digital nature of computational representation is precisely what enables this illusion—or else call it a working model—of immaterial behavior. While signals (voltage differentials, let us say) degrade as they traverse a computer's architecture, just as they would with any physical phenomena, they do so within certain predictable tolerances. There are resting places within the transmission process where the operating system pauses, evaluates the signal, checks for errors, and corrects them before passing the reinvigorated signal further down the symbolic line, where it eventually gets delivered to the user in its "perfect and original" form. Reading data from a hard drive is a good example: the reality is that hard drives make errors all the time—any drive that did not would be operating at such low data densities and speeds as to be unmarketable. However, every sector of data on the disk includes error correcting codes derived from established formal procedures (the Reed Solomon algorithm is favored). The mathematics generates a bit sequence that serves as a redundant expression of the original data; if the two fail to match up during a read or write task then an error is indicated, and the task is repeated. Users never see such errors, which are detected and corrected in the space of milliseconds. This contributes to the way in which the drive is perceived as an abstraction identified only by an arbitrary volume letter ("C") or an icon on the desktop. Absent are the range of small, localized glitches characteristic of other media—the typo in the newspaper, the scratch on the vinyl record, snow on the TV channel—that remind us of their mundane materiality.[25] Programs may

25.   Lisa Gitelman documents one very telling instance of this phenomenon in "Souvenir Foils: On the Status of Print at the Origin of Recorded Sound." (In *New Media 1740–1915*. Lisa Gitelman and Geoffrey B. Pingree, eds. Cambridge, MA: MIT Press, 2003: 157–173). The episode in question concerns a "typo" which may or may not have been intentional on the part of a newspaper compositor who, reporting on Edison's phonograph—a machine that threatened to put compositors out of business by virtue of its new method of recording text—mis-sets the word

crash, files may become corrupted, code will inevitably have bugs, but we don't open the document we were working on yesterday to find that certain characters have been transposed or some sentence has been left behind in the transition from screen to disk and back again.

Think back to Goodman's character strings: the operating system is capable of getting the spelling right each and every time. The concept is similar to telegraphic relays boosting a Morse signal, itself an allographic system. Such a process works because allographic reproduction doesn't demand perfect (autographic) fidelity, but only success within a given range of variation. It is identical in principle to the way we recognize an A as the first letter of the Roman alphabet in a variety of fonts. An A is always just an A and never an A that is almost a B.[26] (Goodman's term for this is "finite differentiation.") John Haugeland offers the example of placing tokens on a chessboard.[27] Were players instructed to place their tokens at some precisely specified distance from the sides of the board, there would always be room for error as the granularity of the measurement increased—it would be impossible to successfully place the token exactly 0.43747 inches from the nearest edge of the square, as in his example (10). Or even if it was possible to do so once or twice with painstaking care and heroic effort, it would be impossible to repeat with any predictable reliability. The task is fundamentally autographic in nature, since there is only one condition for success with no tolerance for variation. If, however, players were instructed to place tokens in a certain square on the grid, say three up and two across, then the process is possible to repeat almost effortlessly since, assuming good faith effort on the part of the participants, their actions will always be within the formal tolerances for error (it doesn't matter where in the square the token goes, so long as it is placed in the appropriate

---

"type" as "tpye" in a sentence describing the new textuality of the machine, which "is not in tpye [sic], but in punctures" (168). As Gitelman notes, "The typographical error is exactly that, graphical. It produces an unpronounceable 'utterance,' which remains viable only on the page, seen and not said" (168).

26. For a good discussion of this phenomenon, see James Elkins, *The Domain of Images* (Ithaca: Cornell University Press, 2001).

27. "What Is Mind Design?" in *Mind Design II: Philosophy, Psychology, and Artificial Intelligence*, ed. John Haugeland (Cambridge: MIT Press, 1997): 1–28.

Figure 3.10 Allographic as opposed to autographic representation. Autographically, the position of the topmost pawn noticeably varies in each image. Allographically, its positions are equivalent to one another by virtue of occupying the same square, a finite and discretely defined—that is to say, digital—space. Images courtesy of Kari M. Kraus.

square of the grid). Perfection is not only possible but effortless and commonplace, as is shown in figure 3.10.

These two properties of digital computation—its allographic identity conditions and the implementation of mathematically reliable error detection and correction—are what ultimately account for the immaterial nature of digital expression. My point is not that this immateriality is chimerical or nonexistent, but rather that it exists as the end product of long traditions and trajectories of engineering that were deliberately undertaken to achieve and implement it. The computer's formal environment is therefore a *built* environment, manufactured and machined, and it has as its most basic property the recursive ability to mimic or recapitulate the behaviors of other formal environments.

This is, of course, the significance of the Universal Turing Machine, the set of mathematical and mechanical procedures defined by the British mathematician Alan Turing in a 1937 paper titled "On Computable Numbers, with an Application to the *Entscheidungsproblem*" (decision problem). A Universal Turing Machine is a conceptual machine; it construes, in essence, a symbolic machine designed to manipulate other symbolic machines. But it is also an iconic figure, modeled and visualized with a remarkably consistent set of explanatory conventions because Turing himself took great pains to delineate its operational components. (As Friedrich Kittler and others have noted, Turing appropriated fundamental features of the typewriter as a writing machine, including its finite key configuration and the spatial regimentation of the inscriptive field.[28])

28. Kittler, *Gramophone, Film, Typewriter*, 245ff.

In a paper dense with mathematical references, Turing lingers over the inscriptive particulars of the traditional scene of computation:

Computing is normally done by writing certain symbols on paper. We may suppose this paper is divided into squares like a child's arithmetic book. In elementary arithmetic the two-dimensional character of the paper is sometimes used. But such a use is always avoidable, and I think that it will be agreed that the two-dimensional character of paper is no essential of computation. I assume then that the computation is carried out on one-dimensional paper, i.e. on a tape divided into squares. (75)[29]

"Computing" in this passage must be understood as the human activity of numeric manipulation, not a reference to actual computing machinery. By the two-dimensional character of the paper Turing means to call attention to the way sums are worked in columns, or perhaps long division. His point is that these operations can all be technically conducted serially, in rows rather than columns, and that the adoption of a vertical dimension is merely a concession to human cognitive faculties. We find, then, a curious bit of origami: the two dimensions of an ordinary sheet of paper become the one-dimensional ribbon of a length of tape (having only horizontal direction).

At a very literal level, even Turing's two-dimensional view of paper is an idealization (or a formalization—as is perhaps signaled by the artificial internal divisions introduced by the square grid—since paper is manifestly three-dimensional, with weight, heft, *and* depth in addition to length and breadth. A reduction to one-dimensional tape is an additional formalization, since of course tape has some modest verticality, even if the horizontal is its dominant measure.[30] In Turing's model the one-dimensionality is an expression of the serial nature of the computational array—one symbol always to the immediate left or right of another, with no possibility of vertical transposition. Moreover, the tape itself is understood to be infinite. Thus the final conceit of an infinite tape, overtly immaterial and idealized, is in fact only the latest in a cascade of

29. "On Computable Numbers, With an Application to the *Entscheidungsproblem*," in *The Essential Turing: The Ideas That Gave Birth to the Computer Age*, ed. B. Jack Copeland (Oxford: Oxford University Press, 2004): 58–90.

30. The command line prompt, with its infinite rightward extension, is an emodied legacy of Turing's tape, as is the UNIX bang bang (!!) password convention (typical notation for the start of a Turing Machine tape).

successive formal idealizations, each prior state literalized, concretized, and formally materialized relative to its even more abstract successor.

I am using the word *cascade* here with awareness of Latour's articulation of the concept in *Science in Action*, where it functions as the central dynamic of those "centers of calculation" that accumulate and mobilize inscriptions. The cascade is the process of abstracting inscriptions, via consolidation or tabulation or redaction. Latour's example is a government census in which the raw traces of the primary inscriptions—responses to the questionnaires—are tabulated, summarized, analyzed, and visualized, each successive abstraction taking us further from the original site of inscription but rendering the data more mobile and more malleable: "At each translation of traces onto a new one something is *gained*. . . . demographers can *see* things on the final curve summarizing the census that none of the pollsters, none of the politicians, none of the interviewed people could see before" (emphases in original).[31] The cascade is also, I would argue, the process of siting an inscription in an allographic modality, such that it becomes available for procedural manipulation and formal abstraction. In Latour's terms, this would be called "mobilization," and it is the basic means by which digital computers work. (The 1890 United States census, as it happens, saw one of the first significant uses of computing machinery, Herman Hollerith's punch card tabulator, manufactured by the company that became IBM.) The cascade is most often described in idealized form in computer science textbooks as a tower or stack, using the metaphor of layers to suggest progression through different levels of abstraction—screen level effects, uncompiled source code, assembly language, machine language, voltage differentials, and so forth.

31. Latour, *Science in Action* (Cambridge: Harvard University Press, 1987), 236. For the "cascade," see chapter 6, Part B. I am aware that Latour introduces a caution against the promiscuous use of the word "abstraction" when, as he notes, it becomes shorthand for some conjecture about a quality of mind—the ability to think in the abstract, as the saying goes. Not so, insists Latour, who reminds us of the immediate documentary reality of every stage of the cascade, no matter where in the progression of activities that contribute to a process of abstraction it lies (241ff). The bar graph summarizing the census is possessed of the same documentary reality, is a product of the same kinds of handiwork, as the questionnaire where the data originated. The graph may *abstract*, but it is not in itself abstract or an abstraction. In what follows, I use abstraction to distinguish between relative states of the cascade, where abstraction consists in the difference between one set of computational behaviors and another, when the two behaviors stand in mutual relative relation to one another, typically but not necessarily recursive.

The tower or stack image is commonplace. It is less common, however, to also find the cascade located in the physical processes of storage and deletion, writing and overwriting, that govern computational operations at the level of their actual inscription. The passage that follows is making the point that the deletion of information, which we looked at closely in chapter 1, is intimately tied to the level of physical and formal abstraction with which it is expressed:

The phenomenon of deletion and persistence can happen at any abstraction level. At the abstraction level of file systems, deleted information persists in unallocated disk blocks until it is overwritten. At the abstraction level of magnetic-disk-reading heads, overwritten information persists as analog modulations on the newer information. And at the abstraction level of magnetic domains, overwritten information persists as magnetic patterns on the sides of magnetic tracks . . .[32]

"Volatility," the authors go on to note, "is an artifact of the abstractions that make computer systems useful" (160). This is a key insight, as important to an understanding of formal materiality as Danny Hillis's earlier comment about digital systems restoring signals to perfection at every stage of their transmission. When we combine the two, we can at last locate the dynamic tension—or call it an exquisite equilibrium—between inscription and abstraction, digitality and volatility, that makes computers technically and historically distinctive as writing machines. Information becomes more volatile (and more usable or available) as it becomes more abstract because it is more susceptible to the basic operators of allographic manipulation, deftly pinpointed by Kari M. Kraus as substitution, deletion, insertion, transposition, relocation, and repetition.[33] These are the operations which can be performed with *any* set of discrete units or tokens or symbols. Thus in the case of Mystery_House.dsk we discover on the original diskette the incompletely overwritten remnants of previous software, preserved by the bit-level copy process that created the disk image—a piece of 1980s software culture frozen in allographic amber. Kraus's operations are also all susceptible to algorithmic

32.   Dan Farmer and Wietse Venema, *Forensic Discovery* (Upper Saddle River, NJ: Addison-Wesley, 2005), 159.

33.   Kraus, *Conjectural Criticism: Computing Past and Future Texts*, dissertation (University of Rochester, 2006). See especially chapter 1, "The Beauty of Innuendos." Essentially a semiotics of prediction, Kraus's work is an important and original treatment of the role of allographic manipulation in digital sign systems.

expression, and if they can be implemented mathematically they can become part of the programmed behavior of digital computers as we know them. The Sharpen feature, ubiquitous in image processing software, is a good example. Sharpen is an instance of what is technically known as an area process transformation. It works by multiplying the color value of a pixel by the quantity of its neighboring pixels and then lightening or darkening the pixel based on whether the resulting figure is higher or lower than the sum of the color values of all the neighboring pixels. The result of this algorithmic operation, repeated over the length and breadth of a picture's surface, is that the image as a whole appears to come into tighter focus. Other image processing filters operate in a similar manner, and the most common algorithms (brighten, smooth, emboss, and so forth) are all readily available in textbooks. What we see, then, is an inverse relation between the autographic but illegible signatures of actual computational inscription—the individualized trace of a bit representation as instrumented, say, by magnetic force microscopy—and the computational power that follows from its allographic manipulation in a digital—discrete—format. The latter is what accounts for both the volatility of data and its propensity for proliferation and multiplication, since it is being represented and propagated by allographic mechanisms amenable to the kind of error checking and correction Hillis has noted. Thus the difficulty of erasing or expunging digital information. Farmer and Venema, the authors of the computer forensics textbook quoted above, put it this way: "As we peel away layer after layer of illusions, information becomes more and more accurate because it has undergone less and less processing. But as we descend close and closer toward the level of raw bits the information becomes less meaningful, because we know less and less about its purpose" (9).

At some point then in the inscriptive cascade, information routinely slips from a formal to a forensic materiality and back again. Where exactly does this slippage occur? The answer must be media-specific to individual hardware and software configurations, individual technologies of storage and inscription. But in the case of the hard drive, the most common storage device in use today, it happens in the buzzing nano-gap between the magnetic read/write head of the drive and the surface of the platter below, moving at some 10,000 RPM, the distance separating the two akin to flying a jumbo jet inches above the surface of the earth.[34]

34. This oft-repeated but nonetheless always astonishing analogy is the product of a simple mathematical extrapolation. See http://www.answers.com/topic/head-crash for just one example.

Formal Materiality II: Applications

When working with software, we establish and dissolve formal materialities routinely as digital objects move between different information states. We see this as an object is transformed through a succession of different formats, each one imposing a different computational structure than its predecessor.[35] Digital images, for example, obey and respond to certain logics, behaviors, and constraints that follow from their composition at the computational level. Take the World Wide Web's ubiquitous JPEG (.jpg) image format, a so-called lossy compression format optimized for use with photorealistic images. The JPEG algorithm does its work by discarding ("losing") information that falls below the threshold of human vision. A JPEGed image will typically be smaller in size (and will thus download faster) than its master image, because it quite literally does not consist of as much information. JPEG first divides a given image into 8 × 8-pixel blocks, and then assesses the importance of each pixel in the image's overall composition.[36] These determinations are based on frequency; information (pixel values) that occurs too frequently is discarded as redundant, which is what ultimately reduces the file size of the image. (This is why images compressed with a coarse JPEG setting typically appear granular or blocky; the algorithm is not making subtle distinctions, and thus information above the threshold of human vision is discarded.) Converting visual information into frequency ranges is a good example of what I meant earlier when speaking of computers as symbolic and allographic. The image is not treated as a conceptual whole—what J. J. Gibson would have called a "picture surface"—but rather as a data set, a formal construct whose tokens are susceptible to mathematical manipulation. But although JPEG can degrade an image to the point where its missing data is optically apparent, the algorithm's proper function is to compress the digital object, not to influence its eventual display.

35. See my chapter "The Word as Image in an Age of Digital Reproduction," *Eloquent Images: Word and Image in the Age of New Media*, eds. Mary E. Hocks and Michelle R. Kendricks (Cambridge: MIT Press, 2003): 137–156. The chapter demonstrates ways in which the formal materialities of digital images and machine-readable text can be leveraged in concert with one another in the context of applied humanities computing.

36. The process is called a Discrete Cosign Transformation. A basic explanation of how JPEG works is available at http://dynamo.ecn.purdue.edu/~ace/jpeg-tut/jpegtut1.html.

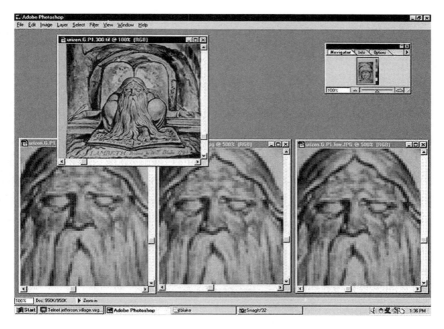

Figure 3.11   The "same" image at 500 percent magnification in Photoshop: a 955K TIFF, a 144K JPEG, and a 37K JPEG. Screenshot by the author.

This is illustrated in figure 3.11, a screenshot from Adobe Photoshop with four copies of the "same" image—one at 100 percent magnification and three at 500 percent magnification. The first of the three images displayed at 500 percent is a TIFF image created from a first generation transparency of the frontispiece to William Blake's *Book of Urizen*, while the middle and right-most images are both JPEG derivatives of the original TIFF (one at a high retention setting, and the other at a low retention setting). All three images appear optically identical, even at 500 percent magnification. But their file sizes differ dramatically: 955K, 144K, and 37K, respectively, a function of the JPEG compression. Therefore, the JPEG derivative is an altogether different image, even if the difference is not optically observable. This is why digital preservationists regard JPEG as a poor choice for serious archival imaging, despite the quick download times that lend it practical value on the Web— precisely because of the formal materiality of the JPEG algorithm, which introduces difference into the image and its derivatives at the level of how much information is retained. Figure 3.12, for example, depicts a TIFF

Figure 3.12 A TIFF (*right*) derived from a JPEG that was created at a very low retention setting (the original TIFF from which the JPEG was derived is at left)—the information discarded by the JPEG cannot be recovered, thereby accounting for the poor quality of the derivative TIFF. Screenshot by the author.

derived from the low retention JPEG used in the previous example, displayed alongside the original master TIFF. Note the muddy quality of the TIFF derivative—the information thrown away by the initial JPEG process is unrecoverable and cannot be used to reconstitute the same "original" image.

A similar way of making this point is by way of the analytical tools included in high-end image processing software such as Photoshop. Figure 3.13 depicts another electronic image file (this time a digital facsimile of a plate from Blake's *Songs of Innocence and of Experience*) opened in Photoshop in two common data formats, GIF and JPEG. To a human observer, these images appear identical. Yet a histogram—a graphic representation of the number of pixels at each of the 256 brightness levels in the image—reveals a profoundly different compositional structure underlying the seemingly identical display of colored pixels. What the histogram shows is that the images are "identical" only in one very narrow and specific sense, that of their appearance to the unaided human eye. Computationally, they show significant differences.

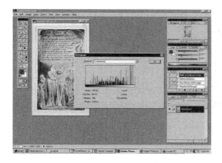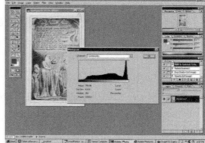

Figure 3.13 The "same" image in GIF (*left*) and JPEG format (*right*), manifesting a radically different computational structure, as evidenced by a Photoshop histogram. Screenshot by the author.

(The difference is accounted for by the different ways in which the GIF and JPEG formats store color information.)

An additional point of interest emerges from the visual glyph that is the histogram itself. Its spikes and valleys can be usefully understood not just as an abstracted projection of the image itself, but as an alternative and equally authoritative rendering of its underlying data structure. The histogram suggests that we would be well advised to evaluate digital images and objects in a number of different informational states, any one of which can be said to constitute the image at a given moment, and only *one* of which is the normative view.[37] That is to say, just as electronic artifacts are capable of endless

37. We can also think about what the JPEG file really represents by looking at the scanning process with which these digital images were first created. The scanner works by using a light source to illuminate a reflective surface (the page or object to be scanned). The scan head traverses the length of the page and, as it moves, light from the page is reflected through a series of mirrors and ultimately focused on a photosensitive diode that translates the light into electric current. The more light reflected, the greater the voltage. A device called an analog-to-digital converter then translates the voltage into digital pixel values, which are in turn stored as byte sequences in a bitmap. We can see that the bitmap itself is thus essentially a digital recording of the amount of light reflected from various points on the surface of the scanned page. This digital recording is what actually constitutes the "literal depiction" of the original object, but the data is useless to us in that form since there is so very much of it (500,000 bytes encoding the pixel values in a typical *Blake Archive* image, for instance). The data must be algorithmically rendered in graphical form for us to view it not as the encoded byte sequences in which it is stored, but as normative visual patterns we can recognize and identify with their source. (It's worth remarking

permutations by virtue of their underlying homogeneity as binary code, so too are they capable of manifesting themselves in a variety of different representational configurations, only some of which may be said to correspond to those representational configurations (say a facsimile reproduction) that we have found to be valuable in our encounters with analog phenomena. Formal materiality emerges out of the process of establishing and transforming these variable representational states such that some are arbitrarily naturalized in relation to others, even as the allographic play of symbolic permutations is itself constrained as a result of prior formal activity (in this instance, JPEG's lossy procedures).

A second example strengthens the point. In 1999 the electronic musician Richard James, aka Aphex Twin, released an EP titled *Windowlicker*. When the CD is played on a computer in conjunction with spectrographic software for visualizing sound waves (a stock feature of most desktop music players) it is possible to discern a demon face, as well as several other images embedded in the track. As *Wired* put it in its coverage of the incident, "Just like the backward messages on vinyl LPs, the face is secretly encoded in the actual sound waves of the music. It is not a separate file on the CD. The image is the aural equivalent of steganography: the practice of hiding secret messages and watermarks in images."[38] The visage, compressed and sunken-eyed, glowers at the user in the bright primaries of computer graphics, like some neo-techno Baal. Yet while its presence amid the audio stream is intentional, the manifestation as it was first reported is an anomaly. As a fan who further pursued the discovery explains, "I started messing around with the settings of the spectrograph program, and after a bit of knob twiddling the mystery revealed itself: the face was supposed to be watched with a *logarithmic* frequency scale, not with a linear scale."[39] The result was quite different, a portrait that is in fact a mild caricature of Aphex Twin himself. Figures 3.14 and

---

here that in computer science, image processing is actually a subfield of signal and information processing.) When we "open" the JPEG file in an image viewer or a Web browser, what we then see is, at least arguably, a visualization of the digital recording that constitutes the literal depiction of the original image.

38. Leander Kahney, "Hey, Who's That Face in My Song?" *Wired News* (2:00 a.m. May 10, 2002 PDT): http://www.wired.com/news/culture/0,1284,52426,00.html.

39. http://www.bastwood.com/aphex.php, emphasis in original.

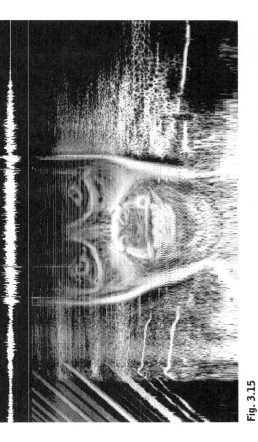

Fig. 3.14

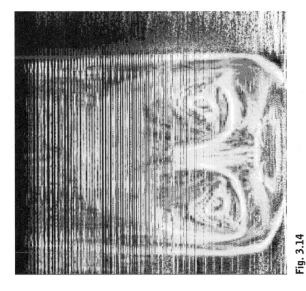

Fig. 3.15

Figures 3.14 and 3.15 The face embedded in the aural data of "#2 (long formula)," the final track on Aphex Twin's 1999 *Windowlicker* EP, when the track is spectrographically visualized using linear and logarithmic frequencies, respectively. *Source:* http://www.bastwood.com/aphex.php

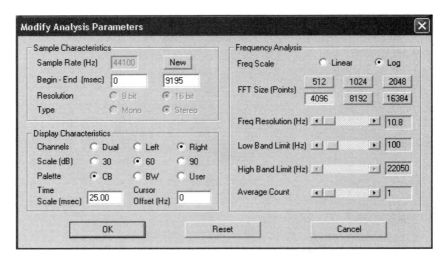

Figure 3.16 Spectrogram settings used to produce the "correct" version of the Aphex Twin face. *Source*: http://www.bastwood.com/aphex.php

3.15 show the two images side by side. Niinisalo, the teenager who found the second image, provides his audience with an self-conscious display of formal materiality by reproducing the control panel of his media player with all of the appropriate settings and parameters so that others can duplicate them (that is, his "knob twiddling") (figure 3.16).

The control panel, as a historically specific interface genre, is itself a compelling testament to the role of formal materiality in our computing machinery. In this instance, the "correct" version of the caricature—produced, let us remember, solely by virtue of the imposition of a specific set of symbolic parameters, as just seen—is materialized as natural and authentic—and intentional—by the formal processes of the spectrographic display, whereas the demon visage is cast as an aberration. I would argue that the tendency to regard one image as correct and the other as deviant is to misapprehend the nature of computers as digital systems, and indeed allographic sign systems in general.[40] But my point here is precisely that the play of code is *not* always

40. Jerome McGann exploits this same cognitive propensity for what I am here describing as naturalization in his visual deformations (his term) of paintings by Rossetti using stock Photoshop filters: "The process invites us to reconsider the critical authority of so-called subjective aesthetic engagement. These strange images evoke our interest exactly because they don't pretend

infinitely fungible and arbitrary—transformations are not always reversible, nor are all transformations always possible or achievable. In this particular instance, for example, the image will not display when the original CD audio track is reproduced as an MP3 recording because the compression (which works in a manner loosely analogous to JPEG) destroys the underlying data structures. Thus the CD audio recording becomes formally materialized in relation to an MP3 rendition of the "same" audio information, since it exhibits a behavioral layer of authenticity that the MP3 does not.

A final example, this time from the domain of textual representation. Since the mid-1980s, markup systems have been routinely used to impose what I am here calling formal materiality on collections of electronic documents. First implemented in SGML and then in XML, these encoding schemas are essentially tools for modeling documents in electronic environments. The formal ontologies of such modeling can range from the simple to the complex, and the implications of a markup language, including the politics and interpretative consequences of markup, have been a constant source of debate in the text-encoding and humanities computing communities for the better part of two decades now.[41] Here is an example of markup, taken from the "header" (a

---

to supply us with a generic response to the picture, something every viewer could agree with (which is what we are offered in iconographical and formal redescriptions). The distortions arrest our attention, moreover, only because we already know the original, which comes back to us through them as if from an unimaginable world or point of view." See McGann's "Imagining What You Don't Know: The Theoretical Goals of the Rossetti Archive," http://www.iath .virginia.edu/~jjm2f/old/chum.html, especially section IV.

41.   The literature here is extensive. A neophyte could do worse than to follow the series of articles that begins with Steven J. DeRose, David Durand, Eli Mylonas, and Allen Renear, "What Is Text, Really?" *Journal of Computing in Higher Education*, 1, no. 2 (1990): 3–26; continues through Renear, Mylonas, and Durand, "Refining Our Notion of What Text Really Is: The Problem of Overlapping Hierarchies," *Research in Humanities Computing* (1996), http:// www.stg.brown.edu/resources/stg/monographs/ohco.html; and finishes with Renear, "Out of Praxis: Three (Meta)Theories of Textuality," in Kathryn Sutherland, ed. *Electronic Text: Investigations in Method and Theory* (Oxford: Oxford University Press, 1997): 107–126. The pages of the journals *Computers and the Humanities, Literary and Linguistic Computing*, and *Text Technology* are all fertile grounds for such debates, as are the proceedings of the annual ACH/ALLC joint conferences on humanities computing. Susan Hockey's *Electronic Texts in the Humanities: Principles and*

section of the file that is a repository for bibliographic metadata) of the electronic edition of the *Book of Thel*, copy F online in the *William Blake Archive*.[42]

```
<objdesc>

<source>

<objdescid>

<objtitle>

<title><hi rend="i">The Book of Thel</hi></title>

</objtitle>

<origination>William Blake

<role>author,</role>

<role>inventor,</role>

<role>delineator,</role>

<role>etcher,</role>

<role>printer,</role>

<role>colorist</role>

</origination>
```

Practice (Oxford: Oxford University Press, 2001) offers an excellent introduction to the field. Jerome McGann has had a major voice; see his *Radiant Textuality: Literature After the World Wide Web* (New York: Palgrave, 2001). Willard McCarty's work on modeling is closely allied, and indispensable; see his *Humanities Computing* (New York: Palgrave, 2005) for a consolidation of his positions. And for the current state of play, see the contributions by McCarty, McGann, and Renear in *A Companion to Digital Humanities*, Susan Schreibman, Ray Siemens, and John Unsworth, eds. (Oxford: Blackwell Publishers, 2005). For markup's most basic precepts, see "A Gentle Introduction to SGML," http://etext.virginia.edu/bin/tei-tocs?div=DIV1&id=SG and elsewhere online, excerpted from the *TEI Guidelines for Electronic Text Encoding and Interchange (P3)*, C. M. Sperberg-McQueen and Lou Burnard, eds. (Chicago and Oxford: Text Encoding Initiative, 1994). For an important recent reading of markup and data structures, see Alan Liu, "Transcendental Data: Toward a Cultural History and Aesthetics of the New Encoded Discourse," *Critical Inquiry* 31 (Autumn 2004): 49–84.

42.   The *William Blake Archive* is available online at http://www.blakearchive.org.

```
<origination>Catherine Blake <role>printer</role>
</origination>
<imprint>
<publisher>William Blake</publisher>
<pubPlace>London</pubPlace>
<date>1789</date>
</imprint>
<compDate>1789
<note>Plates 1 and 8 may have been composed at a slightly
later date (late 1789 or early 1790) than the others. These
same two plates were probably etched later than the others
(late 1789 or early 1790).</note>
</compDate>
</objdescid>
<objInfo>
<printDate>1795</printDate>
<numberobj>8</numberobj>
<objorder>1—8
<note>Bentley plate numbers are used unless otherwise
stated.</note>
</objorder>
<objsize>Plate 1 6.1 x 10.1 cm.; plates 2—8 approx. 15 x 11
cm.</objsize>
<numberleaves>8</numberleaves>
<leafsize>37.1 x 26.9 cm.</leafsize>
<medium>relief etching</medium>
<printingStyle>Relief with rudimentary color printing and
hand coloring. Printed with eight other illuminated books as
part of a large-paper set.</printingStyle>
<inkColor>yellow ochre</inkColor>
```

```
<support>wove paper</support>

<watermark>I TAYLOR/1794</watermark>

<etchedNumbers><note>There are etched numbers—1—6 on plates
3 through 8—but in copy F these are not printed on plates
3, 6, and 8. The etched number on plate 4 is lightly
printed; the etched number on plate 5 is obscured by
washes.</note></etchedNumbers>

<pennedNumbers>none</pennedNumbers>

<framelines>none</framelines>

<binding>Loose.<note>Former binding of half red morocco over
marbled boards retained.</note></binding>

<stabHoles>Stabbed twice through three pairs of holes about
7 cm.

apart.</stabHoles>

</objinfo>
```

Notable here, and even more conspicuous in the markup for the full work, is the prevalence of "object" as a semantic base for a number of the tags. In fact, the Blake Archive markup scheme (properly known as a Document Type Definition or DTD) includes ⟨objdesc⟩, ⟨objdescid⟩, ⟨objtitle⟩, ⟨objinfo⟩, ⟨objorder⟩, ⟨objsize⟩, and ⟨objnumber⟩. These tags define the formal parameters of the virtual "object:" that is, the encoded representation of the physical artifact that is the *Book of Thel*, copy F (housed in the Lessing J. Rosenwald Collection at the Library of Congress). The ⟨objdesc⟩, for example, is the primary container element, grouping information about the work's physical source (including identification, imprint, physical or bibliographical characteristics, and provenance); this followed by the work's sequence of constitutive objects (each individual one of which includes its own encoding for physical or bibliographical characteristics, illustration description, and transcription). Of interest to us here is the fact that the Blake Archive's DTD, and indeed the Blake Archive itself, maintains editorial, structural, and encoded distinctions between works as generic entities (*The Book of Thel*, absent reference to any particular copy), works as particular or discrete artifacts (*The Book of Thel*, copy F), and the individual instances of visual or literary representations that occupy one side of a continuous support (a printed impression from *The Book of Thel*, copy F, a drawing or a watercolor, or a single manuscript page). These distinctions are to some extent realized in the relations and nomenclature of the markup, yet they do not always coexist rationally with one another, nor is the distinction between them always fully articulated. In particular, the word "object" is pressed into service to capture both of the last two manifestations of the work: that is, the work as a particular or discrete artifact, and the work as one side of a continuous support. For example, *The Book of Thel*, copy F, is editorially conceptualized as an object, and is rendered as such in the DTD (all of the constitutive impressions of any given copy are presented within a single object description, or ⟨objdesc⟩, container element). However, the same term is also used to refer to each of the eight printed impressions that comprise *The Book of Thel*, copy F. Likewise, an individual color print, such as "Albion rose," is also an "object" in the Archive's parlance—an object both in the sense of its identity as a particular artifact, and as one side of a continuous support. While the dual uses of "object" may appear to simply coincide in such cases, note that the DTD and the Archive's underlying structure do not allow the distinction to ever truly collapse.

Even more paradoxically, at times when a particular work *ought* to be able to lay claim to these dual uses of "object," its identification as a discrete artifact may be arbitrarily suppressed by the structural constraints of the Archive. The frontispiece to any particular copy of *Europe* (the famous image better known as "The Ancient of Days") can be conceived as an object in the same sense as any particular copy of *The Book of Thel* (that is, as a discrete artifact), in addition to its being an object merely by virtue of its status as one side of a continuous support—yet the Archive only allows the latter, and not the former, identification to take hold. At times then, the object as artifact and the object as one side of a continuous support are distinctions structurally superimposed (as is the case with the painting entitled "Albion rose"), while at other times the two remain structurally (and arbitrarily) disjointed ("The Ancient of Days" never acquires the status of discrete artifact the way "Albion rose" does).[43]

43. Robert N. Essick, one of the Archive's three general editors, comments: "Right—and an interesting aspect of the Archive that also has some grounding in Blake's own history of production. Although he appears to have 'issued' (in some sense—at least 'sold') the *Europe* frontispiece

It would be a mistake to suppose that the DTD's bias toward objectivity (if you will) necessarily yields a strict documentary or material fidelity to the original physical artifact. The Blake Archive makes no attempt to reproduce blank verso pages in the illuminated books, for example, and so—given the definition of "object" as one side of a continuous support—may be said to omit half of the objects in the original work. An "object" in the Blake Archive is thus ultimately an editorial construct, one existing primarily to facilitate the Archive's internal data structures, and only secondarily to evoke the material condition of the physical artifact.

The student of formal materiality will immediately note the fact that markup's fundamental quality is that it models text with more text. This is because computers are relentlessly relative and arbitrary systems. Absent data mining or other forms of predictive pattern recognition, a computer cannot know that a title of a poem is a title or indeed that a poem is a poem without some specific mechanism for explicitly telling the system it is so. The ubiquitous angle brackets in which the so-called tags are enclosed exist to delimit the relationship between the document being modeled and the text employed to describe it, or "mark it up." (Angle brackets were selected for this function because of their rarity in conventional written discourse; indeed, a California job case, as a printer's type drawer is commonly known, does not include them. Markup also has a kind of conceptual antecedent in the so-called ES-Cape codes that were included in the original ASCII character set, a provision that in effect creates an almost infinite keyboard by suspending the literal value of a character when it is coupled with an escape character. This landmark in electronic textual history is the contribution of IBM's Bob Bemer, a name all but unknown in discussion of electronic textual theory.) In any case, what the semantic pressure on the Blake Archive's ⟨objects⟩ should suggest is that an electronic document is being modeled by a cascade of formal or semantic values that materialize it in relation to the electronic environment or sys-

---

as a separate work/entity/object, he did not have copperplate of it separate from the one he used in *Europe*. Thus, I included 'Albion rose' in my separate plates catalogue, but did not include 'The Ancient of Days' since there is no separate copperplate of it (as I argued in an appendix). Thus, the archival distinction has some basis in Blake's methods of production." Personal e-mail to author.

tem that supports it. In this case, certain types of access, representation, and searches are enabled and prohibited by the different renderings of what is and isn't an object in the Blake Archive's formal definition and instantiation of the term.

While the preceding examples have been more or less specialized in their purview, my argument throughout has been that formal materiality is the normative condition of working in a digital environment. We saw this with the Mystery_House.dsk file and its varying presentations in the hex editor and the emulator. Emulators themselves are textbook examples of formal materiality, relying as they do on cascades of virtual machinery to reproduce the functionality of long-gone systems and hardware, the physical limitations of mothballed chips reinstantiated in formally construed mechanisms of control and constraint. Formal materiality inheres in server architectures like LAMP, which uses a cascade of technologies to layer up Web-accessible real-time interactive databases on top of an open source architecture (Linux/Apache/ MySQL/PHP), and it inheres in the Java programming language, which runs its code on a bundled virtual machine that floats on top of the vicissitudes of an individual user's operating system in an effort to provide a uniform and consistent environment in which the code can execute (though as anyone who programs with Java knows, this cross-platform consistency is often more chimerical than practical, as the formal *and* physical materialities of local platforms and environments ineluctably assert themselves). Surely the most mundane manifestation of formal materiality, familiar to all contemporary computer users, is the nested windowing regimens governing their screen space, where the desktop frames a Web browser that in turn frames "pages" or "sites," with each of these environmental layers possessing their own computationally distinct but functionally interdependent architectures, interfaces, and behaviors.

Even formal operations are subject to certain absolute formal limitations; a von Neumann computer cannot compute in reverse, for example. It is by definition a progressive machine.[44] Simics Hindsight, an experimental product for reversible computing that allows programmers to debug their code by stepping backwards through its execution, also works by way of a virtual

44. I am referring to the execution of actual machine-level instructions. Reversible computing should not be confused with CTRL-Z and other common application-level features that allow a user to undo deletions or recover the past history or states of a file.

machine, essentially imposing an extra layer between whatever program is being run and the system's processors, thereby leveraging formal materiality to alter the formal material conditions of computation.[45] Yet forensic and formal materiality must ultimately be understood as interdependent, and it is their interdependence that yields us the kind of factive synecdoches with which we began the chapter. Take once again the notes in *Mystery House*. The notes, and their distinctive behaviors within the game, are an example of pure formal materiality. They behave the way they do because that is the way they have been modeled in the game world. That there were nontrivial programming constraints on the definition of that game world, notably the two-word vocabulary of the parser, reinforces rather than diminishes the point: formal constructs such as parsers and game worlds impose their own self-consistent material conditions as a result of what are ultimately physical limits of computation and media: memory, storage, clock cycles, and so forth. But ultimately the formal materiality of the notes resolves to a forensic trace, the mechanically moving arm of the VersaWriter, an autographic hardware device. The earlier game remnants and crack tags, by contrast, have their origins in the forensic properties of magnetic media and the way the physical space of the disk is organized and accessed by the mechanical components of the drive. Yet the data remnants are preserved and presented formally, transmitted as an artifact of the bitstream copy process that produced the disk image, and revealed as a result of the hex editor being wielded like a magnifying lens or, maybe more aptly, the kind of magic lens one now finds implemented as an interface element. Jerome McGann has influentially used the figure of the double helix to describe his genetically intertwined strands of linguistic and bibliographic codes; I regard forensic and formal materiality as akin to the unique monodimensionality of the Möbius strip, at once separate and coextensive in the cascade of abstractions that is a von Neumann architecture. Engineering that paradox, and more importantly making it mundane, is the technological triumph of the stored program computer.

45. Simics Hindsight is a product of Virutech, http://www.virtutech.com/. A white paper is available here at http://www.virtutech.com/pdf/wp_hindsight_20050304.pdf. As the white paper explains, "It is not possible to run a computer backwards. So when debugging a program, whenever a point of interest has passed, it is gone. The only way to go back is to restart the program from the beginning. This makes debugging very inefficient, since the programmer is investing a lot of effort each time for small amounts of incremental information."

Coda: Making Difference

Computers are built machines. They are machines built and made to routinely instantiate the kinds of digital or symbolic environments in which formal materiality as I have been describing it can be activated and exploited. Yet computers also generate heat, which must be dissipated. The copper traces in the CPU, some 30 miles of them in a standard PC, are responsible for 75 watts of heat per square centimeter, creating temperatures of up to 140 degrees Fahrenheit inside the case; most often this heat is dissipated by a simple fan, the same device that cools other sites of industrial labor. This is not the forensic imagination, but rather a forensic fact. Yet there is a potential danger or objection in that the hard-boiled realism of forensics collapses too readily into a kind of naïve scientific positivism. That's not where I want to go with this book. Ultimately I want to resist the notion that forensics gets us deeper into the computer, lower down to the essence, closer to the soul of the machine. First and not least, computer forensics is carried out *with computers*, so there is a kind of Heisenberg principle at work;[46] this is in fact an important legal and professional consideration, in that an investigator must always prove that digital evidence has not been altered in the course of its collection and examination by digital means. This is nontrivial: computers are finite state machines in a state of constant flux, and even if what an investigator thinks he or she is doing is benign, in the background, as one authority puts it, "processes are steadily eating away at the prior state of the computer."[47] Forensic method uses hashing algorithms to ensure that digital evidence presented in court is mathematically identical to what was originally collected at a crime scene. The odds of producing identical hash values are approximately 1 in 2^{160}; by contrast, the odds of two individuals possessing equivalent DNA are greater, and the odds of two individuals having matching fingerprints are much greater. Electronic objects can therefore be proven legally and mathematically—that is to say, *formally*—identical. At the same time, *forensically*, they remain individual and discrete as interventions in a physical substratum. As the erase bands on the MFM images show, the forensic principle of individualization—that no two objects in nature are ever exactly alike—

46. Dan Farmer and Wietse Venema, *Forensic Discovery*, (Upper Saddle River, NJ: Addison-Wesley: 2005), suggest the aptness of invoking the Heisenberg principle (7).

47. Farmer and Venema, *Forensic Discovery*, 143.

holds true for the phenomenon of data remanence. Formally or allographically identical, forensically or autographically individualized and discrete: this conundrum becomes the methodological lever with which to pry open the relentless symbolic cascade of computation and understand what is unique about computers as writing technologies—that they are material machines dedicated to propagating an artificial environment capable of supporting immaterial behaviors.

If I had to choose one word to describe what computer forensics brings to the theoretical discourse on electronic textuality, that word would be "difference". I would like to think I use a hex editor the same way that maverick bibliographer Randall McLeod uses the mirrors of his homemade collator to gleefully *not-read* books upside down: he is able to observe the text "tranceforming" itself by escaping the "missionary position" of normative reading.[48] By looking at the books upside down, he is looking for difference, a difference that gets made here as patterns of discrepancy in his visual scanning of the now not-read text. One reason for documenting the use of the hex editor in such detail as I have is to serve as a primer for bibliographical or forensic practice in future studies. Or to put the matter more plainly, the bibliographer and textual critic of the future may well need to know as much about hex editors, hashes, and magnetic force microscopy as he or she now knows about collation formula, paleography, and stemma. For practical reasons to be sure, but also to allow the bibliographer and textual critic to be textual sophisticates when confronted with the texts and objects of our digital culture.[49]

48. See McLeod, "From 'Tranceformations in the Text of *Orlando Furioso*,'" *New Directions in Textual Studies*, ed. Dave Oliphant and Robin Bradford (Austin: University of Texas Press and Harry Ransom Humanities Research Center, 1990): 61–85; and for a quick overview of his technique, Daniel Zalewski, "Through the Looking Glass," *Lingua Franca* (June 1997), http://linguafranca.mirror.theinfo.org/9706/fieldnotes.html.

49. Preservation specialist Abby Smith puts it this way: "Just as book conservators should learn as much as possible over the course of their careers about how books have been produced and consumed over the centuries, and as film archivists need to know as much as possible about the original production and exhibition of films, so must preservation experts of the present and future master the creation and dissemination of digital information." See "Preservation in the Future Tense," *CLIR Issues* 3 (May/June 1998): 1, 6.

4

Save As: Michael Joyce's *Afternoons*

At any rate, after someone asked me to inventory the choices again and decided to browse, [Charles] Bernstein, characteristically and quite wonderfully, asked the woman to click "that icon up there on the right of the screen with the picture of the apple."

When I offered my admiration for his choice and suggested that he had unerringly found the choice outside (inside, actually) the system, the margin and boundary of the text, I took over the mouse and dropped the menu for him. "Fine," I said, "what would you like?"

"Can we see your private correspondence or something?" he asked.

—MICHAEL JOYCE, COMMENTING ON A PUBLIC READING OF *AFTERNOON* AT SUNY BUFFALO, IN PRIVATE CORRESPONDENCE DATED FEBRUARY 16, 1991, NOW AVAILABLE IN THE MICHAEL JOYCE PAPERS AT THE HARRY RANSOM CENTER AT THE UNIVERSITY OF TEXAS AT AUSTIN[1]

The question must be put: *What will remain of the electronic age concerning the realm of art?* It is evident that the first two cycles have

---

1. Letter from the Michael Joyce Papers, Harry Ransom Humanities Research Center, University of Texas at Austin, addressee unknown. All references and citations to material in this collection are by permission of Michael Joyce and the Harry Ransom Center.

not found a place in our storehouses for cultural goods, the museums, and even less have they found continuing cultivation, research and communication.

—JÜRGEN CLAUS, "EXPANSION OF MEDIA ART: WHAT WILL REMAIN OF THE ELECTRONIC AGE?" (1984)[2]

—UNIVERSAL GUI ICON FOR "SAVE"

Revealing statements about electronic textuality turn up in all kinds of places. The Department of Defense's Clearing and Sanitization Matrix, which we looked at in chapter 1, is just such an example. The colophon to the copy of Michael Joyce's *Afternoon: A Story* currently running on my computer—the work generally regarded as the first full-length piece of hypertext fiction—is another. Here is that colophon almost in full:

This fifth edition of *Afternoon, a Story* reflects Eastgate Press changes in jacket copy and front matter only. The fourth edition involved Storyspace changes to suit Macintosh © Systems 6.07 and above. The third edition (first published by Eastgate in 1990) changed text windows and typefaces and made minor fixes of links and texts, all differing from the second edition (1989) which took advantage of certain changes to Storyspace to add new links and create a few new places. The first edition of *Afternoon* was distributed quite informally to a number of Storyspace beta-users and interested writers and scholars beginning in 1987. Like most electronic documents, it has grown wings and tentacles. The second edition was distributed to some subscribers to *IF, The Journal of Interactive Fiction and Creative Hypertext*, (edited by Gordon Howell); and a few copies were also distributed at Hypertext '89, the Second ACM Conference on Hypertext, Nov, 1989, Pittsburgh, PA. Each edition includes notice of copyright and none may be copied or distributed without written permission. This definitive edition is published and distributed by the Eastgate Press [street address and contact information omitted].[3]

2. Ars Electronica catalog statement (1984), emphasis in original. Available online at http://www.aec.at/en/archives/festival_archive/festival_catalogs/festival_artikel.asp?iProjectID=9332.

3. *Afternoon: A Story*, fifth edition (for Windows) (Watertown, MA: Eastgate Systems: 1992). Storyspace reader 1.0.7. The lexia is entitled "copyrights and editions." Windows XP.

From this we can see that *Afternoon* has been released in multiple versions and editions, and that it has been exposed to a wide range of editorial interventions and authorial revisions in the course of its relatively brief publishing history. Yet even the foregoing statement, diligent though it is in enumerating the "wings and tentacles" of this unruly electronic document, does not tell us everything we need to know. Eastgate Systems, for example, has assigned *Afternoon* its own edition numbers, so that the first Eastgate edition corresponds to what is described as the third edition above, and my own copy, *Afternoon's* fifth edition, is identified on its electronic frontispiece as the third Eastgate Press edition. Moreover, I am currently running my *Afternoon* on a Windows machine, and the work was originally developed and released for the Apple Macintosh; in its catalog Eastgate discriminates between so-called Macintosh and Windows "editions," when what they really mean is that *Afternoon* has been *ported* between the two platforms, probably more than once. Selections from *Afternoon* have also appeared in print, in the *Norton Anthology of Postmodern American Fiction* (1997), and subsequently online at Norton's Web site, which deploys an elaborate Java-based interface to approximate some of the special features of the original Storyspace software. This online version (and port) is identified as the sixth edition of the work by its own colophon, which is otherwise identical to the one I have reproduced above. There are at least two foreign language translations of *Afternoon*, Italian and German.[4] None of this considers the possibility that copies of *Afternoon* have been individually altered by their owners and put into circulation, intentionally or otherwise, but in any case apparently in violation of the copyright clause that, together with other

4. Based on the fifth edition of the work, the Italian translation is by Alearda Pandolfi, Filippo Soresi, and Walter Vannini and was distributed by Human Systems of Milan in 1993. The package included a 90-page softbound book with various digitally themed works, including Lorenzo Miglioli's *RA-DIO* and "Bit Generation," as well as an interview with Joyce. Published under the ELETTROLIBRI imprint, it came with $3\frac{1}{2}$-inch diskettes for both Mac and PC. The diskettes also included the hypertext version of *RA-DIO*, described as the first work of hypertext fiction by an Italian author. Vannini provides a fuller account of the project here: http://www .electronicbookreview.com/thread/internetnation/ellettrolibri. The project received significant notice in the Italian press. (The bound book, however, was apparently a concession to the booksellers.) The German translation exists as a hard copy of the complete translated *Afternoon* manuscript, with handwritten emendations, among the materials at the Ransom Center. There is no date or attribution—I do not know if it was ever published.

stabilizing gestures such as "definitive edition," is still another noteworthy feature of the colophon.[5] The truth is there are many *Afternoons*, even if the literal textual differences between them may prove slight; and indeed it is Joyce's own personal habit, when naming folders and subfolders to store backup copies of the work on his personal file systems, to use the plural locution "Afternoons" (wings and tentacles stirred animate by these routine desktop chores).

The colophon, meanwhile, has still more to tell us. Most immediately, it situates this electronic work in a profoundly social setting, ranging from Joyce's interactions with the audiences of various journals and conferences to his publisher at Eastgate (and Norton). Here then is Jerome McGann's social theory of texts, and here is John Seely Brown and Paul Duguid's social life of information. While Joyce is indisputably *Afternoon*'s author, the text has had other actors, including (as we will see) in one instance a literal coauthor, whose identity is apparently unknown to Joyce. Moreover, the Storyspace software with which *Afternoon* is read is overtly coauthored by Joyce, and by Jay David Bolter and John B. Smith originally, and now by Eastgate's Mark Bernstein, who maintains the code. Storyspace has its own version history, separate and distinct from that of *Afternoon*. Its stability in turn depends upon that of the Macintosh operating system, as can be seen from fourth edition of *Afternoon*, whose immediate catalyst, as stated before, was Apple's release of System 6. Finally, like *Agrippa* albeit in a more sedate register, the colophon demonstrates that *Afternoon* is an electronic object that enjoys intimate relationships with various physical artifacts in the world—the changes in packaging, cover art, and storage media (from $3\frac{1}{2}$-inch diskette to CD) have paralleled *Afternoon*'s electronic edition history, and these too must be considered in the textual and reception history of the work.

Afternoon's colophon thus dramatizes many often-unacknowledged elements of textual transmission in electronic environments. Yet why is it that in critical discussions of a text that is often celebrated for its fluid postmodern identities—"a story that changes every time you read it," in Joyce's own oft-

5. Deena Larsen encourages her readers to do exactly that with her Storyspace hypertext *Marble Springs*, and multiple versions, edited and expanded by her readers, are extant. See Jane Yellowlees Douglas, *The End of Books—Or Books Without End: Reading Interactive Narrative* (Ann Arbor: University of Michigan Press, 2000), 141.

Figure 4.1 Some of *Afternoon's* desktop icons (not reproduced to relative scale), from the first, third, and fourth editions, and the 1992 Windows edition. The fourth edition icon was published in color (blue tinting with the letter "a" in red). Screenshot by the author.

stated formulation[6]—do we typically bracket these kinds of revisions and variations, these editions, versions, translations, and ports of the text? Consider just the changes wrought to *Afternoon's* desktop icon, the one constantly visible aspect of the text that is first (and last) before the eyes of all who open (and close) Joyce's electronic tale of Peter and Wert and Lolly and Nausicaa (see figure 4.1).

"Because human beings are not angels," writes Jerome McGann in his introduction to *The Textual Condition*, "our symbolic exchanges always involve material negotiations." Texts are "produced and reproduced under specific social and institutional conditions, and hence [. . .] every text, including those that may appear to be purely private, is a social text. This view entails a corollary understanding, that a 'text' is not a 'material thing' but a material event or set of events, a point in time (or a moment in space) wherein certain communicative interchanges are being practiced."[7] If, therefore, according to the cosmology of *The Textual Condition*, all spoken or scripted texts are the product of human and not divine endeavor, then—it stands to reason—so too are electronic texts, and "[c]onsequently, a theoretical study of them will necessarily be materialist in character and constrained to negotiate itself through the study of highly particular cases" (177). Such is my objective in what follows. How can we construe and construct the "material negotiations" that constitute the versions of the text commonly known as *Afternoon: A Story*, and what does it mean to do so when even as strict a materialist as Friedrich Kittler insists, "All code operations . . . come down to absolutely local string manipulations, that is, I am afraid, *to signifiers of voltage differences*" (emphasis in original).[8] To

6. Joyce's *Of Two Minds: Hypertext Pedagogy and Poetics* (Ann Arbor: University of Michigan Press, 1995), 32.

7. *The Textual Condition* (Princeton: Princeton University Press, 1991), 3, 21.

8. Kittler, "There is No Software," *Literature, Media, Information Systems*, John Johnston, ed. (G+B Arts, 1997), 150.

which we might add, locally stored bits on physical media. These questions have become especially acute given that Joyce's literary "papers"—comprising some fifty archival boxes of correspondence, journals, notes, records, and other printed matter, as well as 400-odd floppy disks, several hard drive images on DVD, and a laptop—are now housed at the Harry Ransom Humanities Research Center at the University of Texas at Austin, a shift in physical and institutional location that brings practical questions of editing and accessioning these materials into sudden and sharp curatorial focus. My objective is not just to put the relevant bibliographical history on record, but to consider what electronic textual artifacts have to tell us about the nature of textual transmission writ large, and conversely what textual studies has to teach about the textual condition of electronic objects.

Engineering Intention

A self-avowed "postmodern classic," *Afternoon* is the single best-known work of the nascent electronic literary canon. Nearly every serious critic in the field has found occasion to write about it at one time or another.[9] The most common position sees the text as massively self-referential: "*Afternoon* is about the problem of its own reading," observed Jay David Bolter in 1991, a statement encapsulating many of the critical arguments produced before and since.[10] Af-

9. Some of the most influential: Espen Aarseth, *Cybertext: Perspectives on Ergodic Literature* (Baltimore: Johns Hopkins University Press, 1997), 86–96; Jay David Bolter, *Writing Space: The Computer, Hypertext, and the History of Writing* (Hillsdale, NJ: Lawrence Erlbaum, 1991), 123–127; George P. Landow, *Hypertext: The Convergence of Contemporary Critical Theory and Technology* (Baltimore: Johns Hopkins University Press, 1992), 113–119; Terence Harpold, "Conclusions," in *Hyper/Text/Theory*, George P. Landow, ed. (Baltimore: Johns Hopkins University Press, 1994): 189–222, and Jane Yellowlees Douglas, "'How Do I Stop This Thing?': Closure and Indeterminacy in Interactive Narratives," also in *Hyper/Text/Theory*: 159–188; and various essays by Stuart Moulthrop, especially "Hypertext and the 'Hyperreal,'" in *Hypertext '89* (New York: Association for Computing Machinery, 1989). Douglas's doctoral dissertation ("Print Pathways and Interactive Labyrinths: How Hypertext Narratives Affect the Act of Reading," New York University, 1992) is generally recognized as the most detailed close reading of *Afternoon* on record. For a more recent exemplary reading, see Jill Walker's "Piecing Together and Tearing Apart: Finding the Story in *Afternoon*" in the ACM Hypertext '99 Proceedings and online at http://huminf .uib.no/~jill/txt/afternoon.html.

10. Bolter, *Writing Space*, 127.

ternoon was one of the works at the center of the close coupling of hypertext writing to poststructuralist literary theory that characterized academic discussions of electronic writing in the late 1980s and early 1990s, nowhere more overtly than in the pages of George P. Landow's *Hypertext: The Convergence of Contemporary Critical Theory and Technology*.[11] (Though it could be argued that even at the time this "convergence" was oddly out of step with mainstream literary studies, where high poststructuralism had all but been eclipsed by various strains of cultural criticism, cultural studies, and the New Historicism.) Nonetheless, *Afternoon* and other hypertexts of the era were routinely presented as startlingly literal manifestations of the classic postmodern precepts of the decentered author, the empowered reader, and the writerly text. More recently, Espen Aarseth has described *Afternoon* as a "game of narration," and offers it as a paradigmatic example of ergodic literature, a work that demands nontrivial effort to be read.[12]

Bolter suggests that "Reading *Afternoon* several times is like exploring a vast house or castle. The reader proceeds often down the same corridors and familiar rooms. But often too the reader comes upon a new hallway not previously explored or finds a previously locked door giving way to the touch" (125). We have another mystery house then, but this time with a funhouse twist: the house, or more properly the text, possesses faculties that seem to work to discourage any sense of a normative, stable interaction with the narrative. *Afternoon* thus walks a fine line: though it depends on the reader's active engagement, that engagement is achieved by way of exquisite control—or craft—by the author. For every newly trodden hallway, or door that opens, there is a finely tuned mechanism of links and constraints meticulously wrought and revised. Jane Yellowlees Douglas introduces the term "intentional network" to capture the manner by which a reader's interaction with a hypertext is, seemingly paradoxically, contingent upon strong authorial intent:

If I am in hot pursuit of the answer to a question, confirmation of a hunch, or the opportunity to end my reading, I need to be at least as concerned with the structural details and nuances of the hypertext as I do its content. Even when I am reading casually, the intentional network—made up of guardfields and defaults, link labels or

11. Now in its third edition as *Hypertext 3.0* (Baltimore: Johns Hopkins University Press, 2006).

12. Aarseth, *Cybertext*, 94.

icons and window titles, hot words and cognitive maps—shapes the options I can choose and the trajectory of my reading.[13]

The effect Douglas is describing is a by-product of the fact that a hypertext is a mechanism, what Aarseth calls a cybertext—the scriptons on the screen arrive there as a result of a set of procedural transactions by which certain textons are promoted to screen-level scriptons in accordance with reader choice and the underlying programmatic logic of the work. To read the work effectively, one thus has to learn how to *use* it, and this implies knowledge of or conjecture about the author's intentions. Ultimately, however, Douglas seeks to deflect any question of conservatism in this resurgence of authorial intent, and points out that to the extent hypertexts are complex systems, their readings will always be emergent, manifesting in ways equally unknown and unanticipated by author and reader alike. ("There we match minds," is how Joyce puts it in his introduction to *Afternoon*.)

Yet there is also a kind of latent Romanticism that manifests in much of the writing about the experience of reading (or playing) *Afternoon*. "Every reading of 'Afternoon'," suggests Bolter, "can be a new afternoon, or the reader can choose to pick up the fiction where he or she left it in the last session. The impermanence of electronic literature cuts both ways: as there is no lasting success, there is also no failure that needs to last. By contrast, there is a solemnity at the center of printed literature—even comedy, romance, and satire—because of the immutability of the printed page" (130). The opposition between the sepulcher-like "solemnity" of the immutable printed page and the playfully impermanent (one might say impertinent) electronic text that is always (re)making itself anew is, it seems to me, a species of the same medial ideology we confronted in chapter 1. Indeed, the tendency to elicit what is "new" about new media by contrasting its radical mutability with the supposed material stolidity of older textual forms is a misplaced gesture, symptomatic of the general extent to which textual studies and new media theory have failed to communicate. In a 1999 essay "Cyberspace, Virtuality, and the Text," Marie-Laure Ryan took stock of the descriptive markers that had accumulated in more than a decade of critical writing about electronic textuality. In her first column—print—Ryan includes such words as "durable," "linear," "centered," "tree structure," "unity," "order," "monologism,"

13. Douglas, *The End of Books*, 134.

"sequentiality," "stolidity," and "static." In her second column—the virtual—she opposes these with "ephemeral," "spatial," "decentered," "rhizome structure," "diversity," "chaos," "dialogism," "parallelism," "fluidity," and "dynamic."[14] Ryan herself is not necessarily endorsing these categories; she hedges her bets. On the one hand she notes that the features of electronic text derive "to some extent" from "the inherent properties of the medium" (102), as well as the existence of "natural and elective affinities of electronic writing for postmodern aesthetics—natural, because of the transient substance of electricity itself" (103). This is what Richard Grusin calls the "autonomous agency of the medium" (quoted by Ryan; 102) and its efficacy is not to be underestimated. Yet Ryan also notes the imposition of a certain set of cultural practices on the medium, the interests and *ideologies* (her term now) of a particular avant garde community of writers and critics who were instrumental in propagating and publishing particular views of hypertext in particular academic venues at a particular historical moment—all of which contributed to the set of generic descriptors enumerated above. In the end, Ryan wants to argue for textual pluralism—printed works assuming the properties of the virtual and virtual texts that are somehow stable and static—despite the fact (she returns to the point) that the electronic medium remains "inherently" more hospitable to a "virtual, postmodern" aesthetic than does print (104).

In the specific case of *Afternoon*, what I have been calling a medial ideology may be exacerbated by the fact that the typical Storyspace map views, which display a graphic overview of the text's node and link structures in a variety of diagrammatic configurations, are disabled (the software calls this limited presentation format the Readingspace or Page Reader). Thus there is no experiential sense of the text as a whole or gestalt, only individual screens that inexorably accumulate as the mouse clicks and clicks...and clicks. Yet the number of readings, while very large, is not literally infinite and those readings will always be governed by the programmed conditions of the text—its formal materialities—as they are manifested in the work's link paths and other determinate structures (like guard fields). These structures have themselves, however, proven unstable and subject to revision in the course of *Afternoon's* publication history—as we will see.

14. Marie-Laure Ryan, "Cyberspace, Virtuality, and the Text," *Cyberspace Textuality: Computer Technology and Literary Theory*, ed. Marie-Laure Ryan (Bloomington: Indiana University Press, 1999), 101–102.

It is important from the outset to understand that *Afternoon*, as a hypertext, is not of or on the World Wide Web. It was written with a piece of software known as Storyspace, predating the Web by roughly half a decade. Storyspace, which was programmed in PASCAL, functions as a local executable—that is, as an application you install—rather than as networked hypermedia accessed through a browser.[15] The effects Bolter describes above—"a locked door giving way to the touch," for example—are a direct reflection of the unique capabilities of Storyspace as an authoring environment. In this case, it uses so-called guard fields, which can control access to a particular portion of the text based on what the reader has or hasn't already read. Because understanding Storyspace is essential to understanding *Afternoon* (and other early works of electronic literature besides), and because a closer look at Storyspace opens windows onto computer culture and software history in the 1980s, it is worth recovering the development of the program in some detail. While its various features and functionality are well known and have been described often enough in the criticism on literary hypertext, relatively little has been said about Storyspace's origins and evolution as software.[16]

Storyspace was a product of the early 1980s personal computer boom. At the time, Joyce, whose first novel *The War Outside of Ireland* (1982) had just won a regional literary prize, was interested in exploring what he termed "multiple fictions," the concept that would eventually be made manifest as "a story that changed with every reading," the mandate with which Joyce wrote *Afternoon*.[17] He had become a home computer hobbyist, acquiring first an Apple II and later a Macintosh. Early in January of 1982 (the same year "the computer" would be dubbed *Time Magazine*'s "Man of the Year") Joyce wrote to Howard Becker, a sociologist at Northwestern who had read and admired his first novel and whom Joyce has since characterized as his earliest

15. E-mail from Jay David Bolter to author, May 24, 2006 3:48 PM. Bolter adds: "But it really doesn't matter that much, since Storyspace is mostly interface, which means function calls to the elaborate Mac toolbox."

16. What follows then is partially intended as a contribution to software history, the new field outlined by Henry Lowood in "The Hard Work of Software History," *RBM: A Journal of Rare Books, Manuscripts, and Cultural Heritage* 2, no. 2 (Fall 2001): 141–161. Also available at http://www.ala.org/ala/acrl/acrlpubs/rbm/backissuesvol2no/lowood.PDF.

17. The subtitle of *Afternoon: a story* may have been intended as a truncated version of this same phrase.

hypertext supporter. Becker was a self-professed Apple evangelist. Because these remarks represent what is apparently Joyce's first extended statement about his own writing in the new medium, they are worth quoting in full:

So I'm writing to ask you what to do after you turn it on. Seriously, I am and have been spending long, timeless nights learning my way around this/that thing, and this night I've turned myself outward for some correspondence, and the shift is salutary I think. I am amazed by how compelling the computer is, how freely I am able to write at it (confined to journals as yet, until I get the fine points of Applewriter down), and how easily time goes by at its terminal. But I am aware of its inwardness, a sense that time spent there is burrowing and silent, somehow geometric. Possibly this really is a function of not having the printer as yet, but I doubt so. I think it has more to do with the utterly elemental quality of the information the Apple handles, the really quite pleasing beauty of the rows of chips when the lid is off, the pleasant geographic satisfaction of memory simultaneously on the disk and in memory itself, the ribbed, grey ribbon that links them. I mean, *this* is seductive technology.

A friend asked whether I wasn't bothered by the fact that there is no paper before me, as now, and I honestly had to answer that, if anything, using the computer seemed a more authentic way of capturing language as I understand it. Words seem more like the hive of electronic hashmarks to me than these carbon strikes before me. It seems right to construe language as a series of switchmarks, loads and unloads, zeros and ones. The form it eventually takes is almost incidental; do we always write down dreams?

(I'm surprised by the weight of the "pleasing" and "pleasant" above, but it's the language that comes. A computer, an Apple especially, is a very clean machine.)[18]

Just as notable, perhaps, is what comes immediately after: Joyce asks Becker whether he has acquired any new games that are worth "ripping off;" thus the abrupt shift from a writer's measured meditation on the seductive new affordances of disk and screen to the unbridled enthusiasm of the hobbyist and geek. Not so much jarring as undeniably human and authentic, the transition captures something important about this moment in electronic literature. For every lyrical expression of promise and possibility, there are equal measures of hard-nosed determination to plumb the technology to its depths and

18. Personal correspondence from Joyce to Becker, January 7, 1982; Michael Joyce Papers, Harry Ransom Humanities Research Center, University of Texas at Austin.

aggressively pursue its potential. Then as now, games were where the new platforms' capabilities were being pushed to their limits, so it is not surprising that Joyce would gravitate toward them.

Indeed, Becker would send Joyce copies of whatever programs he thought might inspire a "budding computer novelist," including copies of popular Infocom interactive fiction like the ZORK trilogy and DEADLINE. "By the time you assimilate these you ought to be ready for anything."[19] In 1984, very soon after they first became available to consumers, Becker acquired a Macintosh. He chafed that there were only two programs for it, MacWrite and MacPaint (and thought the names were silly), but comments that the possibilities of MacPaint "are shocking." (Becker also finds the "disk handling" on the new system "confusing" and notes that it would have been easier with two drives, but that "all the drives Sony can make for them are going into computers so there aren't any second drives to buy, not yet anyway."[20] Again a measure of how dramatically physical storage can affect the affordances of computing.) He sends Joyce a printed screen dump of some crude graphics rendered with MacPaint, interspersed with text in a riot of variable fonts: "That's how you can draw if you don't trust your own hand like I don't."[21] This document, a typical-looking artifact of early desktop publishing, would have immediately alerted Joyce to the fact that the Macintosh offered something very different from the monochrome command line interactions he was then familiar with.

In the midst of this Joyce had also begun corresponding with Natalie Dehn, a researcher at the Yale Artificial Intelligence Lab, after reading an account of her work in a computer magazine.[22] This correspondence was to prove as important as Becker's. Dehn, who was working on computer story generators, became an intellectual sparring partner with whom Joyce sharpened his earliest conceits of multiple fictions. Eventually he arranged to spend a sabbatical year at Yale (1984–1985), under the auspices of the lab's director, Roger Schank. Dehn also put Joyce in touch with Jay David Bolter, a classicist

19. Becker to Joyce, February 22, 1984, MJP.

20. Becker to Joyce, March 10, 1984, MJP.

21. Becker to Joyce, August 3, 1985, MJP.

22. As Joyce recounts in his *Of Two Minds: Hypertext Pedagogy and Poetics* (Ann Arbor: University of Michigan Press, 1995), 31–32.

at the University of North Carolina at Chapel Hill, who had himself recently spent time at the Lab tinkering with software designed to facilitate the writing of interactive fiction.

Dehn's work involved writing programs (one was entitled AUTHOR) to automatically generate stories based on what the program could surmise of the user's intentions. The narratological method was relentlessly linear, in keeping with the branching decision models that were then the mainstays of artificial intelligence research. Dehn was a proponent of creativity by constraint, the idea that one best modeled human authorship by forcing the program to choose amongst mutually exclusive paths or narrative directions. In a letter dated October 1, 1983 (which he subsequently annotated with "Early, Important"), Joyce dissents from this view with the following:

> Here it is in a nutshell, I think. You collapse *directions* into *stories* in what I think is an unfortunate but telling fashion. The decision to pick one path and then to go back isn't likely to be the one taken at all. More often than not, in my experience, the author, sensing two directions, will attempt to keep them open within the pathway of one story. In fact, story to me means something quite like this, i.e., an account of multiple possibilities within the "plot" and "character" and whatever else that presents itself.[23]

In large measure the software Joyce began developing with Bolter in early 1984 was about engineering just such story spaces. By this I mean it was about building a formal computational environment that could support the kinds of story structures that were in keeping with Joyce's ideas about multiple fictions and variable constraint, the origins of the intentional networks identified by Douglas. While the body of creative work that has been produced with Storyspace is most often associated with patterns like the rhizome or network, and consequently suitably postmodern figures like Deleuze and Guattari, the extant documentation makes it clear that the ideas for the program clearly and explicitly owed just as much to traditional hierarchical data structures like trees (see Marie-Laure Ryan's lists of categories earlier in this chapter).

23. Personal correspondence, Joyce to Natalie Dehn, October 1, 1983, the Michael Joyce Papers, Harry Ransom Humanities Research Center, the University of Texas at Austin, pages 1 and 2.

The single indispensable source for the early history of Storyspace is Joyce and Bolter's report to the Markle Foundation, which funded Storyspace for a crucial development year in 1985.[24] Today Storyspace is usually described as a tool for spatial or topographic writing, but there are several early concepts and articulations in the Markle report that had less endurance. In particular, Storyspace was conceived first and foremost as a "structure editor," and as a tool designed to facilitate what Joyce and Bolter would call "text processing," by way of explicit contrast to word processing (itself still novel to many with the advent of home computing). Here is how they articulate the concept of a structure editor:

The program currently represents structure as a map or network of rectangular cells and straight lines. Cells are units of text that may range in size from one character to 30,000. The author creates cells, labels them, positions them on the screen using the mouse, and attaches text. Stacking cells inside other cells indicates hierarchical relationships, while drawing and labeling lines from one to another indicates associate links. The author may then use the created structure to control or review the presentation of the text. (Markle 4)

The conceit of text processing, meanwhile, apparently came from Umberto Eco's theories of the open text and the idea that a literary work was a field of relations in which a reader could be invited to intervene and interact in a controlled or calibrated manner. "Text processing makes texts transparent, inviting readers to consider parallels, explore multiple alternate possibilities, and participate in the uncertain process of discovery and creation" (Markle 8). Explicit literary inspirations named in the report include the novels of Sterne, James Joyce, and Cortezar. Joyce and Bolter were also familiar with the existing tradition of hypertext through figures like Vannevar Bush and Douglas Englebart. And they compare Storyspace to oral narrative and to jazz improvisation (Markle 10). Also noteworthy is the fact that Storyspace was originally

24. The full title of the document hereafter referred to as the Markle report is "Storyspace: A Tool for Interaction, Report to the Markle Foundation regarding grant G85105 'to study methods for creating and presenting interactive compositions for video, print and computer media by developing a microcomputer-based "structure-editor".'" Signed by Joyce and J. David Bolter, it is dated March 1986 on the final page. The copy I consulted is part of the Michael Joyce Papers at the Harry Ransom Humanities Resarch Center at the University of Texas at Austin. All further references to the Markle report are to numbered pages in this document.

attractive to the Markle Foundation because of a program officer's interest in creating interactive video dramas using laserdiscs.

From the outset, Storyspace accommodated two different kinds of data structures: hierarchical trees, which represented the overall organization of the text, and associative nodes or clusters, inspired by the mathematical figure of the graph. "More particularly, [the structure editor] involved combining the relatively familiar and efficient hierarchical data structure known as the tree with the less familiar but more robust data structures known as networks or graphs" (Markle 13). Tree structures would have been familiar to both Joyce and Bolter from their activity at the Yale lab, as well as (in Bolter's case) the work of colleagues at UNC (John B. Smith was experimenting with a tree-based editor known as PROSE [Markle 19]). Joyce and Bolter both agreed that a text processor needed to support structures related to the "top level goals" of the work, as well as a form of clustering "which involves the author's awareness of sub-goals, remindings, and perceptions of potential orders" (Markle 16). The latter seems most like the current idea of a postmodern hypertext ("remindings" is a term that originated with the Yale lab's Roger Schank), but it should be emphasized that Storyspace was not developed with exclusively avant garde audiences in mind—it was repeatedly touted for its potential for business, organizational, and other kinds of writing. Likewise, and perhaps even more importantly, both Joyce and Bolter were convinced that hierarchical and networked structures continually informed one another in any piece of writing, and that a structure editor had to be able to facilitate these interactions. "Thus, in designing and creating a graphic structure editor, we were faced with the complex question of how best to represent the two primitive working levels of goal and sub-goal, i.e. hierarchy and cluster, while at the same time disclosing and preserving the dynamic, multiple and transitory working levels which devolve from these two primitive levels" (Markle 17). The point, then, is that Storyspace has significant grounding in a hierarchical data model that is absent from, or at times (as we see with Ryan above) presented as overtly antithetical to, the rhizomatic networks of postmodern hypertext theory. In my own terms, these two data structures instantiate two different and distinct formal materialities, which can be located in relationships expressed by the structure editor.

The tree structures in Storyspace were adapted from a series of software experiments by Bolter that began with a program he called simply TEXT, then renamed TALETELLER and later TALETELLER2 (Markle 19). The latter name actually stuck until 1985. The subsequent shift in nomenclature to Storyspace is worth lingering over, both for the obvious transition from an oral to a visual or spatial paradigm and for the way in which it redistributes agency from the software itself (as the tale teller) to the user (the software provides a venue or space for stories), reinforcing the move away from any pretension of artificial intelligence and toward extending the author's own cognitive capabilities—a tool for thought, in Howard Rheingold's then-current phrase. The key interface concepts—particularly stacking cells inside of other cells, which lent the screen a kind of third dimension—were all explicitly inspired by Joyce and Bolter's experience with folders on the Macintosh desktop, which in 1984–1985 was novel to them and any other personal computer user. Likewise, the ability to copy cells was also inspired by copying folders on the Mac.[25] It is especially revealing that the influence of the Mac desktop was apparently complemented by a hands-on exercise in what Jerome McGann would much later call "imagining what you don't know." Prior to the arrival of the team's first Macintosh, Bolter undertook to port TALETELLER2 (as the program was still then called) to the command line environment of the IBM PC. In the process, the two were able to reverse engineer detailed design specs for the functionality of a graphic interface, through a kind of negative capability (not unlike William Gibson, imagining his cyberspaces free of the constraints of any actual contact with computers). "This largely impoverished implementation thus generated a series of design expectations about potential graphical features" (Markle 19).

While both kinds of structure were clearly foundational to the way the software was designed and developed, Storyspace has since been celebrated chiefly for its networks of associative links, which seemed postmodern and could be aligned with such tropes or figures as the rhizome.[26] Illustrations of Storyspace in critical and theoretical writing from the late 1980s and 1990s nearly always depict it in the "map view," but this was only one of first three, and then four, spatial configurations available, including both a tree and an

25. For evidence of the Macintosh's influence on Storyspace, see the Markle report, pages 5, 19, 23, 26.

26. Janet Murray, discussing *Afternoon* and Stuart Moulthrop's *Victory Garden* (both Storyspace hypertexts), refers to this as the "rapture of the rhizome" and also aligns the rhizome with the figure of the labyrinth. See her *Hamlet on the Holodeck: The Future of Narrative in Cyberspace* (New York: Free Press, 1997), 132–134.

outline view. At some level then the network map is visually more compatible with a certain perceived aesthetic, or ideology, of electronic text, retroactively naturalizing it by privileging it as an apparent default. Yet there is nothing in the software's original documentation to suggest such was the case. The Markle report also suggests that guard fields, one of the most powerfully allusive Storyspace features associated with "serious" literary hypertext, owed their functional origins not to network models of text but rather to tree structures. When Bolter began adding the functionality allowing subtrees to be switched in and out of parent trees, it became clear that each node would require a unique identifier. Once that had been implemented, "the names themselves became available for either limiting access to certain cells, or determining a potential order (perhaps using the filter) for interactive presentation." At that point the software became capable of "guarding an audience's experience of the text" (Markle 32), something with which Joyce had long been interested in experimenting.

Guard fields, as they came to be known, are one of the most distinctive features of Storyspace, and their aggressive employment is central to *Afternoon*.[27] Yet guard fields also have at least a superficial resemblance to the kind of attribute-possession found in interactive fiction. (Joyce recalls that this similarity was first pointed out to him by a student.[28]) The Markle report itself states: "Bolter's programs TEXT and TALETELLER, while essentially concerned with creating interactive fictions of the Adventure type, nonetheless included overt tree structures and linking mechanisms. Joyce's early design documents (in the form of program pseudo-code) suggested extensions to the linking mechanism (for instance the ability to 'guard' certain links beyond the kind of attribute-possession which characterizes adventure games)" (19). The report further amplifies that the idea of a guard field, in its "earliest, simplest level had evolved from the kinds of attribute lists common to adventure game programs (which check to see, for instance, whether a would-be

---

27.   "Guard fields are simply logical conditions which describe what must be true for the link to be followed," explains *Getting Started with Storyspace for Windows* (Watertown, MA: Eastgate Systems, 1996), 78. Typically the conditional takes the form of a prerequisite for spaces already visited. The effect is similar to the kind of if/then conditionals that hold sway in traditional interactive fiction: "There is a bear here. If you have the honey pot, then you can get past the bear. If not, then the bear eats you."

28.   E-mail to author, May 17, 2006 12:07 PM.

wizard has earlier collected a wizard's hat or magic staff)" (44). In my view the exact source of the inspiration for guard fields is of less interest than the fact that the same two data structures that were foundational to Storyspace are also the basis for interactive fiction, which typically builds its game worlds through organizing lists and sublists of entities, which function as trees in their geometry and directed graphs or as networks in their grouping and associations.[29] While the behaviors, interactions, affordances, aesthetics, poetics, and motivations of the two styles are quite different, the presence of common data structures is relevant for students of electronic literature. The point bears emphasizing because of the schism that subsequently arose between interactive fiction and link-node hypertext, created when some observers felt that the former was either too commercial or too game-like (and insufficiently literary or "serious") to qualify as meaningful electronic literature.[30]

By 1988 Joyce and Bolter, by then also joined by UNC computer scientist John B. Smith, had formed a startup they called Riverrun Ltd. and had approached Broderbund, one of the major commercial software publishers of the era. Storyspace was taken quite seriously at Broderbund before it was eventually dropped in early 1989 because of what was perceived to be a weakening software market, as well as lingering confusion over exactly what the tool did and who its potential audience was.[31] In the interim, there had been a serious effort to articulate what it meant to "market hypertext successfully" (as the

29. For a detailed explanation of the role of tree structures and networks in interactive fiction, see David Graves, "Second Generation Adventure Games," *The Journal of Computer Game Design* 1, no. 2 (August 1987): 4–7, also available at http://teladesign.com/tads/authoring/articles/graves1.html. "One can create a model of the world as lists of containers: cities contain houses, houses contain rooms, rooms contain things, and things contain other things. The traditional method for representing complex relationships of objects is through lists of lists, also called trees."

30. Nick Montfort documents what he describes as the "digital literary divide," particularly as manifested in the academic reception of electronic literature, in his *Twisty Little Passages: An Approach to Interactive Fiction* (Cambridge: MIT Press, 2003), 8–13.

31. Harry Wiker to Joyce, February 27, 1989, the Michael Joyce Papers, Harry Ransom Center, University of Texas at Austin. Among other details of the severance, Riverrun was told it needed to return the Mac Plus and Photon hard drive Broderbund had lent them for the project (letter from Joanne Bealy to Joyce, February 27, 1989). Here we see a hard drive (then a still novel technology) being made visible as a significant commodity.

title of one internal report has it), leading to suggestions to de-emphasize (but not eliminate) the overt emphasis on hypertext itself and make Storyspace into something more like a brainstorming or note-taking tool. Potential markets were dutifully identified in the academic, corporate, and medical sectors.[32] One page of legal pad jottings from roughly the same time contains the following notes: "Make more compatible for general consumer/Emphasis moving away from HT [hypertext] w'out taking HT from product."[33] (Ironically, Eastgate Systems, the eventual publishers of Storyspace, are now well known for Tinderbox, a personal information management system that embodies much the same goals.) After Broderbund, Riverrun entered into talks with Mark Bernstein, a computer entrepreneur they knew from the annual ACM Hypertext meetings as the individual behind Eastgate, a small company specializing in hypertext systems research. The contract licensing Storyspace's development and distribution to Eastgate was signed December 17, 1990.[34]

In retrospect, we can see that Storyspace emerged out of a thick tissue of influences and ideas that included literary experimentation and postmodern theory (notably that of Eco), but also interactive computer fiction, artificial intelligence and story generators, word processing, desktop publishing and the then-new GUI conventions of the Mac, hypertext systems research, and interactive videodisc technology. Along the way, the software—the result, let us remember, of a two- and three-way collaboration between a novelist, a classicist, and a computer scientist, mediated by printed and electronic mail, phone calls, and face-to-face meetings—had been nurtured by sabbaticals, funded by a foundation grant, become the object of (routine) legal proceedings to transfer rights, was at the center of a failed marketing pitch to a major commercial software vendor, and finally came to roost at what was a combination small press and high-tech start-up. Whatever the fate of its executable code in the years to come, Storyspace has left behind a forensically replete trail of notes, correspondence, journal entries, proposals, bug reports, legal documents,

32. This report, from the Riverrun partners to Broderbund executive Alex Hogue, is available as an undated document in the Michael Joyce Papers, Harry Ransom Center, University of Texas at Austin.

33. The Michael Joyce Papers.

34. The Michael Joyce Papers.

marketing material, and technical documentation.[35] Henry Lowood claims, "Historians of software clearly will have to venture into every niche, nook, and cranny of society in ways that will separate their work from the work of other historians of science and technology. It has become far more difficult to locate the edges of computing as a discipline and to map the boundaries of its impact on society than for most other technical and scientific fields."[36] As the bootstrap work of theorizing digital culture draws to a close, further case studies of specific hardware and software implementations, and of the micro-events in the commercial and institutional environments in which those implementations are developed and deployed, are going to be essential.

Afternoons

Work proper on *Afternoon* began in March 1987.[37] Joyce was perhaps inspired by a remark from his old friend Howie Becker, who told him after seeing Storyspace, "One thing that will really help nerds like me see how to use this will be a couple of good examples, spelled out in real detail, and included on the disk. Like a story by you as you developed it here."[38] Significantly, there is no mention of *Afternoon* in the Markle report (dated a year earlier, March 1986), but Joyce had copies of the first edition to show at the ACM Hypertext meeting in Chapel Hill in November 1987. A journal entry dated June 4, 1988 comments, "What is not recorded here, but exists in a series of papers, letters, and what-have-you is the experience of succeeding at what I set out to do before Jay and I first contacted each other. 'To write a novel that changes each time you read it' came to be the story, 'Afternoon,' which will likely be

35. As Henry Lowood notes, we cannot always count on being so fortunate. Increasingly digital objects are developed within an exclusively digital setting with documentary material, such as correspondence, also born-digital (in the form of e-mail exchanges or chat sessions). See "The Hard Work of Software History," 148–149, wherein he recounts an anecdote about Justin Hall composing an essay on his word processor, auctioning the rights to it electronically on eBay, and then emailing it to the winning bidder, an electronic magazine that published it (exclusively) online.

36. Lowood, "The Hard Work of Software History," 149–150.

37. As indicated in the interview Joyce gave to Walter Vannini for his 1993 Italian translation of *Afternoon* from Human Systems (Milan). The writing took "very little time."

38. Becker to Joyce, October 3, 1985, the Michael Joyce Papers.

the centerpiece of S[tuart] Moulthrop's first disk magazine."[39] While work on the project initially took no more than half a year, the seeds had clearly been planted much earlier; the collection at the Ransom Center includes a newspaper clipping from the *Jackson Citizen Patriot* dated January 28, 1978, showing a photo of figures in goggles and snowsuits gazing at the wreckage of a burning snowmobile (see the lexia in *Afternoon* titled "winter").[40] Some of the best details of the text's actual composition process are to be had in a letter from Joyce to Sandra Kroupa, the Book Arts Librarian at the University of Washington, whom Joyce gifted with diskettes containing copies of both the first and second editions of *Afternoon* (1987 and 1989), as well as a single precious manuscript page:

[B]ecause afternoon was composed entirely on the computer screen, there is no manuscript. However I did make working notes of the links between different parts of the story as I was shaping them. Only three such pages remain to my knowledge, the simplest of which I am sending here along with Xerox copies of the front and back of the two pages I've kept for my sons. From what I can tell, however, it involves the final(?) mapping for a central complex of screens of the fiction surrounding the screen "yesterday" and has the advantage of being written on the reverse of a scrap paper sheet including a dated memo from 1987.[41]

While it is tempting to linger over the detail that *Afternoon* was composed entirely electronically, at the same time this description reveals a much more heterogeneous scene of writing, both more intimate and more implicated in a complex documentary setting and the rhythms of a working day. The ability to sketch freehand, to jot notes on what surfaces are at hand (like the back of a memo), and the way in which these surfaces are part of a larger, domestic environment—one of the manuscript pages at the Ransom Center features a prominent coffee cup stain—suggest a kind of hybrid textuality, fingers first

39. Journal, June 1987–August 1989, the Michael Joyce Papers, Harry Ransom Center at the University of Texas at Austin. Note the mention of Moulthrop's "disk magazine," the casual nomenclature revealing again a more visible role for storage technology than is typically the case today.

40. The Michael Joyce Papers.

41. Letter from Joyce to Sandra Kroupa, May 25, 1992, the Michael Joyce Papers. Joyce contacted Kroupa because of her efforts to build a collection of artists' books. The other two manuscript pages Joyce refers to above are now in the papers at the Ransom Center.

gripping a pencil, now tapping at keys. This point is more than merely recherché, for it has implications not only for how we think about electronic textuality, but also what it means to preserve it. The scene of writing we can reconstruct on the desktops both of and around Joyce's Macintosh is also, I would argue, a familiar one to the student of writing, who knows that Christian saints were often depicted in paintings at work in their studies, surrounded by a mass of books, papers, implements, and furnishings or other specialized tools designed to facilitate reading and writing. Despite the electronic pedigree of the actual text, *Afternoon's* story space and its written remainder extend well beyond the edge of a screen.

Joyce gave out several dozen copies of what has since become known as the first edition of *Afternoon* at the ACM Hypertext conference in late 1987. A second edition, which was the basis for the first commercial edition published by Eastgate Systems in 1990, was apparently distributed at the 1989 Hypertext meetings in Pittsburgh. A comparison of the first edition of *Afternoon* with a copy of the first Eastgate edition (the third edition proper) reveals several immediately observable differences:[42] the third edition includes a 20-kilobyte bitmapped graphic on its electronic frontispiece; the number of textual nodes has increased marginally, from 536 to 539;[43] the number of links, however, has increased by nearly a hundred, from 854 to 951. The electronic size of the work has also grown, from 235 kilobytes in the first edition to 375 kilobytes in the third. There are a number of minor textual variants. The spelling of "crysalis" in the "winter" node has been corrected to "chrysalis." The spell-

42. In the course of my work on *Afternoon* I had occasion to examine close to twenty copies of the work, from all editions except the second. Four of these copies were first editions, and one was the Human Systems Italian translation (based on the fifth edition). Two were for Windows, the rest for Macintosh. To access the files, I used a hex editor and various versions of Storyspace running in both the Mac Classic environment and OS X. I also inspected the online edition ("sixth edition") at http://www.wwnorton.com/pmaf/hypertext/aft/index.html and the printed excerpts in the *Norton Anthology of Postmodern American Fiction*, Paula Geyh, Fred G. Leebron, and Andrew Levy, eds. (New York: W. W. Norton, 1997), 576–580.

43. The additional nodes are either administrative or vestigial in nature. Two of them, "copyright and editions" (which contains the text of the colophon quoted at the beginning of the chapter) and "dedication" are paratextual; two more, "backlink" and "backlink3" contain neither text nor links and appear to be artifacts of the text's composition. (Note that since there is a difference of only three—not four—nodes between the two editions, at least one node from the first edition must have been removed.)

ing of "temperment" in "winter 2" has been corrected to "temperament." And there are several dozen more such changes—all typos, misspellings, and the occasional piece of punctuation (perhaps the most amusing of these is the correction of "pantyhose" from "pantyhouse" in the "Siren" lexia).[44] While these changes are trivial (accidentals, in the parlance of textual criticism), their very plainness—one can almost conjure Joyce's fingers on the keyboard as he backspaces and edits at some later date—bespeaks the diachronic nature of electronic objects. A more substantive textual variant is to be found in the lexia titled "moon," where the phrase "god rest his soul" has been added to the parenthetical aside that begins "my friend joel, for one." Still another change is more difficult to evaluate. *Afternoon* contains a sequence of four nodes titled "echoing," each presenting a distinctive visual arrangement of the word "echoing" repeated across the screen in a manner reminiscent of concrete poetry. One node in this sequence has had its title changed from "echoing" to "ecoing." This node also contains the text of the word spelled "ecoing," suggesting that the orthography is intentional—Umberto Eco?—but one cannot be sure. On the whole, it seems that changes to the "text itself" have been minor and inconspicuous over the course of the various editions.[45]

44. Collation was done by using linear transcripts of the text extracted from first and third editions of *Afternoon* that had been created using ResEdit. These transcripts were then subjected by me to a number of different file comparison utilities, including UNIX's "diff."

45. That is, with one colorful and well-known exception that has become part of *Afternoon* lore. The first edition included a node entitled "Jung" that contained no inbound links and just a fragment of text: "Man never perceives anything"—a truncated quotation from Jung himself. Joyce has speculated that the node was the vestigial remnant of an abandoned piece of the text. This node became known as the "Jane's space" because Jane Yellowlees Douglas was the first to notice it and call it to Joyce's attention. In later editions of *Afternoon* several additional lines of text have been added. I have written about the apparent mystery surrounding the Jane's space or Jung node—Joyce claims not to know the identity of the person or persons responsible—in my earlier "Editing the Interface: The Textual Condition of Electronic Objects" *TEXT* 14 (2002): 15–51. It is worth noting here, however, that the changes in content correspond to the different editions that have been released and thus serve a pragmatic function, useful to the textual scholar in dating and distinguishing them. In the first (1987) edition, Joyce had written: "Man . . . never perceives anything"; in the third (1990) edition, Joyce added, on a new line, "and only Jane Yellowlees Douglas has read this screen." By the fourth (1991) edition an unknown person had added (also on a new line): "That's not true, so have others." And by the fifth (1992) edition an unknown person had added (again on a new line): " 'To be born again, first you have to die.' *The Satanic Verses*".

The changes to the link structures are more far-reaching. All of the extant documentary evidence suggests that Joyce's efforts toward revision were concentrated not in the language of *Afternoon* but in the links, paths, and guard fields constituting the "intentional network," those formal mechanisms that govern a reader's interactions with the work. This is dramatically exposed in the two manuscript pages now archived at the Ransom Center. Each is covered with Joyce's handwritten notes, on both sides of the page (figure 4.2).

Joyce generally uses an arrow "→" to indicate a link, and symbols for various operators, which became standard Storyspace conventions to delimit guard fields: an ampersand "&" to indicate an AND condition, a vertical bar or pipe "|" to indicate an OR condition, a tilde "~" to indicate a condition that must *not* have been fulfilled, and quotation marks to name lexias (pipes and ampersands and tildes also being standard programmer's notation). Thus the sequence: ~"her hand" & ~"white dress" written in Joyce's notes describes the logical conditions governing a guard field; in this case that neither of the two specified lexias can have been visited. Nearly all of the writing on the manuscript pages is pseudocode of this sort. Some notes are crossed out. One of the pages contains a vertical list of lexias that corresponds to a portion of the default sequence one encounters by reading *Afternoon* simply by striking the Return key: "I want to say," "I want 1.," "I want 2.," "asks," "yesterday," "Werther 3," "Die," "He, he says," "a bet," "The odds," "Whom," "Love," "Thank you." A student of *Afternoon* could spend many hours attempting to reconstitute aspects of the text's creation and composition from these cryptic jottings, but their main significance now is to underscore the extent to which the links and guard fields were a major focus of Joyce's creative attention.

That contention is reinforced by the example of one of the key switch-points in *Afternoon*, a node (lexia) titled "I call." Jane Yellowlees Douglas goes so far as to say: "To penetrate the narrative to its furthest extent, to realize most of its possibilities, I need, in a sense, to experience the place 'I call' in each of the readings. . . . Of all the places in *Afternoon*, 'I call' has the largest number of paths branching out from it—ten—making it, significantly, a place both physically and literally central to the structure of the narrative."[46] If one chooses to read the work in its default mode (that is, simply

46. Jane Yellowlees Douglas, "'How Do I Stop This Thing?': Closure and Indeterminacy in Interactive Narratives," *Hyper/Text/Theory*, ed. George P. Landow (Baltimore: Johns Hopkins University Press, 1994), 167–168.

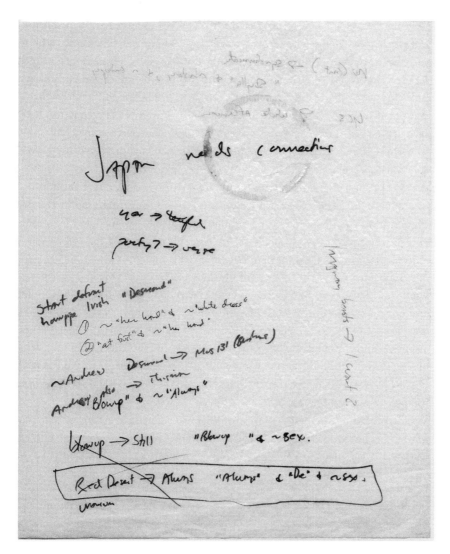

Figure 4.2 One of three surviving manuscript pages for *Afternoon*, including coffee mug stain. From the Michael Joyce Papers, Harry Ransom Humanities Research Center at the University of Texas at Austin.

striking the return key to proceed from node to node rather than selecting links), then, as Douglas notes, the narrative dead-ends at this point—the return key produces no further progression from the "I call" node (165–166). Readers are forced to either abandon their reading of the text or to follow a link—"a word that yields," in Joyce's parlance.[47] The "I call" node, which is composed of about 150 words detailing Peter's attempts (Peter is the text's primary narrator) to telephone various persons who may or may not know something about a car crash that may or may not have involved his ex-wife and son, does not change in its linguistic content from the first edition to the third. But a comparison between the two editions does reveal the addition of one new link: there are ten in the third edition, but only nine in the first (figure 4.3). The new link, titled "under lying value," is anchored by a reference in the text to the character Wert; it yields access to a remote region of *Afternoon* that opens up important new plot developments (which in turn present the reader with still more permutations of choices). This area of the text would not have been previously accessible without a far more prolonged and circuitous reading of *Afternoon*. The addition of a new link to the "I call" node may seem like a modest enough revision, yet Douglas, perhaps Joyce's most attentive and accomplished reader, was struck by the difference: "... when one reaches 'I call Lolly.' I don't know what it is, but I swear to God it reads like an entirely different series of stories. It really jumps to life now right from the first foray into the text . . ."[48]

The preceding discussion serves to illustrate changes to *Afternoon* that cannot be accounted for by the putatively "writerly" nature of hypertext as such. Rather, the variants and revisions I have been enumerating are indicative of the

47. Readers familiar chiefly with the Web convention of signifying links by different colors and underlining should understand that links are not visually distinguished from the surrounding text in *Afternoon*. The instructional booklet that accompanies *Afternoon* explains: "The lack of clear signals is not an attempt to vex you, but rather an invitation to read inquisitively, playfully, or at depth. Click on words that interest or invite you."

48. E-mail from Douglas to Michael Joyce, dated 4:54pm EDT 11 October 1990, provided to the author by Joyce. Note that in this statement Douglas identifies the node as "I call Lolly" rather than simply "I call." *Afternoon* in fact contains lexias of both names, yet it seems clear, given her strong sense of its centrality to the narrative, that Douglas is here referring to changes in "I call" rather than "I call Lolly" (which did not in fact change between the first and second or third edition). Moreover, given that the last line of "I call" is "I take a pill and call Lolly," it seems plausible that Douglas would have referred to the lexia in its entirety as "I call Lolly."

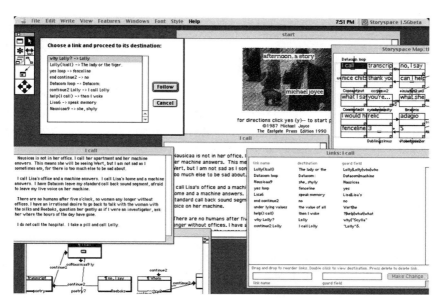

Figure 4.3 Comparison showing two versions of the "I call" node. On the left, open in Storyspace 1.5, is a copy of the 1987 first edition of *Afternoon*. Vertically from the top of the screen we see the list of links available, the text of the node, and the map view. On the right, open in Storyspace 2.0.3, is a copy of the 1990 third edition of *Afternoon*, or first Eastgate edition, showing the title screen, map view, text of the node, and list of link paths available. Notice the addition of the link "under lying values" with the destination "the value of all" (fourth from the bottom). Operating system is Macintosh OS X Panther. Screenshot by the author.

textual condition of all electronic objects, that "material event or set of events" which, for a critic such as McGann, constitute the "social text" that is produced under "specific social and institutional conditions." The power of such a position, illustrated by attention to the kinds of bibliographic particulars I have been enumerating, is that it recovers works of electronic literature from deceptive strata of pure virtuality and restores them to a temporal and historical situation usually belied by the sheer superficiality of the screen. To some extent, the social electronic text resides in physical objects and materials: the manuscript pages, for example, with their coffee cup stains and indentations where Joyce's pen has pressed, or a diskette containing one of Joyce's personal copies of *Afternoon*, the label signed by the author. In response to a question about whether "there will be the equivalent of bibliophilia in relation to CD-ROMs or floppy disks," Derrida offers this: "Probably. Some particular draft that was prepared or printed on some particular software, or some particular disk that stores a stage of a work in progress—these are the kinds of things that will be fetishized in the future" (28–29).[49] But formal materiality, as I have described it in the previous chapter, also serves to fetishize via the computational distance (or torque, or simply effort) necessary to attain access to certain kinds of electronic objects, or to access certain objects in certain ways. In my own case, the first time I successfully opened a first edition of *Afternoon*, I was exquisitely self-conscious of something very much like bibliophilia, precisely because I had to couple the file itself with the right Macintosh operating system and the right version of Storyspace, thereby imposing a formal regimen on the binary object that was *Afternoon*, which then led it to execute, consume system resources, and ultimately present itself for my inspection and manipulation. This kind of access and recovery will, I suspect, ultimately prove more enduring then a collector or connoisseur's sensibility, which seeks to acquire and possess—as William Gibson has his joke in his recent novel *Pattern Recognition*, Stephen King's Wang.[50]

While the account of the various editions of *Afternoon* in the colophon is matter-of-fact, the question of how many *versions* of the work exist is more difficult. Part of the issue is terminological. One might reasonably expect to speak about versions of the work in terms of different readers' experiences with the mutable pathways and multiple fictions of the text, those "locked doors giving way to touch," that make any given encounter with the *Afternoon* unpredictable and difficult to duplicate. In the critical literature, the tendency is to use "version" in this sense more or less interchangeably with "reading" and "contour," the latter a word Joyce himself introduced and evolved to define the sense of an emerging narrative in hypertext.[51] "Contours," he writes,

49. In "The Word Processor," an interview with Derrida conducted by Béatrice and Louis Seguin for *La Quinzaine Littéraire* in August 1996. Reprinted in Derrida's *Paper Machine*, trans. Rachel Bowlby (Stanford: Stanford University Press, 2005): 19–32.

50. Wang, of course, being the brand name of a word processor popular in the 1970s. It was King's first computer. See William Gibson, *Pattern Recognition* (New York: Putnam, 2003).

51. For instance, in this passage by Douglas: "[*Afternoon*] may well resolve into unimagined combinations and sequences during any single reading, since hundreds and even thousands of possible *versions* of the text exist—many of which Joyce has, doubtless, never so much as envisioned" (139; emphasis added). In *The End of Books—Or Books Without End? Reading Interactive Narratives* (Ann Arbor: University of Michigan Press, 2000).

"are the shape of what we think we see as we see it but that we know we have seen only after we move over them."[52] Elsewhere he is more clinical: "Contour is one expression of the perceptible form of a constantly changing text, made by any of its readers or writers at a given point in its reading or writing. Its constituent elements include the current state of the text at hand, the perceived intentions and interactions of previous writers and readers that led to the text at hand, and those interactions with the text that the current reader or writer sees as leading from it" (214). Contour is also about the pleasures of the text: "Contours are discovered sensually," Joyce remarks in the same passage. (Consider that in regard to the *Afternoon* icon, a stylized representation of the female erogenous zone.)

Yet textual scholars tend to mean something rather different when they speak of versions. "The root cause of any version is revision," John Bryant contends in *The Fluid Text*, wherein he is able to demonstrate that the question of versions is more complex than might first appear.[53] What is the threshold by which mere variants in a text promote the text to the status of a new *version* of the work? What are the relationships between the physical or documentary incarnations of the work and its version history? Can evidence from a single witness imply the existence of multiple versions? Can one infer the existence of a version without its having a locatable basis in an actual document? Who authorizes and adjudicates versions? Authors? Publishers? Editors? Can a particular version ever be so radical and wrenching as to constitute a whole new work, rather than merely a version of a previous one? How are versions to be edited and exhibited to readers? Bryant himself comes down squarely on the

52.   Joyce, *Of Two Minds: Hypertext Pedagogy and Poetics* (Ann Arbor: University of Michigan Press, 1995), 207. By far the most complete discussion of contour as trope in early hypertext theory and writing is Dave Ciccoricco's "The Contour of a Contour" in the *electronic book review*, which teases out the genealogy of the word through Joyce and others' work throughout this period: http://www.electronicbookreview.com/thread/electropoetics/tropical.

53.   John Bryant, *The Fluid Text: A Theory of Revision and Editing for Book and Screen* (Ann Arbor: Michigan University Press, 2002). For those unfamiliar with the general tenor of recent debates in textual studies Bryant offers a concise overview, in the process driving home the point that textual fluidity is not a phenomenon unique to electronic media. But while his subtitle may suggest that the book also addresses its arguments to first generation electronic artifacts like *Afternoon*, in fact Bryant's overt observations about new media are limited to a proposal for electronic editions of those printed works he considers candidates for fluid text editing.

side of qualitative rather than quantitative changes, and specifically Peter Shillingsburg's notion that a revision constitutes a new version of the work if it engenders for it a new *function* (81–82). Also, no version of a text can ever manifest revisions so massive or profound as to—ontologically—no longer be a version of the work in question (85–86). Bryant goes on to delineate the characteristics of the fluid text version: versions may be either physical (literally distinct documents) or inferred from the evidence available on one or more extant documents; a version of a work can always be linked to another version; versions are revisions of the work, and they may be initiated, either deliberately or inadvertently, by the author or by some other agency like an editor or the public at large; versions do not depend on the authority of the author to be authorized as versions; versions are manifest by their degree of difference from other versions—"a version always makes us aware of the distance between itself and its linked partners," as Bryant usefully puts it (89); versions entail some reconceptualization or reimagining of the work in question; versions are partly defined by their rhetorical impact on their audiences; and finally, versions are constructed critically by virtue of other artifacts in the documentary field, meaning that the existence of a version is always, in the end, arguable (88–90). If we step back from this delineation, what we have then is an account of versioning wherein a version itself is always critical, contingent, relative or relational, functional, rhetorical, and perhaps above all, consequential. A version is not an inferior derivative of some legitimized and sanctioned work, nor is it simply a collection of observable variants. Versions are the textual differences that make a difference.[54]

The question of versioning *Afternoon*, therefore, is not a question of its multiple fictions and its contours, and it is not necessarily conterminous with the editions as specified in the colophon. Nor is it strictly a question of the versions of Storyspace and its associated Reader utility, though we will examine the role of versioning in software development in the next section. As a textual scholar, I would version *Afternoon* as follows:

- The first version of *Afternoon* is conterminous with the 1987 first edition, and was created using Storyspace 3.3 (as the software was then versioned by Riverrun Ltd.).

54. I am of course following the lead of Gregory Bateson, for whom "information" is (famously) "the difference that makes a difference."

- The second version of *Afternoon* is conterminous with the 1990 Eastgate Systems edition for Macintosh, also corresponding to the third edition of the work (and forward). It was created using Storyspace 1.0 and its descendents as marketed by Eastgate Systems. The justifications for designating a new version are numerous revisions to the text and the link structure (as discussed earlier), implementation with a new version of Storyspace, the addition of a bitmapped graphic on the frontispiece, and commercial packaging and distribution.

- The third version of *Afternoon* is conterminous with the 1992 Eastgate Systems edition for Windows, also corresponding to the fifth edition of the work, and was created using Storyspace for Windows. The justification for designating a new version is the alterations to the interface and its behaviors as a result of porting to the Microsoft Windows environment.

- The fourth version of *Afternoon* is conterminous with the online edition published by W. W. Norton in 1997. This new version is justified by significant changes to appearance, behavior, and the code base as a result of porting to a Web-based Java environment.

As authorities such as Kenneth Thibodeau have stressed, digital preservation is inseparable from questions of access.[55] Readers will notice that my versioning falls largely along the lines generated by the different means of access implied by different publishers, ports, and platforms. This is not the only way an electronic work can be versioned; for example, I have not chosen to regard the Italian translation as a separate version, but rather to associate it with my second version. Moreover, if one were to bracket all questions of access and distribution, there would still be perfectly sufficient technical and editorial grounds on which to distinguish between the first and second versions, and sufficient technical grounds on which to distinguish between all four (figures 4.4, 4.5, and 4.6).[56]

55. Kenneth Thibodeau, "Overview of Technological Approaches to Digital Preservation and Challenges in the Coming Years," *The State of Digital Preservation: An International Perspective*, Council on Library and Information Resources, pub107 (2002), online at http://www.clir.org/pubs/reports/pub107/thibodeau.html.

56. Joyce, in a letter to author Robert Coover dated September 2, 1991, comments "I am interested and not entirely surprised by your preference for the earlier, editable *version* of 'Afternoon'" (emphasis added). Joyce is presumably referring to the first edition, which was distributed without benefit of the Reader utility.

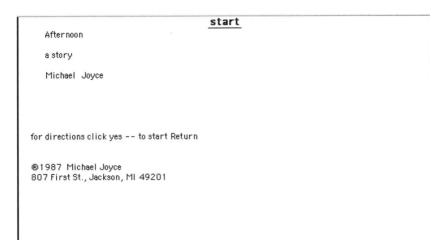

start

Afternoon

a story

Michael Joyce

for directions click yes -- to start Return

®1987 Michael Joyce
807 First St., Jackson, MI 49201

Fig. 4.4

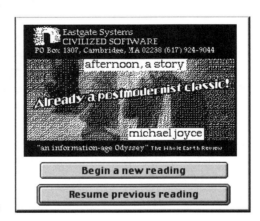

Eastgate Systems
CIVILIZED SOFTWARE
PO Box 1307, Cambridge, MA 02238 (617) 924-9044

afternoon, a story

Already a postmodernist classic!

michael joyce

"an information-age Odyssey" The Whole Earth Review

Begin a new reading

Resume previous reading

Fig. 4.5

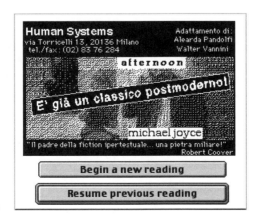

Human Systems
via Torricelli 13, 20136 Milano
tel./fax: (02) 83 76 284

Adattamento di:
Alearda Pandolfi
Walter Vannini

afternoon

E' già un classico postmoderno!

michael joyce

"Il padre della fiction ipertestuale... una pietra miliare!"
Robert Coover

Begin a new reading

Resume previous reading

Fig. 4.6

The Web edition published by Norton in 1997 that I have versioned separately from the others requires additional comment. In addition to brief printed excerpts in the *Norton Anthology of Postmodern Literature*, arrangements were made to publish a limited edition of *Afternoon* online. So as not to compete with the commercial version available from Eastgate, readings of the text would be limited to 15 lexia, or screens, in any given sitting. (Initially access to the online *Afternoon* was restricted to those who could enter a password contained in their copy of the printed anthology, but this restriction has since been removed.) The idea was to allow students to read *Afternoon* in a way that was faithful to distinctive aspects of the original work, but in a setting accessible through a desktop Web browser.[57] While one suspects that the exercise was ultimately minor in its pedagogical impact, it reveals much about the process of porting a work between two environments as radically different as Storyspace and the networked hypermedia of the Web. Indeed, the Norton *Afternoon* represents what is almost certainly the most ambitious porting of a Storyspace hypertext to date.[58]

Figure 4.4, Figure 4.5, Figure 4.6   Three title screens from *Afternoon*: the 1987 first edition, the 1991 second edition (Eastgate), and the 1993 Italian translation (Human Systems) based on the 1992 third edition (all for Macintosh). The front matter for *Afternoon* is particularly interesting to track over time, not only for the addition of the graphic but for the way paratextual material accumulates, including advertising blurbs and publication information. *Afternoon* also has an ISBN, though it is not included in the electronic body of the work. Screenshots by the author.

57.   Jane Yellowlees Douglas's Eastgate hypertext "I Have Said Nothing" is also excerpted online at the Norton site, in a simple HTML-only implementation. Unlike *Afternoon*, no attempt is made to recreate the behavior of guard fields or other Storyspace functionality: "Unfortunately, it's presently virtually impossible to replicate on the Web the system of guardfield conditions that enabled readers to see as options only those paths which took them to destinations that had some meaning, some relevance due to where they'd already been. Nor is it possible for readers to explore the full complexity of the narrative—or the possibilities for interaction that accompany each segment—in this excerpt." See http://www.wwnorton.com/pmaf/hypertext/ihsn/are_we_reading.html.

58.   Porting is the process by which software and electronic objects are migrated from one platform and operating system to another. Sometimes porting is simply a matter of mechanically recompiling software code for a different interpreter. Other times the process is more complex and invasive, involving substantial revision to an application's underlying source code. Stephanie

To recreate the guard fields and word-based links of *Afternoon*, the programmer on the project, Justin Edelson, built a custom Java/Javascript engine. Any encounter with the Norton *Afternoon* is therefore preceded by repeated warnings about appropriate browser configurations. At a minimum, a reader encounters the following: *"afternoon* makes heavy use of JavaScript. You MUST view the site with a Java-enabled browser. This site is thus best viewed with Netscape 3.0 and 4.0 or Internet Explorer 3.0 and 4.0" and "As of September 1997, this hypertext is known to be compatible with the following browsers {four are listed, together with recommended operating systems}.

Strickland, for example, writes the following about the Mac port of her Storyspace hypertext *True North*, originally written using Storyspace for Windows: *"True North* had to be completely redone to make a Mac version, since it was written in a beta version of Storyspace for Windows. They are two really separate works in my view. I had believed, again naively, that a simple 'translation/migration' that Eastgate could do, would create this version. . . . The functionality of those two is(?) certainly was, entirely different. To me as a writer, more different than pastels vs. oil, though maybe not as different as sculpture vs. painting. I had planned the Windows version to make use of the capabilities I discovered it to have. I had to do workarounds galore in the Mac to match the functionality of the Windows version—and I couldn't really, at that point, exploit the extra functionality that was Mac alone. . . . There was no way to map the features 1:1. You had a certain backward glance in the Mac maps you could ask for, whereas you had an index like access to 'titles' in the Windows; you had a keyword search in the Windows. . . . I also struggled against the program because I was making a metaphoric use of the maps (on several levels, shape, naming, etc.), but it was entirely too hard to get the maps to display at a proper size (that should have been readily available, if one had any sense of integrating visuality. Storyspace never did, imo.) Mac was better at the visuality, as I recall; on Windows getting the map in view was often a problem, and certainly getting the right magnification." E-mail to author, Aug 6, 2005 8:26 AM. Porting is a sister process emulation, the practice of building software tools that are designed to reproduce—emulate—the look and feel of another operating system. A colorful example is the thriving high-tech subculture devoted to creating emulators for old video game platforms. These emulators allow games originally programmed for, say, the Atari 2600—an 8-bit gaming system popular in the early 1980s—to run under a 32-bit operating system such as Windows. Emulation software arguably operates within the same horizon that textual scholars recognize as facsimile editing, since the emulator actually allows a contemporary computer system to execute code originally intended for an antiquated platform.

Other browsers may work and you, the reader, are free to try other browsers, but only the above are **known** to work" (emphasis in original).[59] Readers are then further enjoined: "Additionally, users of Netscape Navigator should turn link underlining off." Thus one difference between the conventions of *Afternoon* and the common browser is immediately made manifest. Correspondence between Joyce and Edelson reveals the range of challenges associated with the project. There are structural issues: "'cooler' I know is is [sic] just an internal dummy page but the text should make the point that the original afty [*Afternoon*], which you are careful to represent here, did not show it links." There are also vestigial interface conventions to be considered: "the directions in this space 'a hypertext' are accurate historically but confusing, since pressing the Return key does nothing. (a similat [sic] set of questions accompanies the refernces [sic] to Mac interface and the original toolbar in 'read at depth')." There are variants to be corrected: "Text is munged. The sentence ⟨Pupa or seed when you mix the images so, you dilute the vision. And the Too much, really.⟩ should read ⟨Pupa or seed pod ... when you mix the images so, you dilute the vision. And the banner. ... ? Too much, really.⟩"[60] And so on. Edelson himself comments at length on the process in response to my inquiry:

I was responsible for porting the text from its more or less original state into the HTML/Java/JavaScript version available on the Norton web site. It was an interesting project, especially in that, even in 1999 (and 2006 for that matter), the navigation used by _afternoon_ are still inaccessible to the web publisher without custom development either on the client or the server.

afternoon uses a linking structure based on words, whereas traditional web links are based on location. In addition, each screen or page within _afternoon_ has a 'default' link. These two features feed into each other as every word is a link and if a word doesn't have a defined link, the default link is followed. In addition, _afternoon_ uses conditional links based on what screens/pages the reader has already seen.

[...] The notion of default links is totally lacking in web browsers; even though the HTML LINK tag can be used to indicate a default link, the browser support

59. The text quoted here is from http://www.wwnorton.com/pmaf/hypertext/ and http://www.wwnorton.com/pmaf/hypertext/aft/index.html respectively.

60. The three foregoing quotations are all from e-mail from Edelson to Joyce, Aug 28 1997 09:53:25, Michael Joyce Papers (electronic files).

Figure 4.7 Cover page to the Norton online edition of *Afternoon* programmed by Justin Edelson. *Source*: http://www.wwnorton.com/pmaf/hypertext/aft/index.html

simply isn't there. And although modern browsers do expose a "history" object through JavaScript, privacy concerns have limited its usefulness.[61]

Edelson's comments thus reveal the wholesale overhaul of the text's mechanism that was required for porting the iconic hypertext of the Storyspace era to the online setting of the World Wide Web (see figure 4.7).[62] In particular

61.   E-mail to author, Dec 1, 2006 9:09 AM, in which Edelson is revising comments originally sent at an earlier date.

62.   A different, but no less interesting set of issues was encountered by Deena Larsen in preparing to port electronic poetry by William Dickey, originally authored in Hypercard, to the Web. Larsen comments: "In HyperCard, there is no difference between cursing over a hotspot [link] and cursing over any other spot. Dickey loved this. He thought it was important to distinguish between hotspots and non hotspots merely by the meaning in the imagery—and having people search and click for the next page was very important. If I translate correctly, I would need to incorporate the 'non hand' or unchanging cursor [i.e., the simple pointer]. Outside of technical difficulties [. . .] we have reader difficulties. It is not fair to expect a reader to intuitively

they expose distinctive aspects of the formal materiality of the Web, whose seemingly anachronistic "pages" are not merely a function of nomenclature, but are built into the document object modeling the Web's protocols and browser software support.

If versions denote textual differences that make a difference, what difference does it make to enumerate the various versions of *Afternoon*? In his 1957 Sandars Lectures in Bibliography, Fredson Bowers cuttingly observed: "[I]t is still a current oddity that many a literary critic has investigated the past ownership and mechanical condition of his second-hand automobile, or the pedigree and training of his dog, more thoroughly than he has looked into the qualifications of the text on which his critical theories are based."[63] While scholars in more established areas of literary study do typically acknowledge differences between versions of a work and their rationale for choosing a particular version or edition, anecdotal evidence suggests this happens less frequently in the nascent field of electronic literature. *Afternoon* is typically cited without any acknowledgement or awareness of the differences between its versions, or even the fact that multiple versions exist. For example, it is often assigned a publication date of 1987, referring to the date of the first edition, when it is probably more likely that the scholar is working with one of the commercial editions available from Eastgate. Thus the impulse to historically situate *Afternoon* as the "first" hypertext fiction is at odds with the fact that the first version of it is not widely available. In my view a fully adequate scholarly citation for *Afternoon* would specify the text's edition (according to the colophon), Storyspace software version, platform, and operating system; for example

---

understand that you can click anywhere without seeing a [pointing] hand. Readers are used to hand equals hotspot, line equals nothing [i.e., no link]. And they won't change these expectations for Dickey's work—anymore than they would agree to read backwards for the Jabberwocky. So, do I deliberately ignore the author's intent (and this was a major issue with Dickey) in favor of writing conventions that Dickey never knew (he died before the Web took off) or do I incorporate the author's intent and lose the audience?" E-mail to author, May 17 1999. I have covered Larsen's innovative editorial work on William Dickey more extensively in my "Editing the Interface: Textual Studies and First Generation Electronic Objects," TEXT 14 (2002): 15–51.

63. Bowers, *Textual and Literary Criticism* (Cambridge: Cambridge University Press, 1959), 5.

Afternoon, a story, 5th edition (1992), Storyspace Reader 1.0.7, Windows XP.[64] (Careful versioning citations of this kind are routine in software documentation and bug testing, where specification of exact builds and operating systems is essential.) The general flattening effect whereby all versions and editions of *Afternoon* are assumed to be more or less homogenous is, in my view, symptomatic of still commonplace attitudes toward electronic textuality among the critical community, which assumes electronic objects exist absent of any meaningful diachronic dimension. As we will see in the next section, however, there are communities and constituencies in information technology for whom the view that electronic objects did *not* exhibit temporal or diachronic behavior would itself seem alarming and dysfunctional.

64.   In my article "Editing the Interface: The Textual Condition of Electronic Objects," I published a provisional vocabulary for versioning and describing electronic objects based on the example of Fredson Bowers's magisterial *Principles of Bibliographical Description*, 2nd edition (Princeton: Princeton University Press, 1986), the authoritative work in a field devoted to describing books as physical artifacts. I proposed the terms *release, layer, version, object, state, copy,* and *instance*, and covered each of them with reference to the specific example of David Blair's *WAXWEB*, a massive, multiplatform, iteratively versioned hypermedia network. At the time I wrote: "My first thought in what follows was simply to retain Bowers's terms, and suggest how one might distinguish between the different editions, impressions, states, and so forth of an electronic object. This terminology, however, soon proved inadequate. Bowers's definitions of terms are (as one might expect) absolutely dependent on the material specificity of their medium— that is their great strength. The disjunctions between the material conditions of printed and electronic objects are, I believe, too great to bridge by way of Bowers's strict formulations. There is simply no clear analogue, for example, to an 'edition' in electronic media, defined by Bowers as 'all copies printed at any time or times from one setting of type,' nor is there any analogue for an 'impression,' one single 'complete run of sheets' from one setting of type. It is true that I could have evacuated these definitions of all of their minute particulars, retaining only the shell of the term's original usage—equating settings of type to versions of code, for example—but finally it seemed more effective to introduce a new set of terms, conceived expressly for the electronic medium" (45–46). While I stand by the need for such a descriptive vocabulary and think my effort here was a robust first attempt, it seems clear the task must be a collaborative community-based one, undertaken by a collective of scholars with a shared stake in the outcome. One such example is the Electronic Literature Organization's Preservation, Archiving, and Dissemination initiative (PAD), of which I have been a part since its inception in 2003. See http://eliterature.org/programs/pad/ for working papers and other materials.

Versioning and the Long Now of Software

Versioning is a hallmark of electronic textual culture—as a thriving industry of content management systems, file comparison utilities, and so-called version control or concurrent versions systems, the archetype of which, Concurrent Versions System (CVS), originated at about the time Joyce was writing *Afternoon*.[65] A Dutch computer scientist working on a large distributed programming project devised a repository structure that would allow him and his students to collaborate without inadvertently overwriting one another's code.[66] While most prevalent in software development, especially open source projects with their often globally dispersed contributors, a version control system like CVS (or its heir, Subversion) is capable of managing any kind of data, textual or otherwise. A version control system retains every state of every file checked in or out of the repository, and is capable of stepping back through the resulting decision trees to access the data at any point in its revision history. In essence, what these systems represent are temporal extrusions of the immediate documentary event on a user's screen.

Most people encounter versioning not through sophisticated repository structures like CVS, however, but through increasingly commonplace features of workplace productivity software. Since the debut of Word 97, users have had the ability to track changes in their documents, the software automatically logging each and every addition and deletion, as well as changes in formatting—all date- and time-stamped to the second (figure 4.8). (Expressly designed to facilitate collaborative work, the Track Changes feature in Word 97 is one concrete manifestation of the millennial corporate doxa of teamwork as articulated by Alan Liu.[67]) At some point in the editing cycle, the entire history of changes is meant to be either accepted or rejected, removing them from the textual strata of the finished document. In fact, a common workplace gaffe is to send a client or correspondent an electronic copy of a document with the *view* of the changes turned off, but the changes themselves not yet

65.   Versioning and variants are also an integral aspect of computer virus detection and analysis, and anyone who works in one of those fields takes the phenomenon of an electronic object mutating and changing over time as a matter of course.

66.   See http://www.cs.vu.nl/~dick/CVS.html#History.

67.   See Liu's *The Laws of Cool: Knowledge Work and the Culture of Information* (Chicago: University of Chicago Press, 2004).

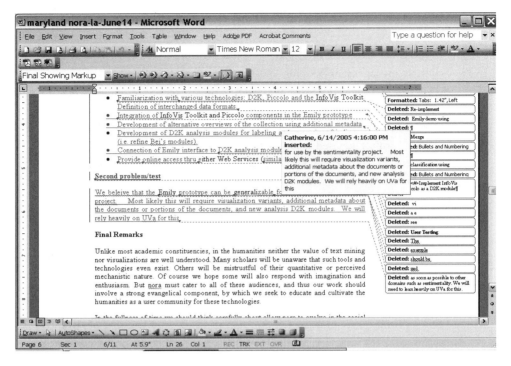

Figure 4.8 MS Word's Track Changes feature in use. Screenshot by the author.

accepted or rejected—thereby displaying the word-by-word *processing* of the text to its intended recipient as soon as the view of the changes is turned back on in their own copy of Word.[68]

Likewise, an online information resource such as *Wikipedia* renders its editing and revision process publicly transparent in a way that a printed encyclopedia never could, by retaining the version history of the document and giving users access to the full text of all previous versions (with editorial com-

---

68.   Similar risks accrue when electronic documents are migrated from one format to another. For example, a public National Security Agency report titled "Redacting with Confidence: How to Safely Publish Sanitized Reports Converted From Word to PDF." See http://www.fas.org/sgp/othergov/dod/nsa-redact.pdf. Likewise, according to Michael Caloyannides in *Computer Forensics and Primary*, Word's "fast save" option works by appending changes to the original copy of the document, rather than by writing the new document to disk in its entirety. "A savvy recipient of this saved document (in the form of a floppy disk or an electronic attachment to email) will have the benefit not only of the last version of the file but also of all of the interim versions" (26).

mentary on each). Coupled with terabyte-scale storage options, version control systems offer a glimpse of a radically different model of electronic textuality, one in which the state of a document and its relation to prior and past states is pitilessly available and exposed, perhaps laying to rest the kind of concerns raised by no less a textual sophisticate than David Greetham in regard to the limitations of electronic writing:

> I think we can already recognize that in an electronic environment it is difficult to see how the secure parental genetic features necessary to the project of recension could not become irrevocably blurred and yes, 'contaminated' in the shifting multilevel and idiosyncratic traversal of a hypertextual coding of relationships. All parent-child affiliations would become contingent and temporary, the product of an individual and nonreplicable linearity that would be no more than the onscreen "history" of a series of "visits" to certain "sites."[69] (118)

CVS architectures exist precisely to instantiate those parent-child relationships; that is, to enforce linearity and enable programmatic recension—as literally, inexorably, and grindingly absolute as their dendritic logics can allow. Indeed, Track Changes and similar methods of document versioning embody, more or less literally, the precepts of a school of editorial method known as *genetic editing*. Originating in Germany and France, genetic editing seeks to expose the writing process by rendering variants directly in the body of the edited text rather than in an apparatus or some other marginal locale (often this requires elaborate typography, punctuation, and formatting). Whereas the editors of a so-called eclectic text might pick and choose amongst various surviving versions to manufacture a text that is in keeping with the author's putative final intentions (but corresponding to no historically extant document), and whereas editors of the social or documentary stripe might pick one particular historical manifestation of the text to foreground as the material basis of their edition, a genetic editor treats the text as a kind of dynamic field, wherein all variants are recorded and reproduced. The most famous example of this approach is undoubtedly Hans Walter Gabler's edition of *Ulysses*, which delivers a "synoptic text" consisting of the original manuscript text of each page of the novel side by side with the genetic text, which displays the eruption of every known variant in any other manuscript or edition of the work.

69. David Greetham, "Phylum—Tree—Rhizome," *Huntington Library Quarterly* 58 (1996): 99–126.

This is, I would argue, essentially the textual model underlying a feature like Track Changes, where the reader can toggle between a clear reading view of his or her document (presumably as it embodies his or her current intentions) and its revision history, where every change (or variant) is duly exposed for consideration.

The disadvantage of the genetic approach for scholarly editing is, as John Bryant notes, that it engenders an ironic flattening effect, whereby every variant, no matter how trivial, is elevated to the status of a legitimate editorial (and typographically visible) event, with the result that the very idea of a "version," as a meaningful distinction among texts, becomes obscure: "the equal valorization of variant and version in geneticism tends to reduce all versions to an indiscriminate continuum of intentionality that impedes rather than furthers the study of versions."[70] Likewise, Track Changes, while adept at preserving document history, is not capable of discriminating between versions of a text in a more critical or qualitative sense; in effect, it lacks the ability to determine "*this* is a major revision, those are just some minor tweaks..."[71] Finally, while the genetic text aims to expose the writing process, Track Changes ultimately seeks, as the revisions are accepted or rejected, to collapse it and produce a singular, immaculate textual product. The point, however, is that from a computational perspective, a feature like Track Changes is no more or less natural to the medium than a model of word processing where changes take effect instantly and all on-screen edits are consigned to a textual oblivion. It is merely different, the imposition of an alternative formal materiality on the writing process as it is modeled by the universal machine called the computer, in response to the demands of new workplace practices. So then, as easily as electronic documents obscure or efface their own histories, so too can they be made to reveal them. In practice, users encounter a variety of document technologies capable of extruding simple and complex version histories from their data on a daily basis. They range from the CTRL-Z keystroke command to Track Changes, Merge, and analogous features in word processing and other productivity software (and their granddaddy, the UNIX "diff" command), to the repository architectures of versioning systems, and finally to the

---

70. Bryant, *The Fluid Text*, 75.

71. The inverse of this problem is to be found in automated plagiarism detection, a rapidly expanding area of document science characterized by the use of algorithms to detect texts with a significant degree of similarity.

high-end cryptographic signature and watermarking technologies that serve to authenticate the integrity and provenance of an electronic object. All of these are ultimately formal rather than forensic individualization mechanisms, meaning that they rest upon algorithmic operations and the states of the computer's internal symbolic environment rather than interventions in any material substrate. From this perspective the poststructuralism that has held sway over discussions of electronic writing since the late 1980s is a demonstrable medial artifact, one that had more to do with its moment (and marketing) than with the fundamental nature of electronic textuality. By contrast, an industrial-strength CVS environment is perhaps the ultimate realization of the kind of document science that has been practiced since the first stemma were printed in 1827 to display the relationships amongst a group of Swedish legal manuscripts.[72]

Consumers of electronic culture inevitably encounter some species of versioning through numbered releases of software. At a superficial level, these numbers testify to the fact that software vendors turn obsolescence into a selling point. But the fact that seemingly arbitrary numbers can become part of a product name and take on iconic significance in such an exquisitely brand-conscious industry also suggests the extent to which the acceptance of versioning has penetrated the popular imagination. The practice of branding software packages by year only heightens the effect, since users of Windows 2000 in the year 2005 are reminded of the creeping antiquity of their systems in the most familiar and humanistic of chronological registers—the calendrical annual. But of course version numbers are not simply marketing devices; they play an integral role in the internal management of a software project, and the numbering schemes typically come with their own highly evolved internal conventions and schemas. According to *Wikipedia*, "In most commercial software, the first released version of a software product has version 1.0. Numbers below 1 mean alpha or beta versions, i.e., versions for testing purposes or internal use, or versions that aren't stable enough for general or practical deployment. In principle, in subsequent releases, the *major* number is increased when there are significant jumps in functionality, the *minor* number is incremented

72.   See Robert J. O'Hara, "Mapping the Space of Time: Temporal Representation in the Historical Sciences," *New Perspectives on the History of Life: Systematic Biology as Historical Narrative*, ed. M. T. Ghiselin and G. Pinna (San Francisco: California Academy of Sciences, 1996): 7–17. My thanks to Kari M. Kraus for this reference. A stemma is a tree diagram that displays the genealogical relationships among extant witnesses of a text.

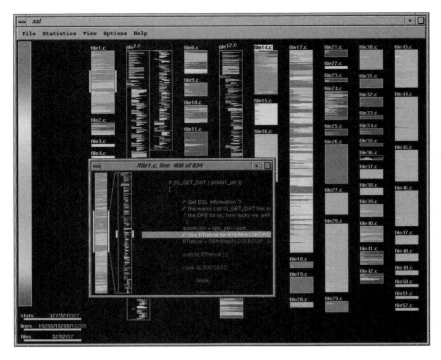

Figure 4.9 SeeSoft, a tool designed to visualize the collaborative and temporally-evolved status of software code. *Source*: http://www.itl.nist.gov/iaui/vvrg/emorse/papers/soa/DocumentVisualization

when only minor features or significant fixes have been added, and the *revision* number is incremented when minor bugs are fixed."[73] Versioning thus exposes the cumulative labor that attends a piece of software. Software projects themselves are often collaborative. They are also iterative, revised and refined as they are tested and explored; in an era of globalization they are frequently distributed, with people in different physical places inhabiting different time zones and adapting different rhythms of work; they are also incremental, with certain features knowingly planned for a later date precisely because they are always open to revision. A visualization tool such as SeeSoft illustrates the point (figure 4.9). Each horizontal "line" represents a line of the program and colors are assigned to various features, in this case the date of origination—

73. http://en.wikipedia.org/wiki/Version, accessed May 22, 2006.

one color being older lines of code, another more recent. Alternate features include date of change, identity of authors of different parts of the code, and so forth. The existence of tools like SeeSoft testifies to the existence of user communities for whom the history of electronic objects is of more than academic interest; in fact, the diachronic dimension on display is emblematic of the normative state of working with electronic objects.

Yet software is also ineluctably part of a proleptic *now*, what Joyce himself has dubbed the "anticipatory nextness" of electronic culture, "each screen unreasonably washing away what was and replacing it with itself."[74] Alan Liu, in his *Laws of Cool*, sees the shift as even more wrenching, aligning it with a millennial upheaval in the nature of knowledge work and the knowledge economy, the "post-industrial now" anticipated by Schumpeter and realized daily on our twenty-first century (flat) screens as "the self-evident presence of information" (8). An electronic document is literally created anew each time it is accessed, symbolically and procedurally reconstituted from the analog bit representations recorded by storage media (magnetic or otherwise), and so it comes to us bearing no forensic traces of prior use, no visible signs of lived experience or worldly contact.[75] This is the jumping-off point for an instinctively appealing strain of human-computer interaction (HCI) research that attempts to invest digital documents with visual cues corresponding to analog wear and tear—"object-centered interaction histories," in the parlance of the field. Noting such serendipitous occurrences as the book whose binding cracks open at an oft-referenced page, or favorite recipe cards accumulating the most dog-ears and stains, the researchers seek to "display useful graphical abstractions of the accrued histories of the documents themselves."[76] These take the form of scrollbars or other devices that serve as visual indicators of the amount of time spent editing or viewing different portions of a document. The infinite elastic space of the scrollbar, perhaps the most universal and iconic aspect of

74. Joyce, *Of Two Minds*, 233.

75. David M. Levy offers a useful account of this phenomenon, comparing it to a book that must be published—indeed, whose printing press must first be constructed from scratch, the type cast and set, the pages printed—each and every time it is opened. See his *Scrolling Forward: Making Sense of Documents in the Digital Age* (New York: Arcade Publishing, 2001), especially 137–157.

76. See William C. Hill. et al., "Edit Wear and Read Wear," *CHI '92 Conference Proceedings* (Reading, MA: Addison-Wesley, 1992): 3–9.

electronic word processing, thus becomes colonized by human labor and attention through the rote acknowledgment of keystrokes and mouse events. As appealing as it is, however, the point is that this HCI work is exactly a *formal* materiality, a visual regimen imposed by the programmatic logic of an artificial environment that interprets use or attention in purely quantitative terms.

This line of HCI research is also only a more overt and literal—a more visible—instantiation of the fact that a digital document encodes a remarkable and potentially incriminating amount of self-knowledge. Every operating system employs its own intricate methods for tracking the history and composition of the objects it maintains, and portions of this information are routinely made available to users. On Windows systems, for example, this documentary information is known as an object's "Properties." A user can tell at a glance the name of a file, its format and default application, its location in the file system, and its size; the user is also provided with date and time stamps that certify (to the second) the moment of the object's local creation, the last time it was modified, and the last time it was accessed, as well as various attributes defining the object's relationship to the operating system as a whole (whether it can be revised or whether it is "read only," for example). The word processor in which I am writing this chapter can reveal to me the exact number of minutes I have spent editing it, and with the installation of additional software I or some other agency could count the number and pace of my keystrokes, including mis-strokes that need to be backspaced and corrected. As storage capacities increase, different versions of the file will be saved—every version, by default. That these values can be faked or rendered inaccurate by the formal environment of the machine (a wrongly set system clock, for example) is incidental insofar as electronic documents, as human productions of human technologies, exist in space and time and have histories, and those histories, themselves formal configurations of the system, are recoverable through formal manipulation—whether it takes the form of the Properties window of a word processor, the doctored scrollbars of Edit Wear/Read Wear, or more exotic forensic tools. In short, electronic objects are *functionally* defined by enormous amounts of documentary information, and in a far more systematic and regularized manner than manuscripts and books. Computer operating systems are characterized less by their supposedly ephemeral nature than by the exquisite precision of their internal environments.

Cruft and bloat, two loosely related pieces of programming slang, likewise indicate the diachronicity of electronic objects. Tellingly, cruft is thought to have originated with physical hardware, specifically the piles of antiquated, unfathomable machinery visible through the windows of Harvard's abandoned Cruft Hall. Most hacker jargon dictionaries identify it with dust, a substance that accumulates without visible agency. A writer for *Dr. Dobb's Journal* is more lyrical: "When you spot a class interface that is no longer used by any client, but that nobody dare delete, that's cruft. It is also the word 'seperate [sic],' added to a spellchecker's private dictionary in a moment of careless haste, and now waiting for a suitably important document. Cruft is the cruel corruption and confusion inevitably wrought by time upon all petty efforts of humankind."[77] All petty efforts of humankind, *including software*—despite the fact that one of the "great fascinations" of software, as Martin Campbell-Kelley points out, is its "invisibility and intangibility."[78] The conventional wisdom is that software is a kind of black box, the container for a delicate but inviolate system that must be held in suspended animation in order to function as intended. In fact, programming is messy business, and the inside of the black box often resembles a construction site, with spare parts and blueprints left lying about in plain view. The following colorful remarks, from an independent software developer commenting on software engineering at Microsoft, make this point vividly:

What originally started as a rather feeble but lucky attempt to get on the [object-oriented] bandwagon, the [Microsoft Foundation Classes] soon became something you'd like to see Steve McQueen kill. Patches and work-arounds and bugs and more bugs, and bloat and more bloat. [. . .] Microsoft's RegClean, a popular product for fixing corruptions in the MS Windows Registry is another case in point. When this application was originally introduced I downloaded it and wondered about its size. It weighed in then at nearly a megabyte. Similar applications out there were 20 [kilobytes] and hardly more. What was inside this monster? I opened it and looked inside.

Remember all those stories about how surgeons in the old days just threw their rubber gloves inside the patient's stomach before sewing them back up again? Well

77. See "The New Adventures of Verity Stob" (August 2002), http://www.ddj.com/184405140.

78. Campbell-Kelley, *From Airline Reservations to Sonic the Hedgehog: A History of the Software Industry* (Cambridge: MIT Press, 2003), vii.

here you had it. There were humungoid bitmaps never used. There were dozens of icons never referenced. There were tens of kilobytes of entries in the string table that had no meaning for the application whatsoever.[79]

The technical references to object-oriented programming, registries, bitmaps, and string tables are not important, and neither is the rhetorical salvo lofted at Microsoft. Instead, I reference these comments because they go a long way toward demonstrating the extent to which software applications are built mechanisms, with parts and components and structures and substructures, all of which are put together deliberately over time. Even if one does not understand the specific terminology or follow the precise issues at stake, it is clear from the preceding passage that software engineering is ultimately a process of engineering and design. Software is, in short, a species of artifact. If we accept this, then we should also accept that those of us who study artifacts like books may one day also want or need to study software—first learning some of the terminology and technical issues—out of the conviction that our intellectual perspectives are unique and valuable.

The textual practices embodied by a CVS stand in marked contrast to the "version" of electronic textuality that is perhaps better known in literary and artistic circles, largely as a result of first-wave hypertext theory. At no time is this more obvious than when comparing the figures of the tree—the basic data structure of any versioning system—and the rhizome, or network. That Storyspace embodied both from the first is no surprise, given that it was also intended to support a rudimentary versioning system for its authors: "That is, a number of writers could share access to a publicly distributed text (or medium) while control of access could easily be adapted to keeping track of individually tailored versions, or keeping track of proportional authorship of documents created through allowable borrowing of segments from publicly shared versions" (Markle 32). The same story spaces that modeled evanescent postmodern theory, in other words, could also, at least in principle, be made to enforce just the kind of versioning protocols that were then emerging in the software development industry.

Concurrent version systems, word processing features like Track Changes, file comparison utilities, and visualization tools like SeeSoft all speak to the existence of communities for whom electronic textuality means something

79. R. A. Downes, "The Bloatware Debate," e-mail distributed to *RISKS-LIST*, April 30 1999.

other than the ground effects of Web surfing, a self-reflexive activity in the most literal sense in that it accumulates in the browser's History file, as though "history" on the Web did not exist outside of any one user's single, subjective browsing experience. (The temporality quivering around the date of access, a prominent feature of MLA-style citation of Web resources, reflects precisely an anxiety over the general absence of externally accessible version histories on the Web.) Perhaps inevitably, it has now become fashionable to version even the Web itself, as we speak of "Web 2.0," teeming with social software, intelligent agents, and semantic links. The extent to which the network is an agent of its own "remindings" (to take us back to Roger Schank's term) is a topic to which we will turn in the next chapter.[80]

Coda: Austin's Afternoons

It is late February, 2006. I am at the Harry Ransom Humanities Research Center at the University of Texas at Austin, where the Michael Joyce Papers are in the process of being cataloged and accessioned. The collection is not yet available to the public, but the curator has graciously agreed to accommodate me (and my deadlines) anyway. A series of electronic mail exchanges to plan the visit, an (electronic) plane ticket, and my body is transported 1500 miles through space to be deposited in Austin, where I am to spend a week examining materials both physical and virtual. Every morning before I am granted access to the Hazel H. Ransom Reading Room I must present valid photo ID; I am allowed to bring my laptop inside with me, and pencils, but no pens. The physical part of the Joyce collection resides in archival (or acid-free manila) folders, in turn housed within Hollinger boxes, some fifty of them, which I am able to request by exchanging handwritten paper slips with the collection staff. The first accession of virtual materials have been lifted from the almost 400 diskettes comprising their original storage media and uploaded to an electronic repository system known as DSpace. They are online, but can only be accessed from a dedicated laptop (not my own) located in the Reading Room. The digital objects in the DSpace repository are what are known in the trade as BLOBs, Binary Large OBjects. DSpace knows how to manage both item-level metadata and access to these files, but it does not facilitate the use of them. To actually work with the *Afternoons* or with any

---

80. For other recent work on that topic, see Lisa Gitelman, *Always Already New: Media, History, and the Data of Culture* (Cambridge: MIT Press, 2006), especially chapter 4.

other material it must first be downloaded to the desktop of the Ransom Center's laptop, where I use what means and know-how I can to make cranky old binaries execute on the up-to-date operating system. Sometimes I am unsuccessful. I suggest the addition of a hex editor, emulators, and other forensic tools to the utilities already available on the computer. Since DSpace maintains the integrity of a master copy of every file, I can do what I please with the derivative I download to my local desktop—hack at it, tweak it, break it. (This is not covered in the instructional video all new users of the collections are required to watch the first time they are admitted to the Reading Room.) In any case, the working arrangement has my own laptop computer, on which I make notes, positioned off to one side of me, the Ransom's laptop with its pipeline to DSpace off to the other side, and whatever physical documents I am examining laid out in between. Such is the discourse network I have erected. I am forbidden, of course, to make copies of any of the electronic materials; screenshots must be printed out and paid for as though they were Xeroxes. At the end of every work day I leave the Ransom Center and cross busy Guadalupe Street to a coffeehouse that offers public WiFi service. I log on and immediately copy and paste my notes into an e-mail message that I send to myself, the bits beamed into the late Austin afternoon to be sprayed across the surface of a hard disk spinning in the silo of a server farm I will never see.

I understand that I was the first patron to access electronic files on deposit at the Ransom Center in the Reading Room. I will not be the last. Yet all texts are hybrid, mediated, relative. In *The Textual Condition* (in the essay of the same name) Jerome McGann writes: "IF TEXTS ARE TO BE PRODUCED CRITICALLY, WHETHER THROUGH WRITER, READER, OR EDITOR (ALONG WITH THEIR SURROGATES) THE TEXTS MUST EMPHASIZE THEIR RELATIONS, AND THEIR RELATIVITIES" (93; capitals in original). Catherine Stollar, the archivist at the Ransom Center charged with processing the Joyce materials, describes the painstaking process of cataloging the original diskettes, loading them on vintage Macintosh hardware, extricating the files from the diskettes one by one, verifying their contents, indexing them on a spreadsheet, checking for viruses (using software calibrated to detect then-contemporary digital pathogens), wrestling with corrupt boot sectors, identifying archaic file extensions, associating resource forks, sorting duplicates, hashing the collected files to ensure their electronic integrity, and uploading them, with newly generated metadata, to the DSpace repository that organizes the collection into hierarchies based on the functional series of "Works," "Academic Career," "Correspondence," and so on.[81] There are some 211 MB of data (much of it text) and 4,800 files in the first accession alone (Kiehne 10). This is without a doubt the most comprehensive and systematic act of digital preservation in the field of creative born-digital literature to date, and the insights gleaned from the process will be relevant for some time to come. For example:

One of the first issues that we noticed, while working with Joyce's digital records was the fact that many clues that one uses when working with paper documents are not present in the electronic environment. For example, when the author did not explicitly insert his name in the text and the document was not clearly perceived as being his, we could not count on handwriting analysis, letterhead, type of paper, ink color, ink type, smell, type of copy, and other clues that are generally applied in the paper contexts. We were completely dependent on the language that was used and the content of the file, which sometimes could be quite misleading. In some cases it took two people working through the documents more than once to try to find more clues to identify not only the author, but also what the file actually was. (Kiehne 13)

There is in fact a subfield of computer forensics known as software forensics that deals specifically with identifying the authorship and intended function of software and other electronic objects through such "soft" factors as code style, commenting habits, and similar practices.[82] Moreover, had Joyce so chosen (unlikely though it would have been at the time), he could have

81. As recounted in detail in Thomas Kiehne, Vivian Spoliansky, and Catherine Stollar, "From Floppies to Repository: A Transition of Bits. A Case Study in Preserving the Michael Joyce Papers at the Harry Ransom Center" (May 2005), unpublished paper.

82. See Robert M. Slade, *Software Forensics: Collecting Evidence from the Scene of a Digital Crime* (New York: McGraw Hill, 2004). Slade defines software forensics as "the analysis of program code, generally object or machine language code, in order to make a determination of, or provide evidence for, the intent or authorship of a program" (5). He specifically identifies Biblical Criticism, stylistics, and more dubious textual critical practices, such as cumulative sum techniques (cusum), as precedents of and influences on the analysis of software code. The field originated in virus detection and countermeasures. "Evidence of cultural influence exists right down to the machine code level. Those who work with assembler and machine code know that a given function can be coded in a variety of different ways, and that there may be a number of algorithms to accomplish the same end" (9).

digitally signed and cryptographically authenticated his files. The point, once again, is just how hard it is to pin any absolute or essential characteristics onto electronic content; rather, the emphasis must fall on user habits when working with that content, and the way developers—who have the power to functionally define the nature and extent of those habits—choose to model particular environments and behaviors by way of their software code, consequently imposing a formal materiality.

If the Ransom Center and DSpace represent one end of the archival spectrum, the kind of clean, well-lighted place that serious digital preservation demands, then the Home of the Underdogs (HOTU) represents its opposite. Home of the Underdogs is an abandonware site, probably the most famous one on the Web (it has been online in one incarnation or another since 1998).[83] Abandonware is not free software or freeware; it is software that is no longer being sold or actively supported by its rights holder. Sometimes the rights holder does not even know the software in question exists. Abandonware sites such as HOTU are thus unsanctioned repositories—of questionable legality—for the storage and dissemination of such products, most often games. More than just download sites, they often offer the only real extant documentation of the original work, including screenshots and technical specs. Sarinee Achavanuntakul, the HOTU's founder, describes her motives: "It's important to keep abandonware alive because countless games will be lost without such efforts, since few companies nowadays even know what classic games they own. It's also important because there is now no Project Gutenberg equivalent for games, and games stand a much higher chance than printed materials of being lost without serious efforts."[84] Robert Pinsky's *Mindwheel* (the interactive fiction written by the former poet laureate of the United States and published by Broderbund in 1986) is available on HOTU, currently the only place I know to find it. The network is essential to abandonware distribution, not only in the practical sense of allowing users to upload and download files, but also in establishing a culture of communication around a shared preservation enterprise. They provide modules allowing

83. http://www.the-underdogs.info/.

84. See Daniel Terdiman, "Nostalgia Keeps Games Afloat," *Wired News* (April 8, 2004), http://www.wired.com/news/gaming/gamingreviews/news/2004/04/62975. Project Gutenberg is the long-running grassroots effort to digitize plain-text transcriptions of well-known works of literature and place them into free circulation on the internet.

users to rate, rank, and sort the different offerings. These are grassroots, folk-sonomic undertakings; the forums and bulletin boards on HOTU are alive with user queries relating to the location, identification, documentation, and propagation of obscure programs from all personal computing platforms. This is also the same culture and community of enthusiasts that reliably sees to the creation of emulation and interpreter software to formally reconstitute obsoles-cent platforms and systems. Despite real technical obstacles, digital preserva-tion is ultimately a challenge demanding social (above and beyond the purely technological) solutions. Consigning a file to the open network, a profoundly social setting, is no less a SAVE *as* any command available on our isolate desktops.

5

Text Messaging: The Transformissions of "Agrippa"

[T]he historian does not remain inside of his historiographic language. He does not get outside it, however, merely by producing discourse about documents and artifacts; in doing that he is still inside his discourse. Rather, he gets outside of it just as any scientist gets outside of his discourse: he predicts. But his predictions can scarcely be about events which no longer exist. Rather, he predicts about where he is going to find documents and artifacts and what their attributes are going to be. Thus the proper object of the historian's investigations is not, as he usually imagines, the events of the past, but rather documents and other artifacts whose existence is concurrent with his own.

—MORSE PECKHAM, "REFLECTIONS ON THE FOUNDATION OF MODERN TEXTUAL EDITING"

The struggle for tne text *is* the text.
—RANDALL MCLEOD

Against variance, redundancy. This is the basis of formal theories of information transmission. Claude Shannon, working in the context of applied electrical engineering at Bell Labs just after World War II, put it this way: "The fundamental problem of communication is that of reproducing at one point either exactly or approximately a message selected at another point. Frequently the messages have *meaning*; that is they refer to or are correlated according to some system with certain physical or conceptual entities. These semantic aspects of communication are irrelevant to the engineering problem."[1] This dovetails with Norbert Wiener's understanding: "Messages themselves are a form of pattern and organization. . . . In fact, it is possible to interpret the information carried by a message as essentially the negative of its entropy, and the negative logarithm of its probability. That is, the more probable the message, the less information it gives. Cliches, for example, are less illuminating than great poems."[2] From these two passages, published two years apart, several key points emerge: first, information, in this context, is absolutely devoid of any semantic component. Second, the amount of information carried by a message in transmission is a function of that message's probability—the less likely a message is to be sent, the more information it may be said to bear. Third (and this follows directly from the previous point), an actual message exists only as a function of its relation to a larger system of potential messages. Fourth, information is directly related to entropy—the more entropic or disorganized a system, the more potential information it contains.[3]

Likewise, it is common for textual critics and bibliographers to speak of the "transmission" of a text. W. W. Greg, for example, writing in 1932, asserts that "At the root of all literary criticism lies the question of transmission, and it is bibliography that enables us to deal with the problem" (239).[4] A few lines later he adds that bibliography may be properly understood as "the science of the transmission of literary documents" (239). Toward the other end of the century, Jerome McGann endorses a view of textual criticism that is". . . born of the awareness that texts descend to us through a more or less complex, more or less fractured, transmission history. The business of textual

1.   Claude Shannon and Warren Weaver, *The Mathematical Theory of Communication* (Urbana, IL: University of Illinois Press, 1949), 3.

2.   Norbert Wiener, *The Human Use of Human Beings* (New York: Doubleday, 1956), 21.

3.   N. Katherine Hayles narrates much of this history in *How We Became Posthuman: Virtual Bodies in Cybernetics, Literature, and Informatics* (Chicago: University of Chicago Press, 1999). See especially chapter 3. For an alternative philosophy of information, one which does not jettison semantic meaning, see Donald M. MacKey, *Information, Mechanism, and Meaning* (Cambridge: MIT Press, 1969).

4.   W. W. Greg, "Bibliography—An Apologia," *The Library* 13 (1932): 113–143, in *Collected Papers*, ed. J. C. Maxwell (Oxford: Oxford University Press, 1966), 239–266.

criticism . . . [is] to expose the entire network of transmissive variation."[5] Even a casual survey of the professional literature on bibliography and textual criticism would find these two examples easily multiplied.

Transmit is from the Latin *mittere*: to send. But what do we really mean when we talk about transmitting—sending and receiving—a written text? And what are we to make of words like "error," "corruption," "purity," and "verification", all of which are also conspicuous in the language of textual criticism and bibliography? Information theory has occasionally manifested itself as a trope in theoretical writing about textual scholarship, perhaps most blatantly in several essays by Randall McLeod.[6] Indeed, the correspondences between the two disciplines can sometimes be striking. Greg's famous distinction between accidentals and substantives, for example, can be parsed as an exercise in information theory: "But here we need to draw a distinction between the significant, or as I shall call them 'substantive,' readings of the text, those namely that affect the author's meaning or the essence of his expression, and others, such in general as spelling, punctuation, word-division, and the like, affecting mainly its formal presentation, which may be regarded as the accidents, or as I shall call them 'accidentals'" (21).[7] Likewise, many of Shannon's statements about information theory might not seem out of place in *Studies in Bibliography*; when he jettisons semantic content from the

5. McGann, *The Textual Condition* (Princeton: Princeton University Press, 1991), 50.

6. See especially Randall McLeod, "From 'Tranceformations in the Text of *Orlando Furioso*,'" *New Directions in Textual Studies*, ed. Dave Oliphant and Robin Bradford (Austin: University of Texas Press and Harry Ransom Humanities Research Center, 1990): 61–85 and "Information on Information," *Text* 5 (1991): 240–281. Perhaps the most brazen commingling of cybernetics and textual studies is to be found at the conclusion of D. F. McKenzie's famous dissent from the precepts of Greg-Bowers bibliography, his 1969 "Printers of the Mind," in which he writes: "Bright lights will cast deep shadows, and I must confess to a feeling of mild despondency about the prospects for analytical bibliography . . . wherever full primary evidence has become available it has revealed a geometry of such complexity that even an expert in cybernetics, primed with all the facts, would have little chance of discerning it" (60). See *Studies in Bibliography* 22 (1969): 1–75. Here "cybernetics" functions as a kind of transcendental signifier, the sheen of the word generating its own aura and authority as the limit case for what is possible. But that hardly does justice to the term's true pedigree during the previous twenty years, in which cybernetics and information theory had enjoyed a tremendous popular vogue throughout the United States, Europe, and the Soviet Union.

7. W. W. Greg, "The Rationale of Copy Text," *Studies in Bibliography* 3 (1950–1951): 19–36.

information signal, he would seem to mirror this well-known statement of Greg's: "I start then with the postulate that what the bibliographer is concerned with is pieces of paper or parchment covered with certain written or printed signs. With these signs he is concerned merely as arbitrary marks; their meaning is no business of his."[8] Fredson Bowers seemingly echoes Greg: "What is important is that the impressed symbols which are letters and words are treated in a physical and not in a literary way."[9] And the correspondences go deeper still. Bowers, as the most influential bibliographer of the postwar period, spent World War II as a naval intelligence officer in

8.   Greg, "Bibliography—An Apologia" in *Collected Papers*, 247.

9.   Bowers, "Bibliography, Pure Bibliography, and Literary Studies" in *Essays in Bibliography, Text, and Editing* (Charlottesville: University Press of Virginia, 1975), 42. An example of this kind of analytical bibliography is Bowers's successful identification of the five different compositors for the first edition of Hawthorne's 1828 romance *Fanshawe* (for which no manuscript survives). It is this volume in the Centenary Edition (Columbus: Ohio State Press, 1964) that Bowers may have had in mind when in a later letter he referred to "'breaking the code of the two different systems of compositor marking' in two of Hawthorne's books" (quoted in Tanselle, "Life and Work," 34). Let us briefly consider it as a case study in bibliography and information theory. The primary evidence involves first edition variants in spelling, capitalization, or punctuation: "or" vs. "our" in the endings of words, "grey" vs. "gray," "Doctor" vs. "doctor," and so on. In all, Bowers identifies twelve such variables on which to base his case: "No two workmen differ from each other in every respect in the evidence noticed. Moreover, the significant points of variance do not occur in the stints of every one of the compositors. Nevertheless, by observing the different combinations of twelve pieces of evidence, selected as representing the general stylistic practice of an individual workman, but in each of which at least one other workman differs, some specific conjectures may be made despite the dearth of Hawthorne manuscripts from this period that would have assisted in identifying variants stemming from Hawthorne's own irregularities" ("Bibliography, Pure Bibliography" 319). From this Bowers is able, with high confidence, to assign individual responsibility to compositors A–E for all but the last twenty-five pages of the book. It is my contention that Bowers's methodology here generally parallels the basic tenets of Shannon and Wiener's information theory, whereby a message is a probabilistic outcome of a set of statistically predictable potential messages. Bowers is able to justify emending his text of *Fanshawe* on the basis of characteristics observed in the later Hawthorne manuscripts. *Fanshawe*'s five compositors, for their part, are not so different from the human gun-pointers that Norbert Wiener viewed as an integral component of the fire control systems in his cybernetic solutions for target acquisition: "It is essential to know their characteristics, in order to incorporate them mathematically into the machines they control" (*Cybernetics* 6). In both cases, human and mechanical actors are tightly coupled agents in a feedback loop.

Washington, DC, where he supervised a group of textual scholars and former students who worked as military cryptanalysts (several of whom, such as Charlton Hinman and Stephen Parish, went on to influential scholarly careers themselves).[10] As Bowers's biographer would later observe of the bibliographer's stint as a cryptanalyst: "the goal of both activities is to find meaningful patterns in what at first seem to be chaotic data, and the bent of mind required for both is obviously similar."[11] Norbert Wiener, for his part, was raised in the house of his father, Leo Wiener, a Harvard philologist specializing in Eastern European languages and literatures.[12]

Like the historian in Peckham's example earlier, the textual scholar does not study the past so much as the patterns of its transmission and transformation as they are manifest in the documents and artifacts of the present. ("Transformission," McLeod's term, is an amalgam of the two words: "And since we don't have texts that aren't transmitted, transformission should cover most everything."[13]) "Transmission," in fact, is a word that occupies a special place in the lore surrounding the *Agrippa* project, since it was the name of a

10. For Bowers and his naval career, see G. Thomas Tanselle, "The Life and Work of Fredson Bowers," *Studies in Bibliography* 46 (1993): 1–154. Hinman, meanwhile, was the inventor of the Hinman Collator, a machine he contrived to aid in the collation of the 79 *First Folios* at the Folger Shakespeare Library (sometimes described as a "mechanical detective," it would have been a familiar tool to forensic document examiners—the CIA and FBI both purchased them). For the definitive account of Hinman's invention and its various influences, including his exposure to automated techniques for analysis of aerial photography during the war, see Steven Escar Smith, "'The Eternal Verities Verified': Charlton Hinman and the Roots of Mechanical Collation," *Studies in Bibliography* 53 (2000): 129–161. For Hinman, Bowers, and the import of their work as cryptanalysts, see Jeffrey Masten, "Pressing Subjects: On the Secret Lives of Shakespeare's Compositors," *Language Machines: Technologies of Literary and Cultural Production*, eds. Jeffrey Masten, Peter Stallybrass, and Nancy J. Vickers (London: Routledge, 1997): 75–107.

11. Tanselle, "The Life and Work of Fredson Bowers," 34.

12. As a result, Wiener was certainly aware of textual scholarship, as is demonstrated by a passage in *The Human Use of Human Beings: Cybernetics and Society* (New York: Doubleday, 1956) where he comments on the "scientific interest" in language by "textual criticism" and the problem of authenticating "holy texts:" "What has been learned for the maintenance of true religion has been carried out as a literary discipline, and textual criticism is one of the oldest of intellectual studies" (86). See also Wiener's biography by Steve J. Heim, *John von Neumann and Norbert Wiener: From Mathematics to the Technologies of Life and Death* (Cambridge: MIT Press, 1980).

13. McLeod, "Information on Information," 246.

pivotal event in the text's eventual release—indeed, its literal transmission, its *transformission*—out onto the public Internet, though possibly not in the way originally imagined or intended. As a work and text, *Agrippa* is intensely self-reflexive about its own artifice and artifactual dimensions, and both the poem and representations of the original book object have been transmitted and remediated to such an extent as to today constitute an intricate synchronic system amid the electronic networks of the contemporary Web. As an electronic work designed to efface itself, yet paradoxically one of the most available objects on the Web, "Agrippa" reminds us that preservation is ultimately a social domain, where actions and agency can serve to trump purely technical considerations. The next two sections are given over to documenting the textual conditions of "Agrippa," both past and present, its transmission and concomitant transformation.

Transmission

The text of "Agrippa" became available online on the morning of Thursday, December 10, 1992, when it was uploaded as a 10-kilobyte ASCII file to MindVox, a New York City–based electronic bulletin board run by Patrick K. Kroupa, aka Lord Digital.[14] Its first public mention does not appear to have come until a day later, when users who logged into the board's crowded Vox forum—where news of general interest was placed—would have seen the following note, from "The Chemist," posted on December 11 at 09:00:07 AM: "It's online right now, no explanation, there it is." A day after that, the person who claimed chief responsibility was heard from:

```
From: Templar
Posted: Sat, 12 Dec 1992 11:40:09 AM
Subject: AGRIPPA

Yes, ladies and gentlemen, I am proud to present, after much
controversy, the full text of William Gibson's AGRIPPA to the
users of MindVox first!

Look for it in the uploads directory ...
```

14. Patrick K. Kroupa, e-mail to author Tue, Jun 17 2003 12:50:26 −0400. Kroupa states "I got the cleartext at roughly 2am, wrote Agr1ppa at 3am, and released both the next day."

```
Enjoy ...

—T[15]
```

The nature of the "controversy" to which Templar (the poster) alludes, together with the circumstances surrounding the text's movement across the network from this point forward, capture a cross-section of online textual transmission at a moment just prior to the release of the NCSA's Mosaic Web browser.[16] Though rumors of Gibson's latest publishing project had been circulating for almost a year, before the events of December 1992 only its author and a handful of others would have read "Agrippa." Within days, the text had been spread far and wide across the network, and was read by thousands.

Immediately after MindVox, the initial points of availability for "Agrippa" were FTP servers and anonymous mailers. Its progress was only slightly slower in what would have been the expected venues, USENET news and listserv e-mail. A garbled copy of the text (a botched cut-and-paste job from the original MindVox file) had been sent to the FutureCulture listserv and then to alt.cyberpunk as early as December 11, but was not further circulated. A corrected copy was then posted to FutureCulture, and by December 13 the following message had appeared in the alt.cyberpunk newsgroup: "Re: all the requests to post/send AGRIPPA....It is on ftp sites...it is available via auto-mailers....The real version is propagating, the incorrect version does not seem to be. Thus, there is no reason to publically [*sic*], obviously subject onesself [*sic*] to obvious copyright violations if it is not necessary."[17] Further

15. Recovered from MindVox BBS archives no longer publicly available online, during exclusive access granted on June 13, 2003 by Patrick K. Kroupa.

16. The Web itself had been in existence since late 1990, when Tim Berners-Lee began circulating the draft specifications for HTTP and HTML and launched the first Web server at CERN, cryptically named nxoc01.cern.ch. At the time it was overshadowed by now largely forgotten network services such as WAIS and Gopher. Prior to the advent of Mosaic, the Web would have been accessed (browsed) using a utility such as Lynx, which operated in a text-only, command-line environment. Mosaic (which was programmed by Marc Andreessen, then an undergraduate at the University of Illinois) was the first browser to render the Web in the graphical configuration to which we are accustomed today; it was soon to be followed by its commercial cousin, Netscape.

17. Andy Hawks, post to alt.cyberpunk newsgroup 1992-12-14 19:34:17 PST.

complicating matters was the release, nearly simultaneous with that of "Agrippa," of a text by Kroupa on MindVox called "AGR1PPA" (note the numeric "1")—best understood as a kind of parody, though its author would deny its having any relation whatsoever to Gibson's "Agrippa." "AGR1PPA" was also widely circulated, and no doubt conflated with "Agrippa" by some unknown number of hapless readers.[18] Meanwhile, over on FutureCulture— then a premier salon for the cyber-chic—Gibson's "intentions" for his self-consuming poem and its subsequent reappearance online were being hotly debated (and in the midst of this some wag began posting phony messages attributed to "William Gibson"). By early January 1993, a mere three weeks later, the text was being regularly uploaded to alt.cyberpunk and breathless announcements that someone had "finally" got hold of a copy were being flamed as old news.

The precise manner in which the text of the poem made its way to Mind-Vox does not appear to be widely known and has never been authoritatively discussed. Gerald Jonas, in an article reprinted in Victor J. Vitanza's popular *Cyberreader*, told countless readers that it was an "international legion of computer hackers" who had "broken the code" (289).[19] Gibson himself, in interviews, has offered only vague statements: "[S]omeone got a hold of a copy of the thing kind of early on, cracked the supposedly uncrackable code and posted the poem on the Internet, where it remains to this day . . ."[20] In the pages that follow I have documented the textual transmission of "Agrippa" as best I could, drawing extensively on online sources such as the Google Groups USENET archive and public listserv digests, as well as correspondence with some of the principals, notably MindVox's Patrick Kroupa and publisher Kevin Begos, Jr. As we will see, electronic media are to a remarkable extent

18. "Agrippa" was an instant magnet for satire and parody. In addition to Kroupa's "AGR1PPA," there was this aborted version by "Scotto:" "I hesitated/before untying the bow/ that bound this book together./Then I decided,/why the hell not,/it cost me a couple hundred dollars . . ." Andy Hawks on FutureCulture spoke of parodying the poem (Wed, Dec 16 92 16:20:28 MST), and a complete (and rather impressive) leetspeak version was posted to Future-Culture on December 21 by "Zorgo:" "1 HESiTated/bEf0Re unty1ng tHe B0w/tHAt B0uNd th1s B( )0K t0g3th3r." And so on, for all 300 lines.

19. Gerald Jonas, "The Disappearing $2000 Book," in Vitctor J. Vitanza, *Cyberreader*, second edition (Boston: Allyn and Bacon, 1999), 287–289.

20. http://www.aint-it-cool-news.com/display.cgi?id=5140.

self-documenting (date- and time-stamps enable precision chronologies of a kind that students of printed texts can only dream of) but in the end it was still necessary to reach out to key individuals for their personal recollections of events.

The complete *Agrippa* project, consisting of Ashbaugh's book of etchings, the diskette containing Gibson's text, and accompanying paraphernalia, was initially announced by Kevin Begos Publishing, Inc., in July 1992. It is doubtful whether anything but a prototype or two existed at the time. A contemporary press account describes the package as follows:

AGRIPPA comes in a rough-hewn black box adorned with a blinking green light and an LCD readout that flickers with an endless stream of decoded DNA. The top opens like a laptop computer, revealing a hologram of a circuit board. Inside is a battered volume, the pages of which are antique rag-paper, bound and singed by hand.

Like a frame of unprocessed film, AGRIPPA begins to mutate the minute it hits the light. Ashbaugh has printed etchings of DNA nucleotides but then covered them with two separate sets of drawings: One, in ultra-violet ink, disappears when exposed to light for an hour; the other, in infrared ink, only becomes visible after an hour in the light. A paper cavity in the center of the book hides the diskette that contains Gibson's fiction, digitally encoded for the Macintosh or the IBM.[21]

The project thus shares some affinities with a genre of electronic writing known as artifactual fiction, where a piece of electronic literature is presented as a found object amid other documentary materials.[22] It is unclear exactly how many copies of *Agrippa* were eventually manufactured, but it was nowhere near the 455 mentioned in early press reports. Various copies in the hands of museums or private collectors are incomplete—some lack the black

21.   Gavin Edwards, "Cyberlit. William Gibson's latest story costs $450, comes on disk, and self-destructs after one reading." *Details*. June 1992. Transcribed by Debaser.

22.   See Bill Bly, "Learn Navigation: Doing Without the Narrator in Artifactual Fiction," *ACM SIGWEB Newsletter* 9.1 (February 2000): 34–37. The term "artifactual fiction" is usually ascribed to John McDaid, who first used it to describe his *Uncle Buddy's Phantom Funhouse*, a 1993 hypertext diskette from Eastgate Systems that comes with a boxful of faux documentary materials. A lesser-known work which displays some striking superficial similarities to *Agrippa* is James T. Downey's artist's book *Binary Dreams*, which he made at the Iowa Writer's Workshop in 1993. It consists of a floppy disk inserted into a disk drive, both bound into a book. The project is documented here: http://www.afineline.org/writings/bookbind.html.

case and LCD readout, others lack the diskette. The Whitney, which lists *Agrippa* in their collection catalog, actually owns only a cardboard mockup and a copy of the original sales prospectus.[23] Begos's plans involved a cascading price list depending on whether one purchased *Agrippa* with reproductions of the Ashbaugh etchings; with the etchings themselves; or a deluxe edition with vellum binding, a custom designed box, and other accoutrements; they were priced at $450, $1,500, and $7,500 respectively. What *Agrippa* eventually became seems to consist in one or more prototypes or mockups that more or less conform to the full press description, plus an unknown number of additional copies in various states of completion. It is questionable whether the IBM version of the disk was ever produced, though the Macintosh version was. Other aspects of the project also went unrealized. Importantly, for example, the ambitious plans for the photosensitive ink never really came to fruition—although according to one collector the illustrations do "fade a bit" and the DNA etchings darken.[24]

By his own account Gibson did not have much involvement in the project beyond contributing the poem itself. He composed his text electronically, and indeed claims never to have made a hard copy—a resonant detail in light of the much-loved bit of lore concerning his writing of *Neuromancer* on a manual typewriter. Gibson was probably working on his Macintosh SE/30 at the time. There is no information available as to the poem's precise date of composition, but earlier that year (21 May 1992, 16:05:30 PST, to be exact), Tom Maddox—fellow cyberpunk author, Gibson confidant, and USENET stalwart—tantalizingly began including the line "I swear I never heard the first shot" in his USENET signature file, attributed to "Wm. Gibson, 'AGRIPPA: a book of the dead'." Pointedly perhaps, his post that spring day was to a thread on rec.arts.books that had arisen in response to some advance publicity for "Agrippa," then erroneously being described as a short story. Maddox's signature file, which he would continue to use throughout the summer and fall, thus marked the first trace of the text on the public Internet, and that line would indeed appear, verbatim, in the version of the poem eventually released from MindVox. By December 14, when "Agrippa" was in general circulation and the poem's audience had expanded exponentially, Maddox had

23. According to Zimra Panitz, Assistant Librarian, Frances Mulhall Achilles Library, Whitney Museum of American Art, e-mail to author Thu, Jun 12 2003 14:39:13 −0400.

24. Peter Schwenger, e-mail to author Sun, Jun 15 2003 15:51:52 −0300.

already changed his signature; yet it was clear, in retrospect, that he was one of the privileged few who *had* heard the first shot, not its online echo afterward.

Early press reports had also mentioned plans for a global "fiber optic" broadcast of "Agrippa," variously timed for "September," "October," "this fall," and from "a barn in Jackson Hole, Wyoming." This event apparently never took place, but it was the embryonic idea for what happened on Wednesday, December 9, 1992 at the Americas Society in uptown New York City. Begos contrived to stage an elaborate networked multimedia performance, something akin to a release party and gallery opening for *Agrippa*, including plans for an electronic simulcast involving other gallery spaces and the Internet.[25] This became the event known as "The Transmission." The complete prototype of the work was on display, and the centerpiece of the evening was a recorded reading of Gibson's text by magician Penn Jillette (of Penn and Teller fame—Jillette was an avid computer hobbyist) accompanied by a big-screen projection of the poem scrolling to oblivion.[26] An NPR story about *Agrippa*, which featured snippets of Jillette's prerecorded reading, had aired earlier in the day. (This was not a complete rendition of the poem, however, as is sometimes reported, and so it was *not* in fact the first public broadcast of "Agrippa.") In the transcript from the NPR show the host, Tom

25. There are several reports of what happened elsewhere around the country that evening. The first is from Mark Taranto, writing on the rec.arts.books newsgroup, 1992-12-14 22:14:59 PST: "[W]hen I met Mike Godwin a couple of months ago, he somehow got me to subscribe to a local BBS called Echo (somewhat similar to The Well). On the night of the reading, Echo broadcasted AGRIPPA. It was done in an interesting fashion, in keeping with the self destructing theme. As Echoids logged off, we were treated to several screens of the AGRIPPA text." Others were apparently not so lucky. According to Paul Rutkovsky in an online newsletter called the FINEART Forum (February 1, 1993, Volume 7.2): "An evening of events centered around the eventual reception of William Gibson's AGRIPPA (A Book of the Dead), programmed for computer viral self-destruction, was a lesson of sorts in telecommunications frustration. . . . the last instructional revision was received two days before the 'transmission.' Disks were sent to the sites stating that the text could not be sent successfully. The original plan of telecommunicating spontaneously with text that would also self-destruct was not going to take place."

26. In a letter to Gibson from October 1992, Begos comments: "I can't remember if I told you that Penn volunteered to do a live, unrehearsed reading of the story at one of the locations in December. His idea was to read the lines off a screen, to an audience, in real time. I like the idea, as it twists the origin of *Agrippa* even further. And if Penn makes 'mistakes', then the story mutates again." See http://agrippa.english.ucsb.edu/letter-from-kevin-begos-to-william-gibson-item-d27-transcription/.

Vitale, is quoted as saying: "Author William Gibson and publisher Kevin Begos both figure that some hacker will crack the self-destructing code and copy the disk or that an unauthorized taping of one of tonight's events will eventually be transcribed and passed along on computer bulletin boards."[27] This was to prove prescient. By the next day, December 10, "Agrippa" was already up on MindVox, and as have we have seen it propagated quickly after that.

Rumors soon abounded as to whether the RSA encryption had indeed been cracked, and if so by whom, and why wasn't the FBI talking to them?—no idle threat, as all of this was transpiring not long after the wave of trumped-up arrests and prosecutions chronicled in Bruce Sterling's *The Hacker Crackdown*. Incidentally, these skirmishes between hackers (so-called) and federal law enforcement culminated in the trial of Craig Neidorf, aka Knight Lightning, who, as editor of the underground electronic broadsheet *Phrack*, had published the infamous (and ultimately innocuous) "E911 Document"—another electronic text with a complex and consequential history, whose transmission, in Neidorf's case, had been interpreted as grounds for federal wire fraud charges. (The case was eventually declared a mistrial, though Neidorf was never officially exonerated.)

When the text of "Agrippa" was first uploaded to MindVox, Templar, as its custodian, prefaced it with a brief introductory note in which he presented the poem as "hacked and cracked" by "-Templar-/Rosehammer & Pseudo-phred." He then added: "And I'm not telling you how I did it."[28] In fact,

27. "Amazing Disappearing Computer Book." NPR, All Things Considered. Host Anne Garrels. December 9, 1992.

28. The complete note, which is almost never reproduced with the text of the poem, reads as follows:

> When I first heard about an electronic book by William Gibson . . . sealed in an ominous tome of genetic code which smudges to the touch . . . which is encrypted and automatically self-destructs after one reading . . . priced at $1,500 . . . I knew that it was a challenge, or dare, that would not go unnoticed. As recent buzzing on the Internet shows, as well as many overt attempts to hack the file . . . and the transmission lines . . . it's the latest golden fleece, if you will, of the hacking community.
>
> I now present to you, with apologies to William Gibson, the full text of AGRIPPA. It, of course, does not include the wonderful etchings, and I highly recommend purchasing the original book (a cheaper version is now available for $500). Enjoy.
>
> And I'm not telling you how I did it. Nyah.

contrary to many colorful claims from that moment forward, "Agrippa" was never really hacked or cracked at all, at least not in any strict computational sense.

I have received two accounts of what really did happen. The accounts differ, and I have no way to reconcile them. According to Kevin Begos, Jr., a group of NYU students representing themselves as documentary filmmakers attended the Transmission at the Americas Society and videotaped the big-screen display of the text that accompanied Penn Jillette's recorded reading.[29] Presumably this group included the person known online as Templar. They then transcribed the poem from their tape, and, within hours, had gotten the text file uploaded to MindVox. This is Begos's understanding of what happened, and it would seem corroborated by a public posting from Templar himself, years after the fact, in which he refers to the work's "first public unveiling in Manhattan" and states "that's where we got the original copy and posted it."[30] There is also evidence that an actual videotape existed, as we will see in the next section. Yet Patrick Kroupa, one of just a few people in a position to really know, discounts this version of events.[31] There is reason to think, however, that Kroupa's recollection of events may not be reliable. Just as this book was going to press, the author was contacted by Rosehammer and Templar, who furnished a full account.

See the Appendix for all of the details. What is clear and unequivocal and agreed upon by all parties is that "Agrippa" was never really "cracked"—one way or the other it simply didn't need to be, and the text's illicit promulgation was effected through more mundane means. It should be noted that

---

Original source, http://riverbbs.net/pub4/ebook/AGRIPP.TXT, which is now only available in GoogleCache. Submitted by me and now archived on *The Agrippa Files* at http://agrippa.english .ucsb.edu/post/documents-subcategories/the-disk-and-its-code/templars-introduction-to-the-first-online-copy-of-gibsons-agrippa-poem-1992.

29. Kevin Begos, email to author Sun, Jun 15 2003 15:43:24 −0400.

30. Posting on Slashdot.org, Friday February 04, 2000 @06:33PM. See http://slashdot.org/ comments.pl?sid=3790&cid=1307101.

31. Patrick K. Kroupa, email to author Tue, Jun 17 2003 12:57:20 −0400. "What is correct is that nobody bothered to ever 'crack' it. The text came from Kevin Begos publishing prior to ever being encrypted."

both Begos's and Kroupa's accounts are consistent with the chronology of events I have established, in which the December 9 Transmission serves as the pivotal juncture in the text's release. Both versions would also seem borne out by Templar's own steadfast refusal to admit the precise methods by which he obtained the poem.[32]

In the introduction in which he claimed credit for the hack, Templar had airily written that the text of "Agrippa" was a "challenge, or dare . . . the latest golden fleece of the hacking community." And so it was, a black box figuratively as well as literally, a perfect-pitch technological glyph that seemed to call out for some delicate or elegant solution for its Rosetta stone. If in retrospect the process by which the poem was brought to light seems anticlimactic—no late night bout of cybernetic jujitsu, no mainframe supercomputers burning away at the encryption with the incalculable energy of their massively parallel clusters and clock cycles—it's also a situation thoroughly anticipated in the staccato rhythms of Gibson's own prose, in the opening lines of the short story "Johnny Mnemonic" published ten years earlier:

I put the shotgun in an Adidas bag and padded it out with four pairs of tennis socks, not my style at all, but that was what I was aiming for: If they think you're crude, go technical; if they think you're technical, go crude. I'm a very technical boy. So I decided to get as crude as possible.[33]

Templar was also a very technical boy. Here he had gone crude, regardless of which version of events is to be believed. Yet he had not necessarily lied or been disingenuous in his use of the terms "hacking" and "cracking." Broadly speaking, these activities do not need to involve a computer, and refer more to a lifestyle ethos than any specific technical procedures. In fact, all of the actions that have been ascribed to Templar are consistent with such venerable if dubious cracker practices as "shoulder-surfing" (looking over someone's shoulder as they type a code or password), "trashing" (scouring trash containers for sensitive documents), and "social engineering" (verbally conning someone out of information you want). Templar's tactics may have been crude, but they were not any less of a hack for being low-tech. Indeed, an important

32. In 2007, Templar did exactly this. See the Appendix.

33. William Gibson, "Johnny Mnemonic," in *Burning Chrome* (New York: Ace, 1987), 1.

part of the hacker ethos involves using the minimum effort to accomplish the desired result, and a brute force crack of the encryption achieved via privileged access to a supercomputer would not necessarily have been considered any more artful. Or as Gibson would put it in the continuation of the lines above: "These days . . . you have to be pretty technical before you can even aspire to crudeness" (1).

The next day the following appeared on MindVox:

```
Subject: AGRIPPA Sterling & Gibson
From: deadboy (The Dead)
Date: Sun, 13 Dec 92 18:43:12 EST
```

According to what went down in IRC a few minutes ago Bruce Sterling was talking to William Gibson today, who is aware that AGRIPPA was cracked and is online [at] MindVox. The real copy is here, Sterling was sent a copy of it and called Kroupa today to relay Gibson's best wishes and say that this was a "planned progression" of his work.

IRC refers to Internet Relay Chat, the forerunner to contemporary chat rooms. Kroupa himself has said that the phone call actually came *before* the text was publicly posted to MindVox, and that it came from Gibson himself.[34] (Gibson, for his part, has never mentioned a phone call to Kroupa or anyone else in any of his public remarks on the subject.) In either case, it seems plausible that Gibson learned of the text's availability either before, or else very soon after, it went up on MindVox, and that directly or indirectly he communicated his approval of that outcome.

34. Patrick K. Kroupa, e-mail to author Sun, Jun 8 2003 21:19:49 −0400. The phone call episode may shed some additional light on the question of how the text was obtained. At first Kroupa's claim—that Gibson called *him*, and *before* the text's release—seems improbable given the very tight chronology of events (for the call would have had to have come some time between the end of the evening's proceedings uptown on December 9 and the text's posting on the morning of December 10). The claim is *not* improbable, however, if one subscribes to Kroupa's version of events all the way through—that MindVox had in fact obtained the text through other means, and not from the reading at the Americas Society. Thus Kroupa's narrative of events *is* self-consistent from start to finish. It does not, however, reconcile Templar's own statement that "we got the original copy and posted it" from the public performance.

In subsequent interviews he was to prove even more expansive:

So, the result of the thing for me, in a funny way, was that I produced a sort of monument to my father, because the piece is a long three-verse poem about my relationship with my father who died when I was very young and I didn't get to know him very well. And it wound up being this permanent ghostly presence on the inter-net, which I couldn't erase if I wanted to. Which is interesting too. There is no place to go and pull the plug on this thing. It sort of lives there. So, it worked out really well. It was quite startling the amount of press it generated on its own. It generated as much commentary as a book.[35]

This last remark is worthy of further consideration. In retrospect, the whole *Agrippa* project—the artist's book as well as the electronic poem—was one of the last great memes of the pre-Mosaic Internet. Gibson's own participation in the project was not without controversy at the time—some thought he had sold out to the art world and that the notion of a collector's edition costing thousands of dollars was unforgivably elitist—but when one reads the early newsgroup conversations there is an almost palpable sense of an audience desperately straining to believe in the idea of a vanishing book and a self-consuming text. Certainly the idea is not new—the Russian poet Velimir Khlebnikov is said to have read the *Temptations of Saint Anthony* by burning each successive leaf for the light to read the next page by.[36] But the irony here is that it is perhaps only through its threadbare material existence, as much conceptual art as anything else, that *Agrippa* even came close to fulfilling its original aesthetic mandate, the "absence of the book" as theorized in the writings of Maurice Blanchot.[37] Put more plainly, the practical failure to

35.   Quoted in http://www.ubu.com/papers/ol/jirgens.html.

36.   Bob Perelman, *The Marginalization of Poetry* (Princeton University Press, 1996), 7. Book artist Keith A. Smith has likewise described plans for a conceptual book whose pages would consist of a series of undeveloped photographic images on film transparencies: "Upon turning each page the viewer will momentarily see the image as it sacrifices itself to protect the remaining pages." See *A Book of the Book*, edited by Jerome Rothenberg and Stephen Clay (Granary Press, 2000), 66.

37.   See Peter Schwenger, "*Agrippa*, or the Apocalyptic Book," *South Atlantic Quarterly* 92, no. 4 (Fall 1993): 617–626. Unlike Liu's attention to the poem in *Laws of Cool*, this excellent essay focuses mainly on the book object *Agrippa*, and does the important work of reconstructing the original theoretical environment for the project.

realize much of what was initially planned for *Agrippa* allowed the project to succeed by leaving in its place the purest form of virtual work—a meme rather than an artifact. Or else (and it is impossible not to reach in this direction) *Agrippa* functioned as a livewire language virus, one that the great patriarch Burroughs would have recognized, as he wrote in a 1971 essay titled "Electronic Revolution:" "I have frequently spoken of word and image as viruses or acting as viruses, and this is not an allegorical comparison."[38] Indeed, a number of early media reports had stated, incorrectly, that the text of "Agrippa" was destroyed by a computer virus (as opposed to its being encrypted; 1992 was also the year of the much-hyped Michelangelo boot virus, the first computer virus to gain widespread public attention[39]). This kind of misinformation was roundly pounced on and corrected whenever it appeared in a forum like alt.cyberpunk or MindVox, but something of the allure of the viral formulation was captured very early on in remarks by Andy Hawks, writing on FutureCulture within days of "Agrippa's" initial release:

So it struck me that a 'Next Phase' in [Science Fiction] lit might be the actual email lists themselves, and all the thousands of people on them—to use the cliché—

38. *Word Virus: The William S. Burroughs Reader*, James Graverholz and Ira Silverberg, eds. (New York: Grove Press, 1998), 312. This viral formulation is by no means original or unique. Lance Olsen, in a creative piece entitled "Virtual Termites," writes: "A metaphor for (un)total recall, as well as a thematic exploration of it, *Agrippa* happens only in a viral gap that literally nibbles away relentlessly at its own boundaries, performs rather than simulates destruction, keeps gnawing onward" (238). See also Liu's *Laws of Cool* for *AGRIPPA* in the context of "destructive art."

39. *The Agrippa Files* offers a facsimile and transcript of a letter from Begos's (anonymous) programmer, alluding to a "fuss" over the supposed fact that "Agrippa" contained a virus, a concern that did not escape the notice of no less a personage than the Electronic Frontier Foundation's John Perry Barlow. This also apparently in the wake of a *New York Times* article by John Markoff on government attempts to clamp down on public access to encryption technology. Whatever else it represented, "Agrippa" clearly tapped into the technorati's intense interest in the subjects of both viruses and encryption at the time it was released. See http://agrippa.english.ucsb.edu/letter-from-the-programmer-may-7-1992-item-d32-transcription/. The instructions printed to accompany the diskette also contain a declaration that the disk does not contain a virus: http://agrippa.english.ucsb.edu/instructions-for-the-diskette-in-agrippa-item-d3-transcription/. However, the early sales prospectus for the work (the only extant copy is owned by the Whitney) clearly states that the disk *does* contain a virus: see http://agrippa.english.ucsb.edu/hodge-james-bibliographic-description-of-agrippa-commissioned-for-the-agrippa-files/#14.

functioning as neurons, synapses, mitochondria. AGRIPPA certainly has pulled together a cloud, an aura of anticipation and predisposition that I've never seen b4 in many years on the Net. . . . I'm only an SF fan, not a lit major by any means, but has AGRIPPA heralded a new form, one that was already in existence, via the lists?[40]

Another poster had likewise suggested that "Agrippa" might best be understood as a piece of emergent performance art, with everyone online, including the crackers "like predictable clockwork automatons," playing a role.[41] Nor was the point lost on early commentators that while the title *Agrippa*'s immediate referent is to a brand of photograph albums, it also hearkens back to Renaissance mage Heinrich Cornelius Agrippa von Nettesheim, whose major work, *De occulta philosophia libri tres* (1531), was an exploration of the Kabbalistic tradition—that is, an exploration of textual ciphers.[42]

While *Agrippa* as an instance of communal Internet art may be the most compelling way of looking back at the events of December 1992, one is struck to find another azimuth from which this text, which ends in the "warm breath" of a typhoon on the Asian Pacific rim, continues to signify. In the original *Agrippa* package, Ashbaugh's artist's book served as the literal receptacle for the diskette as well as the material conceit for the poem, its "Kodak album of time-burned/black construction paper." This is what Charles Sanders Peirce, in the language of semiotics, would have described as an indexical relationship—an essentially physical (rather than merely mimetic) relationship to an original referent.[43] Read "Agrippa" now, and go back to the archives of MindVox, FutureCulture, and alt.cyberpunk, and gradually one begins to find that this electronic text has acquired its own set of indexical relations; the stark contrast between the sparse Courier type in which, often as not, the poem still manifests and the lush graphical interfaces of the contemporary browsers that are now its support is a material connection to the bit-brittle world of bulletin boards, codes, "philes," and "warez" that defined the network prior to the commercial advent of the Web. Alan Sondheim has called this milieu the darknet—a twilight world of command line clients and

40. Andy Hawks, e-mail to FutureCulture listserv Wed, Dec 16 92 15:45:17 MST.

41. Anthony Garcia, e-mail to FutureCulture listserv, Wed, Dec 16 92 12:24:33 CST.

42. See http://fusionanomaly.net/agrippa.html.

43. Kari M. Kraus has written extensively about the importance of indexical relationships in the context of the semiotics of textual reproduction in her dissertation, "Conjectural Criticism: Computing Past and Future Texts" (University of Rochester, 2006).

text-only protocols (Telnet, USENET, IRC, MOO/MUD, Finger, Gopher, FTP). Kroupa himself has written eloquently about the passing of this moment:

Names, places and events all flow together in an infinite virtual landscape where a handle was as real or imaginary as a character you chose to play in that particular timeslice and thoughtscape. Even the players who were consistent with their presence in this non-space, choosing to manifest themselves with one central persona—frequently vented their schizophrenia and imagined into existence scores of characters they'd role-play for a time, and then blip off the face of the matrix as a new mask emerged.[44]

So "Agrippa" is perhaps the best example I know of the capacity of a digital object to take on and accumulate a material, indexical layer of associations, and for that reason, as much as the poetry, it continues to compel. But that capacity is unequivocally present in *all* digital objects, and to show how and why this matters has been the purpose of this book—to cultivate, in Gibson's words, an "awareness of the mechanism."

And the mechanism always becomes visible if you know where to look. In the copies of "Agrippa" available on the Web the poem's final lines sometimes appear like this:

laughing,
in the mechanism.

.

The final dot is not a typo, nor is it an act of authorial punctuation. It is instead the material mark of the electronic mail software that was most likely used to transmit the ASCII version of the poem, as distinctive as the broken serif that allows a forensic document examiner to pinpoint a specific typewriter. The UNIX-based "mail" program uses a period alone on a new line to indicate the end of a file, as does "ed," a UNIX-based line editor. MindVox was a UNIX-based board. To see that mark, the forty-sixth character of the ASCII alphabet, still embedded in the text file a decade later, is to see the mechanism, an artifact of the text's initial transmission—just as the

44. See http://www.phantom.com/staticpage/Media/Mondo2.html.

mechanism-as-trope appears in the poem itself to signify similar irreversible divides in time.[45]

There is a postscript. As of this writing, "Agrippa" is the only one of Gibson's texts licensed for commercial e-book distribution.[46] It is available from a number of vendors, for a fee (usually between $5 and $10), in a variety of popular reader formats, including Adobe e-book, Gemstar Rocket, Palm, and the Microsoft Reader. These are all proprietary and mutually incompatible formats, and in a casual sense of the term might be said to be encrypted; indeed, the irony is that "Agrippa's" disappearing act anticipated current commercial digital rights management (DRM) strategies, which sell a work for one-time use or with a timed expiration window.[47] "Agrippa's" trajectory from text file to the commercial matrix of the Web is also perhaps loosely analogous to the scribal publication of the seventeenth and eighteenth centuries, whereby poems in manuscript achieved widespread circulation from one reader to another in commonplace books before being acquired and printed as a saleable edition.[48] Of course, vastly greater numbers of readers have read "Agrippa" for free on the Internet than have ever paid for one of the e-book distributions. But the key point is that "Agrippa's" afterlife as an e-book should remind us that the term *electronic text* is never rendered homogenous merely by virtue of a text's electronic pedigree, and should instead be understood as a thick constellation of historically visible inscriptive practices, determined both by technical considerations and by market forces.

45. Nick Montfort has pointed out to me that in normal practice the period would not be recorded as character data in any electronic file it served to terminate. It would instead exit the text buffer at the line it was invoked. Why then does it remain intact and visible here? It is impossible to know for sure, but one likely scenario is that the text of the poem was initially prepared for mailing in one file, including the special-function period, but then copied and pasted into a second text file that was propagated in some other way—perhaps by FTP. This second text file would have then retained the period as plain character data.

46. However, several of Gibson's novels have previously been available on CD-ROM from the now-defunct Voyager Corporation.

47. See Jeff Kirvin's "Gone in Ten Hours," *InfoSync* (August 9, 2001): http://www .writingonyourpalm.net/column010827.htm.

48. See Harold Love, *Scribal Publication in Seventeenth-Century England* (Oxford University Press, 1993). According to Love, a key function of scribal publication was to bond "groups of like-minded individuals into a community, sect, or political faction, with the exchange of texts in manuscript serving to nourish a shared set of values and to enrich personal allegiances" (177).

Transformation (and Codework)

"Agrippa," as we have seen, fed off contemporary passions surrounding government controls of encryption technology, and its release on MindVox was overtly motivated by the computer underground ethos of "information wants to be free." Thus the contrast between its encrypted text blocks and the open ASCII character standard used to circulate it could not have been more sharply drawn. Yet while *encryption* is a specialized term in computational practice, referring to the deliberate mathematical obfuscation of information, all digital data is *encoded*, that is to say "in code." The universal ones and zeros of digital representation are always arbitrary symbolic values absent the imposition of some specific formal regimen—packaged and delivered as software—which interprets the codes so that they act upon a programmed formal materiality. As one authority puts it, "[U]nless one has the software to give meaning to those ones and zeros, the data is meaningless."[49] It is likewise important to remember that there is no essential meaning to any given string of binary numbers: as we saw in chapter 3, 01000001 could be the ASCII character code for "A" or it could be the decimal number 65. Or it could stand for something else entirely, as it is always relative to the software that is interpreting it. Abby Smith, working in the specific context of applied digital preservation, puts it this way:

When all data are recorded as 0's and 1's, there is, essentially, no object that exists outside of the act of retrieval. The demand for access creates the "object," that is, the act of retrieval precipitates the temporary reassembling of 0's and 1's into a meaningful sequence that can be decoded by software and hardware. A digital art-exhibition catalog, digital comic books, or digital pornography all present themselves as the same, all are literally indistinguishable one from another during the storage, unlike, say, a book on a shelf.[50]

To this I would only add that the lack of an "object" at the storage level does not imply the lack of an inscription (a formulation in keeping with Kenneth Thibodeau's articulation of the physical, logical, and conceptual levels of digital phenomena). Binary code, in my view—the symbolized sequence of 0s

49. Alexander Stille, *The Future of the Past* (New York: Picador, 2002), 304–305.

50. Abby Smith, "Preservation in the Future Tense," *CLIR Issues*, 3 (May/June 1998): 1, 6.

and 1s—is thus the scripted expression of some particular formal regimen, and the forensic traces of that scripted expression on physical storage media are its inscribed remainder. Digital preservation turns out to be all about "codework," the reading and revealing of codes so that data can be reconstituted in keeping with its original intent. Thus digital preservation, in practical terms, is about identifying and imposing the requisite formal materiality on an encoded sequence of stored bits (what are sometimes known as BLOBs, or Binary Large Objects in the trade, a euphemism that captures the state of the code, which is homogenous and inactionable until it is activated by the requisite formal environment).

In this context, the encryption of "Agrippa" the poem is a dramatization of the eventual fate of all digital objects, which will inexorably be reduced to opaque code blocks, or BLOBs, as they become detached and drift away from their native software environments, and as those software environments themselves become distanced from the hardware running the operating systems that support and sustain them. If *Agrippa* the book aestheticizes the forensic properties of distress and accelerated aging in the postapocalyptic presentation of its physical materials, then *Agrippa* (both book and electronic work) also aestheticizes the formal properties of digital code in a like manner, through a radical acceleration of its obsolescence cycle.[51] Moreover, remember that code is overtly on display throughout the *Agrippa* project, most conspicuously in the pages of the artist's book, where the C-A-T-G text of the bicoid maternal morphogen genomic sequence occupies the bulk of the printed matter. Begos has commented, "The intent was never to reproduce a specific sequence in type or images. The intent was to create a unique and beautiful book—a genetic creation of our own, not a reproduction."[52] Thus the code is first and foremost intended to speak for itself, to be read *as* code. Likewise, there was discussion—it is unclear if the result was ever implemented—about display-

51.   See Alan Liu, *The Laws of Cool: Knowledge Work and the Culture of Information* (Chicago: Chicago UP, 2004), 339–348, and Peter Schwenger, "*Agrippa*, or the Apocalyptic Book," *South Atlantic Quarterly* 92, no. 4 (Fall 1993): 617–626.

52.   See http://agrippa.english.ucsb.edu/genetic-code-item-d2-about/. Raymond Malewitz, in his important Ph.D. dissertation "Cybernetic Textuality: Ephemeral Works of Contemporary American Literature" (University of Virginia, 2007), offers the shrewd and original observation that the prevalence of genetic source code in *Agrippa* serves to individualize the work in a manner akin to the various forensic processes I have been describing in this book. I am grateful to Malewitz for sharing portions of his study with me.

ing the encrypted ciphertext of the electronic "Agrippa" as part of the presentation of the poem. "[L]ines of text can [...] be layered on top of others until the screen fills up," the project's anonymous programmer wrote to Begos during the development.[53] So again, code is imagined and presented, prima facie, for its own unique textual artifice. This makes *Agrippa* (again, both the printed and electronic components) an early exemplar of codework, the genre that has come to be identified with the composition of new media text objects containing either code or pseudocode, sometimes executable and sometimes not, as an integral aspect of their poetics and aesthetic. Indeed, as Rita Raley notes, one important strain of codework (inaugurated by Alan Sondheim) develops a politics "clearly manifest in the genre's thematization of subjectivity, identity, and the body"[54]—concerns clearly not incompatible with the

---

53. See http://agrippa.english.ucsb.edu/last-letter-from-programmer-item-d29-transcription/.

54. Raley, "Interferences: [Net Writing] and the Practice of Codework," *electronic book review* (September 8, 2002), http://www.electronicbookreview.com/thread/electropoetics/net.writing. See also a special issue of the *American Book Review*, edited by Alan Sondheim (22, no. 6 September/October 2001). In my opinion, codework is one of the most innovative areas of electronic literature (and net art) currently being pursued. Yet I have a critique. To the extent that codework operates (as nearly all of it does) at a specific, permeable boundary between the visible natural language of interface and screen, and the formalized but still human-legible syntaxes of higher-level programming languages, it foregrounds that one particular and partial view of electronic textuality. High-level programming languages were developed to free the programmer from the limitations of producing code statements with a one-to-one correspondence to ordered ranks of machine language instructions. All of the well-known advantages of high-level languages—their portability and relative ease of use chief amongst them—follow from this initial design objective. High-level languages encourage a view of electronic textuality that is referential (variables, arrays, and pointers), fluid (branching conditionals), modular (object oriented), and even autopoietic—for example, the original FORTRAN GOTO statement, which would later come to vex no less a luminary than Edsger Dijkstra because it allows a program to ricochet brazenly, creating the potential for infinite loops. Codework thus serves to naturalize this particular view of electronic textuality by virtue of the ease with which codework's aesthetics map to actual coding practices that are nevertheless themselves highly contingent in their ultimate relationship to other layers of symbolic abstractions in a computer. So it is that the one-to-many ethos of high-level languages finds immediate concrete expression in Mez's, aka Mary Anne Breeze's, penchant for polysemic wordplay ("2 polysemicalli m-ploy a fractured wurdset"). Moreover, the sheer inscriptive density of much codework may, paradoxically, serve to dilute the extreme artifice of its representations since the user, desensitized by thickets of alien punctuation and orthography, is lulled into assuming they must be witnessing electronic writing in something close to its natural state.

genetically rendered themes of body and memory in the complete *Agrippa* project. But whereas most literary codework operates at the interface between natural language and high-level programming, scripting, or markup languages (like C++, Javascript, or HTML), "Agrippa's" codework lies in its performance of an actual act of encryption and the way that act fuels the work's overall tension between obfuscation and transmission. Less a text than an ongoing series of textual events over the course of its publication and reception history, *Agrippa*, as a double artifact that is the progeny of both forensic and formal processes, comes closest to a literal embodying of the peculiar nature of electronic objects I have sought to capture in *Mechanisms*: their remarkable staying power and their fugitive abandon. That the more overtly physical and forensic object—the book—is also the more obscure is not so much irony as it is a testament to the efficacy of formal information transmission.

Playing on the word "gate" as both logic gate and Bill Gates, Gary Taylor writes:

Changes in textual practices have always created narrow gates, through which texts have to pass if they are to remain legible. The change from uncial to minuscule script, the great vowel shift, the invention of print—these mutations of the media of representation transformed textual practices so radically that texts which were not translated into the new medium almost always perished, because they had become unintelligible to the textual classes. The change from print to digital technology has been correctly perceived as another such life-or-death gate. Unfortunately it is not a single gate, but a succession of gates, with shorter and shorter intervals between them.[55]

Taylor's argument, which proceeds from his first-hand experiences developing an edition of the Renaissance dramatist Thomas Middleton's collected works (stymied by lack of funding and a succession of problems related to the management and migration of the project's digital file systems), is that the cultural pressures to utilize the newest and most advanced forms of digital technology and the expenses (time, expert labor, money) associated with so doing will affect the scholarly industry by radically constricting the number of texts that are reproduced and pushed through the electronic gates; this will result, ironically, in fewer and fewer texts being preserved at precisely the moment we are witnessing the (theoretical) explosion of the capacity for

55. Taylor, "c:\wp\file.txt 05:41 10-07-98" in *The Renaissance Text: Theory, Editing, Textuality*, ed. Andrew Murphy (Manchester: Manchester University Press, 2000): 44–54.

textual reproduction. Thus the importance of "Agrippa's" initial dissemination as an ASCII text file cannot be overstated: as 8-bit ASCII, it could move effortlessly across bulletin boards, listservs, newsgroups, Gopher, and other network services. (The term *text files*, in hacking circles, refers literally to text in ASCII format, but it was also something like a genre label, one that established an open relationship between information and the technical means by which it is communicated.)[56]

The history of ASCII and other electronic character codes is part of a longer history of sequential, symbolic, and literally digital—*discrete*—transmission protocols, beginning with Samuel Morse's famous code and his perfection of telegraphy on through the 5-bit code devised by Jean-Maurice-Émile Baudot for use with teleprinters and Herman Hollerith's 6-bit punch card-based code.[57] The UNIVAC-1 was the first general purpose computer capable of processing alphanumeric as well as strictly numeric data. In other words, it played host to the first electronic alphabet, a 6-bit character set that mapped more or less directly to a typewriter keyboard. Throughout the 1950s and early 1960s character sets proliferated; IBM, for example, had its own proprietary 8-bit character set called EBCDIC that saw use on mainframe computers well into the 1980s. By the early 1960s, however, the smart people recognized the need for a standard, and so ASCII was born in 1963, and was officially adopted by the American National Standards Institute in 1967. ASCII was (and is) a 7-bit character set.[58] (Paul E. Ceruzzi offers up the suggestion that one of several reasons ANSI adopted a 7-bit rather than an 8-bit code was because it was felt that eight holes, punched across a thin piece of paper tape,

56. Jason Scott, curator of the massive and vital Textfiles BBS archive, writes: "Simply put, they were textfiles of any sort, written to explain in detail an important new computer discovery, a great new concept, or an old piece of knowledge that needed to be passed on. It included stories, poems, songs, ramblings, and long treatises on theories that the writer couldn't possibly have known. They were full of bravado, of half-truths, of promises, and occasionally, of brilliance . . ." See http://www.textfiles.com/statement.html.

57. See http://tronweb.super-nova.co.jp/characcodehist.html. Notably, Morse was inspired by another digital technology, letterpress type, which he became acquainted with in his brother's print shop. Early experimental telegraphs were kludged from artifacts found around the shop. Morse also used the relative numbers of letters in the California job case (the standard compositor's draw) as the basis for the statistical distribution of his code, so that "e," which he observed had the most pieces of type, requires only a single dot to transmit.

58. The best technical history of ASCII is contained in C. E. Mackenzie, *Coded Character Sets, History and Development* (Reading, MA: Addison-Wesley, 1980).

would render the paper weak and vulnerable to tearing.[59] Thus we find that ASCII, which defines the conditions of electronic textuality we know today at absolutely the most fundamental level, is literally informed by the materiality of paper.) Seven bits created 128 binary permutations, ranging from 0000000 to 1111111. The ASCII character set included the twenty-six letters of the Roman alphabet, both lower- and uppercase; the ten Arabic numerals; punctuation marks of the sort that would be found on a typewriter; and a series of "control codes" such as line feed, carriage return, and the bell, that ineluctably tie ASCII to the materiality of one particular piece of hardware, the teletype, which was the default interface device. An "A" was represented by the binary string 1000001. But of course it's more complicated than that. National variations soon proliferated; the character set known as ISO-646 substituted the British pound sign (£) for the dollar symbol, for example. Still, computers like to think in terms of 8-bit "bytes," or octals, as an 8-bit sequence is more properly known. So, given that ASCII couldn't accommodate all of the characters necessary for Western European languages, let alone other languages, it wasn't long before there were 8-bit extensions, which added another 128 characters to the 128 characters of the original 7-bit set for a total of 256. These became codified in the family of ISO-8859 character sets. If you're reading this book in the United States or Western Europe, chances are your Web browser is set to display ISO Latin-1, the variant of 8859 that supports character symbols for the national languages of those countries. There is a recent movement afoot to replace Latin-1 with Latin-9, which also includes the character code for the Euro sign (€). Your browser might display it anyway because it includes native Unicode support, but that's another story. Obviously the sociopolitical dimensions here are enormous, and the proliferation of character sets and encoding standards gives lie to the notion that there is finally any such thing as "plain text" in the electronic sphere. ASCII itself has been heavily versioned, and the original 7-bit standard is now officially known as ANSI X3.4-1986. Any serious student of textual transmission in electronic environments must therefore come to grips with the specifics of character sets and encoding.[60]

59. Ceruzzi, *A History of Modern Computing* (Cambridge: MIT Press, 1998), 152.

60. For a good recent treatment of these issues, see Harry E. Gaylord, "Character Representation," *Computers and the Humanities* 29 (1995): 51–73. For additional support of this argument, see John Lavagnino, "The Analytical Bibliography of Electronic Texts" (presented at the *ALLC-ACH '96* conference, University of Bergen).

So what can such students learn about electronic textuality from the transmission history of "Agrippa" itself? First, despite its being a uniquely volatile electronic object—ephemeral by intent and design—"Agrippa" has proven remarkably persistent and stable over the years. One common belief is that the online text is morphing or mutating. Gibson himself contributes to this perception, commenting: "And the longer it stays [online], the more for some reason it decays. So every year or so, I have a look at it, and I find that lines have changed and it's sort of mutating into something else.... It's like it's being cut and pasted by cyberspace itself."[61] While an appealing idea, and in keeping with both the aesthetics of the work and the supposed ontology of the virtual, in fact there is no evidence that this is actually taking place. I have examined and collated dozens of digital copies that have been in circulation between 1992 and the present, and have been unable to locate any significant textual variation other than in style of graphical presentation.[62]

Some of the perceptions of textual mutation may originate with Kroupa's "AGR1PPA" and the other early parodies; more generally I would view them as manifestations of the same medial ideology that leapt to embrace the conceit of a disappearing book and a vanishing poem. In retrospect, it should not be surprising that the myriad digital copies of the poem manifest perfect stability as they continue to appear and multiply around the network. Given the formal nature of digital transmission, which resolves itself in the form of technologies like packet switching (whereby a file sent across the network is broken up into smaller units that are then reassembled at the receiving end

61.   http://www.aint-it-cool-news.com/display.cgi?id=5140.

62.   Ironically, the sole exception is the copy of the poem online at Gibson's own official Web site: http://www.williamgibsonbooks.com/source/agrippa.asp. It contains two obvious typos. The first is in the closing lines of section III: "torqueflite radio, heather and power steering and brakes, new/w.s.w. premium tires. One owner. $1,595." Presumably "heather" should be "heater". The second is in the closing lines of the poem: "tonight red lanterns are battered. /laughing,/in the mechanism." Presumably the period after "battered" should be a comma— "battered"—as it is any every other rendition I have seen. The punctuation here seems self-evidently incorrect. Mail to the site's webmaster regarding these errors yielded no response. Given the nature of digital duplication, the typos are noteworthy for their suggestion that the text online at Gibson's site originated elsewhere than one of the generic copies now circulating on the Web. Notable instances of the text online also include Alan Liu's copy of the text, which is helpfully line numbered and includes links to some other supplemental materials: http://www.english.ucsb.edu/faculty/ayliu/unlocked/gibson/agrippa.html.

in accordance with checksum and other error checking routines), there is no occasion for the text to slip in the manner of scribal transcription. (What is more likely, perhaps, is that one or more scribal errors were introduced into the original transcription from the video tape, if that is in fact where the online copy originates.) In Goodman's terms, the online texts of "Agrippa" exhibit "sameness of spelling." A substantive variant would have to be the result of someone's deliberate intervention rather than an accident of transmission. No model of digital inscription that rests upon the new medium's supposedly radically unstable ontology can be taken seriously so long as innumerable copies of this particular text remain only a search query away. (Or as Gibson chose to put it, there's no way to "pull the plug.") Indeed, there is a strong argument to be made that digital information can best ensure its own longevity through its unprecedented capacity for proliferation, and textual theory must take this into account.[63] Today, the 404 File Not Found messages that Web-browsing readers of "Agrippa" inevitably encounter—the result of that file no longer residing on the local server where it was originally indexed by the search engine—are more than just false leads; they are latent affirmations of the work's original act of erasure, which allow the text to stage anew all of its essential points about artifacts, memory, and technology.

Second, we have seen that "Agrippa" owes its transmission and continuing availability to a complex network of individuals, communities, ideologies, markets, technologies, and motivations. Only in the most heroic reading of these events is "Agrippa" saved for posterity solely by virtue of the knight Templar. "Agrippa" thus demonstrates what the renowned bibliographical scholar D. F. McKenzie influentially called the "sociology of texts," and from its example we can see that the preservation of digital media has a pronounced

---

63. In the aftermath of September 11, many U.S. government agencies, corporations, and other entities scrambled to remove what they deemed sensitive information from the Web. This proved surprisingly difficult to implement in practice, as copies of files and documents resided in the remote caches and indices of search engines (notably Google), with archival sites like the Wayback Machine, and, of course, in the local file systems of countless individual browsers. See "The Curse of the Cache: Is Google's Memory Too Good?" at http://www .pcworld.com/article/id,110323-page,6-C,google/article.html. Similarly, Lots of Copies Keeps Stuff Safe (LOCKSS) is a Mellon- and NSF-funded project to safeguard digital information through the massive (but controlled) proliferation of redundant copies. See http://www.lockss .org/. Significantly, the title of "locks" is evocative of permanence, but also security and stability.

social dimension that is at least as important as purely technical considerations.[64] Just as textual critics now engage with only a minute fraction of the materials retained by major research libraries, archives, and repositories, so too will they be called upon to contend with only the tiniest samples of the massive assemblages of data and digital information comprising the digital spectrum. But the question of which data sets, and whether the requisite electronic documents will be recoverable in a usable form, is one that relates directly to the scholarly enterprise. Textual scholars should have a voice in these matters, much as Thomas Tanselle has long been an advocate for bibliographers and textual critics in traditional library settings, where he has opposed destructive "preservation" policies that tamper with bindings, dust jackets, and other important kinds of bibliographic evidence.[65] This "social life" of electronic objects (to borrow yet another phrase) has been a key concern throughout this study.[66]

Third, as we have already noted, the electronic text of "Agrippa" is by no means a singular or homogenous entity. In fact, it can be observed to exist in at least four basic electronic states: the clear text copies on whatever unused disks from the original project may still remain; the encrypted text blocks from used versions of those same disks; the ASCII text transcriptions available from the World Wide Web and other network services; and last, the copies of the poem that are for sale in the various commercial e-book formats. Though

---

64. This same point has been made in a far more sobering context in Daniel Beunza and David Stark's ethnography of a World Trade Center investment banking firm returning to business in the aftermath of 9/11. They quote testimony from an executive who recounts survivors from the firm sharing personal recollections about deceased colleagues' family members, pets, hobbies, vacation spots, and so forth in an effort to guess personal passwords that were obstructing access to key systems in the wake of the attack. "[C]risis reveals that any technology is always a *socio-technology*" is how they put it (150). The episode is worth juxtaposing with the account I give of forensic data recovery from the World Trade Center in the preface. See Beunza and Stark, "The Organization of Responsiveness: Innovation and Recovery in the Trading Rooms of Lower Manhattan," *Socio-Economic Review* (2003) 1: 135–164. My thanks to David Kirsch for this reference.

65. See G. Thomas Tanselle, "Bibliographers and the Library," *Literature and Artifacts* (Charlottesville: Bibliographical Society of the University of Virginia, 1998): 24–40.

66. See John Seely Brown and Paul Duguid, *The Social Life of Information* (Cambridge: Harvard Business School Press, 2000).

all of these copies are perhaps identical in the narrow sense of their screen-legible textual content, they represent a cross-section of digital inscription practices encompassing munitions-grade encryption, standardized ASCII, and a ten-year span of proprietary commercial formats, some of them no longer easily accessible. "Agrippa," as a text, is thus no more self-identical than a particular edition of, say, *The Prelude*, and we would do well to begin applying the same documentary rigor and historical precision to electronic media that we habitually bring to bear on other textual productions.

Finally, *Agrippa*'s transmission exemplifies what Joel Spolsky, author of the popular Web log *Joel on Software*, calls the "Law of Leaky Abstractions." Abstraction, according to Spolsky, is the process of representing complex operations in formally simpler terms. This is a basic element of software engineering. His primary example is the TCP (Transmission Control Protocol) packet-switching that delivers information across the network; e-mail (or a copy of "Agrippa") arrives perfectly every time because of the redundant error checking built into the process. This formal simplification overcomes potential complications in the form of limited bandwidth or downed servers. Similarly (the example is also Spolsky's), a file system is a formal abstraction of the physical or forensic nature of data storage on a hard drive, effectively abstracting the mechanical operations of the device. Yet, as he points out, formalization can only extend so far. There is always something outside the (operating) system. A mouse can chew through your Ethernet cable, in which case your e-mail won't get delivered no matter what TCP is doing:[67]

This is what I call a leaky abstraction. TCP attempts to provide a complete abstraction of an underlying unreliable network, but sometimes, the network leaks through the abstraction and you feel the things that the abstraction can't quite protect you from.

67. This example is not as far-fetched as it might seem. Here is advice posted to a public bulletin board for a systems administrator troubleshooting a chronically ailing server: "In between your hardware and software checks, you might want to verify that you have the correct voltage coming in from the outlets you're using. Also check to make sure your ground spike is deep enough; sometimes when it hasn't rained for a while the ground is not reliable (this happens more if it is too shallow). Are you running the whole shebang off one circuit and breaker, or are you spread over two or more circuits? This also might help safeguard operations especially in peak demand periods. While yuou're [*sic*] checking, use a fine emery cloth or very fine steel wool to burnish the prongs on your plugs." http://www.boardgamegeek.com/thread/106498.

This is but one example of what I've dubbed the Law of Leaky Abstractions: **All non-trivial abstractions, to some degree, are leaky.** Abstractions fail. Sometimes a little, sometimes a lot. There's leakage. Things go wrong. It happens all over the place when you have abstractions.[68]

For Spolsky, the Law of Leaky Abstractions becomes a reality to be regretted, and when possible, overcome. He sees it as particularly dangerous in software engineering, as programmers rely more and more on GUI interfaces and object-oriented toolkits or libraries to do their work, at greater and greater removes from the computational ground truth of the code (itself, of course, still at a very great remove from the electromechanical reality of the voltage differentials in the circuitry that the code exists to abstract). Yet the kind of "leaks" Spolsky documents can also be powerfully enabling, and are fundamental to any act of preservation, not least because they are inevitable. In the case of *Agrippa*, it is worth recalling that the text survives because it has been abstracted, with significant loss, from its original source media. Although the tendency now is to regard the diskette as only an arbitrary vehicle for the text that was eventually released onto the Internet, much of "Agrippa's" original textual identity was bound up with the disk as its specific means of distribution. The anxiety over whether it contained a virus is a prime example; a public reaction, medium-specific, which fed the mystique of the work. The instructions distributed with *Agrippa* warned: "You must run Agrippa from the diskette that came with Agrippa (a book of the dead). Also, do not copy the application Agrippa. [. . .] If for any some reason you encounter a difficulty with your disk due to high speed copying processes a replacement disk will be provided. Disks which break down or refuse to run due to attempts at reproduction or disassembly will not be replaced."[69] The plans for the December 9 Transmission included elaborate contingencies for distributing the disks beforehand. Clearly then, in its original artifactual incarnation, the text of "Agrippa" reminded us just how closely electronic culture was identified with these generic black plastic rectangles, the real-world counterpart of the buffed military-style cartridges Gibson was imagining as the storage platforms

68. http://joelonsoftware.com/articles/LeakyAbstractions.html, emphasis in original. Posted November 11, 2002.

69. http://agrippa.english.ucsb.edu/instructions-for-the-diskette-in-agrippa-item-d3-transcription/.

for the weaponized code in his then-contemporary fiction (the act of "jacking in" in Gibson's work has its equivalent in "slotting" a virus).[70]

Ultimately the fascination of *Agrippa* for me is not only that the work is intensely self-reflexive about its own artifactual condition (which it is), but that this very self-reflexivity sets in motion unintended, emergent, distributed events that transform the work in ways that were probably unanticipated but nonetheless clearly licensed by the original project ambitions. For instance, the drawings in at least one copy of the physical artist's book were printed using uncured photocopy toner, in an abortive attempt to realize the concept of the photosensitive images.[71] As one turns the pages they inevitably rub and smear, thus remaking the book in the act of reading. A more significant example is to be found in *Re:Agrippa*, a video composition (5:42 in length) attributed to one "Rosehammer," one of three people credited by Templar for the poem's "hack" in his MindVox posting.[72] An experimental, montage-based work consisting of a test pattern, footage from the public reading, and other sources, it is, as the title implies, a remix or remediation or repetition as well as a response to *Agrippa* (following the standard e-mail convention of using "Re:" for a reply to a message). At one point we read the following text, attributed to Rosehammer: "I feel offering only 100 copies of Agrippa for $2000 each is a form of cultural elitism. And I ponder the legal and social repercussions of making the file available to the public for free." The tape is date-stamped 4/9/93, and while this cannot be independently verified it corresponds with Begos's recollection of the receipt of such a tape some months after the December event.[73]

"Welcome to Re:Agrippa. Prepare yourself for a mindfuck," a voice, presumably that of Rosehammer, intones over and over. Yet the video is not especially mind-blowing; it seems about equal parts art school and MTV. The line "Do not adjust your TV" appears repeatedly, as does the seemingly contradictory statement "This is not TV" attributed to one "Celeb-Hack." (And

70. For example, in his "Burning Chrome," from the short story collection of the same name (New York: Ace, 1986): "'Go for it,' I said, when it was time, but Bobby was already there, leaning forward to drive the Russian program into its slot with the heel of his hand" (168).

71. For more on the toner, see http://agrippa.english.ucsb.edu/hodge-james-bibliographic-description-of-agrippa-commissioned-for-the-agrippa-files/#12.

72. Available here: http://agrippa.english.ucsb.edu/post/documents-subcategories/the-transmission/reagrippa. See also the Appendix.

73. E-mail to author from Alan Liu, Dec 1, 2005 3:22 PM.

indeed it is not: *ceci n'est pas un pipe*.) Characteristic of the hacker ethos, the video maintains a clear distinction between the politically necessary act of liberating "Agrippa" and its attitudes toward the project itself and its creators: "Props go out to my man William Gibson. Props go out to my man Kevin Begos. Props go out to my man Dennis Ashbaugh." We hear a voice, presumably that of Penn Jilette, reading from the poem ("A Kodak album of time-burned black construction paper . . ."). We see Begos at a podium talking about computer networks and the Internet, but the soundtrack is distorted and the visuals overlaid with indeterminate washed-out video footage. We catch glimpses of the poem, scrolling to oblivion while the camera tilts and swoops and pans, at times filming the screen almost obliquely. At 5:25, for a split second, we glimpse the following text, lines 100–102 of "Agrippa:" "A lens/The shutter falls/Forever." This moment, a single video frame, literalizes the act of still photography that is a backdrop for the *Agrippa* concept. The video concludes with an extended shot of a cityscape at night, lines of traffic etching colored strings of light in manner highly evocative of Gibson's fiction, while an authoritarian female voice issues traffic control instructions. "Does the FCC have domain over our minds?" the on-screen text display rhetorically inquires. "I've got to get out of here. I'm trapped," announces a heavily digitally processed voice, the last clear vocal we hear. The footage ends with the attribution: "Produced by: Rosehammer & Templar."

Re:Agrippa offers the only extant documentation of the original video tape from which "Agrippa" may have been transcribed, and to my knowledge the only extant documentation of a performance of the poem itself, however heavily edited and treated. Yet the *Re:Agrippa* I saw is actually a 114 MB video file (named "reagrippa-full-stream.wmv") digitized from the original VHS recording. So when I see the text of "Agrippa" on my screen, what I am really looking at is a digitization of a video that is itself a processed remix of an earlier video recording of a big-screen projection made during a public reading of the poem in December of 1992 (figure 5.1).

Coda: Re: Agrippa

Against variance, redundancy. I know I am repeating myself. As it turns out, the December 1992 transmission of the full text of "Agrippa" on the public Internet was only stage one of its networked apotheosis. Thirteen years later to the day, in December 2005, a second, more deliberate act of "transmission" occurred. Publisher Kevin Begos, Jr. had agreed to make a large number of

Figure 5.1 Title screen of "Agrippa" running on a Mac, as captured by the *Re:Agrippa* video footage. *Source*: http://agrippa.english.ucsb.edu/still-shots-from-reagrippa-video-based-on-dec-9-1992-transmission-of-agrippa-1993/

primary source documents related to *Agrippa*'s project and production history available on the Web site of the Transcriptions project at the University of California, Santa Barbara. There a team led by Alan Liu itemized and digitized them for an online archive dubbed *The Agrippa Files* (which I have been drawing on extensively in the preceding pages).[74]

As Liu notes in his introduction to the site, *Agrippa* was "in danger of being erased by its own legend." The rumors and exaggerations about the work along with the dearth of access to copies of the actual physical book had conspired to create a wild spectrum of beliefs and misperceptions, ranging from the virus meme to the conviction that the whole thing was an elaborate hoax. *The Agrippa Files* themselves are a bracing example of documentary preservation, using high-resolution facsimile images, scrupulous transcriptions, editorial commentary and annotation, serious descriptive bibliography, and compilations of scholarship and secondary sources to contextualize the work.

74.   Available at http://agrippa.english.ucsb.edu/.

In a manner akin to the Michael Joyce Papers at the Ransom Center, we find notes, correspondence, press releases and promotional materials, proofs, prospectuses, drafts, code samples, and other written remainders, both physical and born-digital. Specialized tools allow users to manipulate digital images side-by-side for rapid comparison, and to experience a simulation of the originally planned fading ink effect. What was once distributed is now centralized in a database and state-of-the-art content management system, ready-made for Web 2.0. Yet if some of the mystery or allure surrounding the project and its aftermath has been tempered, the forensically replete spaces of *The Agrippa Files* have at last opened the door for serious scholarship on this important but misunderstood new media artifact.

Inevitably (and also instantly), *The Agrippa Files* themselves were and will be absorbed by the network constructs surrounding them, as the digital "files" are cached and downloaded onto countless individual hard drives (and perhaps set in circulation again despite the copyright prohibitions against it), as well as crawled and cached by search engines, scraped by the Wayback Machine, and brushed by other indeterminate electronic agents. Thus *Agrippa* continues to reinvent itself and prove anew the chipped adage of textual scholar Randal McLeod: "the struggle for tne text *is* the text."

Some 30 months earlier I had begun my own research into *Agrippa*, casting my dragnet over Usenet archives, Google, the Wayback Machine, and such reflecting pools as the Web then offered. From this I constructed the backbone of the narrative presented here. I searched and sifted newsgroups, formulated iteration after iteration of Google queries, purchased a ten-year old transcript from the NPR Web site. Some of my most important lessons about digital bibliography were gleaned from this process: the effortless ease with which certain kinds of chronologies and transmission histories could be established using date and time stamps (recorded to the second); the extent to which the network itself, as a redundantly distributed hard drive, functioned as an agent of preservation. Yet I also found the network cruelly arbitrary: for example, the FutureCulture list archives, maddeningly, are available only from December 16, 1992 forward, meaning that accessible records for this venue exist back to one week *after* "Agrippa's" initial online release.[75] The holy grail was MindVox itself, which persists as a weird, psychedelic Web presence but offers no access to the BBS that was once the core of its identity.[76] Eventually it

75. See http://futurec.taylor.org/archives/1992/.

76. http://www.mindvox.com/cgi-bin/WebObjects/mindvox.

became clear that search engines would take me only so far, and I would need to reach out to certain individuals. Here too the network yielded points of contact, in the form of e-mail addresses scavenged from archived postings and correspondence. Sometimes these contacts led nowhere, as in my efforts to elicit a response from Templar (I still believe I had a current e-mail address). Other times I was rewarded.

An e-mail from a celebrity (or a lover) is more than a possession. The presence of the message also matters, the "From" field stacked democratically amid the other mundane minutiae of one's inbox, the very arbitrariness of its vertical situation in the queue feeding the frisson. This is where the line between the formal and forensic comes nearest to dissolving, in a moment of stochastic contact as close and yet as far as a hard drive's read/write head and the platter passing a nanometer below at 10,000 RPM—or one of Bowers's five anonymous compositors, identifiable only by his idiosyncrasies, hand outstretched for a piece of type, this one and not that one—or the following e-mail, which I was (fortunately) at my computer to receive in real time one Friday afternoon, one June:

```
Subject: Re: Agrippa
Date: Fri, 13 Jun 2003 16:23:26 -0400
From: "Patrick K. Kroupa" <[address removed]>

Sorry do0d, doing 1001 things at once here.

I've put MindVox back online for an hour or 5. I'd suggest
going to the [Search] section, [Subject]: <change to>: [Con-
tains] agrippa

I just did this, I see ... 47 hits. including Templar, Ahawks,
PhiberOptik, etc, etc, to forth and wit. Bruce in there some-
place too, search [bruces]

It's up right now, it'll become a mirage again by 10pm or so.
We cannot handle the hit-rate leaving it online at this exact
moment would generate.[77]
```

Laughing, in the mechanism.

77. E-mail to author.

Coda: The Forensic Imagination

the failure of a property
that has been changed
by an external agent
to return
to its original value
when the cause
of the change
has been removed:
i.e., hysteresis.
the laws of physics assign
proximity
no more meaning
than absence.
yet one word
follows another
—MICHAEL JOYCE, *AFTERNOON*[1]

The copper-jacketed slug
recovered
from the bathroom's cardboard
cylinder of

1. Quoted here from the first edition, the lexia entitled "womb reamed."

Morton's Salt
was undeformed
save for the faint bright marks of
lands
and grooves
so hot, stilled energy,
it blistered my hand.
—WILLIAM GIBSON, "AGRIPPA"

The realm of the dead has the same dimensions as the storage and
emission capacities of its culture. *Media* . . . are always already
flight apparatuses *into the other world*.
—FRIEDRICH KITTLER[2]

We live in a time of the forensic imagination, as evidenced by the current
vogue for forensic science in television drama and genre fiction. Forensics in
this popular sense returns us to the scene of the crime; as a legal and scientific
enterprise forensic investigation has its origins in the same nineteenth-century
era that produced the great inscribing engines of modernity—the gramophone, film, and the typewriter all among them. Even as these technological
media were effacing the last trembling traces of the writing hand,[3] finger*printing* was storing up the marks of individualized bodies in a new classification
and recording system, making those marks both mobile and repeatable. Photography and microscopy, Arthur Conan Doyle's Sherlock Holmes and Samuel
Clemens's extraordinary twins, Francis Galton and (somewhat later) Edmond
Locard—all lend their testimony to forensics as a signature discourse network
of modernity at the juncture of instrumentation, inscription, and identification. But forensics is commemorative as well as juridical, and fundamental to
the arts as well as the sciences. Stephen Greenblatt's ringing opening declaration in *Shakespearean Negotiations* (1988) is justly famous for recalling us to the

2. From the "Introduction" to *Grammophone, Film, Typewriter*, in the translation by Dorothea
Von Mücke originally published in *October* 41 (Summer 1987), reprinted in *Literature, Media,
Information Systems*, John Johnston, ed. (Amsterdam: G+B Arts, 1997), 42. Emphasis in original.

3. I am thinking here of course of some of the particulars of Freidrich Kittler's technohistory,
as remixed in his various writings.

forensic imagination with an unusually distilled confession of intent: "I began with a desire to speak with the dead."[4]

At the beginning of another long, erudite, and ambitious book, artist and cognitive psychologist Michael Leyton describes the detritus one typically finds on a deserted subway platform, mute material evidence of the past impinging on the present. In a crushed can, he sees the press of an absent grip; in a dented trash bin, the impact of a kick from a long-gone limb; in a coffee stain on the concrete, the recollection of a spill; in scuffmarks on the floor, the tread of many feet.[5] This experience, according to Leyton, is emblematic of the human condition: "Like the subway station, the present is a silent chamber that has a history we cannot experience. It is only from the contents of this chamber that we might be able to infer prior events.... We can examine only what we possess in the present, the relics that surround us" (1). We are, as Leyton argues, "prisoners of the present," and this singularity (his term) is absolute: "We shall argue in this book that all cognitive activity proceeds via the recovery of the past through objects in the present" (2).

The recovery of the past through objects in the present is our one recourse, besides spiritualism, to satisfying a desire to speak with the dead. Storage, which I have discussed throughout this book, is all about creating a systemized space in which this activity can unfold. And though he does not use the term, Leyton is speaking here directly to the forensic imagination, for the recovery of the past through objects or relics—or inscriptions—in the present is an accurate enough characterization of forensic method, where individualization, wear (or more properly tribology, the study of interacting services in

4.   The passage, which has been quoted many times, continues: "This desire is a familiar, if unvoiced, motive in literary studies, a motive organized, professionalized, buried beneath thick layers of bureaucratic decorum: literature professors are salaried, middle-class shamans. If I never believed that the dead could hear me, and if I knew that the dead could not speak, I was nonetheless certain that I could re-create a conversation with them. Even when I came to understand that in my most intense moments of straining to listen all I could hear was my own voice, even then I did not abandon my desire. It was true that I could hear only my own voice, but my own voice was the voice of the dead, for the dead had contrived to leave textual traces of themselves, and those traces make themselves heard in the voices of the living." See *Shakespearean Negotiations: The Circulation of Social Energy in Renaissance England* (Berkeley: University of California Press, 1988), 1.

5.   Michael Leyton, *Symmetry, Causality, Mind* (Cambridge: MIT Press, 1992), 1.

relative motion—friction), persistence over time (hysteresis, familiar to us from our study of magnetic recording), and trace evidence collectively name the behaviors and phenomena by which we construct legible records of what happened on the other side of a present singularity, records of a past now as near and now as inaccessible as the opposite side of a subway platform.

If, as Lisa Gitelman says, inscriptions are interventions, then the forensic imagination mines or invades exactly the site of intervention, seeking to reclaim its very grooves and lands as vectors of meaning, identity, and intentionality. We find this invasion literalized in a passage from Nicholson Baker's novel *The Mezzanine*, which has its protagonist contemplating lines scored into the frozen surface of a pond by a pair of skates:

If you made a negative of that image of my skate blade's gorge, you would arrive at the magnified record groove—a hushed black river valley of asphaltic ripples soft enough to be impressed with the treads of your Vibram soles; an image cast from a master mold that was the result of a stylus forced to plow through wax as it negotiated complex mechanical compromises between all the various conceptually independent oscillations that stereophony demanded of it; ripples so interfingered and confused that only after a day with surveying equipment, pacing off distances and making calculations (your feet sparking static with each step) are you able to spray-paint "Bass Clarinet" with some confidence in orange on an intermittent flume of vinyl, as workers in Scotchgard vests spray-paint the road to indicate utility lines beneath. Cobblestone-sized particles of airborne dust, unlucky spores with rinds like coconuts, and big obsidian chunks of cigarette smoke are lodged here and there in the oddly echoless surface, and once in a while, a precious boulder of diamond, shorn somehow from the stylus by this softer surface, shines out from the slope, where it has been pounded deep into the material by later playings, sworn at by the listener as if it too were common dust. That was needle wear.[6]

The conceit of microscopic explorers descending the canyon walls of a record groove to pace its vinyl flooring allows us to linger (literally) amid the materiality of inscribed sound. Conspicuous in this passage are some of the most prevalent aesthetic markers of the forensic imagination: extreme juxtaposition, or oscillation, of spatial and temporal scale; a precision vocabulary that bespeaks an intimacy with industrial procedure and fabrication; beauty in

6. Baker, *The Mezzanine* (New York: Vintage, 1986), 66.

novel proximity to mundane objects, here dust and debris that are revealed as obsidian and "precious boulders of diamond" (reminiscent of James Elkins's work on the aesthetics of scientific images).[7] The fantastic voyage into the record groove also becomes the site of numerous second-order instances of the forensic imagination, whether the footprints left in the vinyl, or the use of a spray paint aerosol to mark and stain, or the "needle wear" whose residue is embedded in the sloping wall. Note too that the scene recounted above is manifestly an outcome of media and instrumentation: it is the *magnified* negative of an "image," while the record is a mechanical copy of a remote wax cylinder original.[8]

The forensic imagination is most clearly activated whenever process collapses into product, a spatial-temporal extrusion whose novel geographies and chronologies leave skate grooves looming like geological formations; shadows, perhaps, of the same sublime cliffs that presided over William Wordsworth's boat stealing in the *Prelude*. Or else think of the so-called bullet-time of time-slice photography introduced to worldwide audiences in the Wachowski brothers' *The Matrix* (1999). Consider too this passage, from William Gibson's 1993 novel *Virtual Light*: "[T]he smell reminded him of a summer job he'd had in Knoxville, his last year in school. They'd been putting condos into the shell of this big, old Safeway out on Jefferson Davis. The architects wanted the cinder block walls stripped just this one certain way, mostly gray showing through but some old, pink Safeway paint left in the little dips and crannies. . . . He'd overhead one of them explaining to the foreman that what they were doing was *exposing the integrity of the material's passage through time*. He thought that was probably bullshit, but he sort of liked the sound of it anyway" (7–8; emphasis in original). Here we see the forensic imagination colliding with the aestheticization (and commodification) of process.[9]

7. Elkins, *The Domain of Images* (Ithaca and London: Cornell University Press, 1999).

8. *The Mezzanine* ends by referencing an article in an obscure Polish industrial journal that purports to document a study employing a mechanical contrivance that stresses shoelaces rhythmically and repeatedly in order to ascertain their break points. The data thus collected answers the protagonist's question of why one shoelace breaks before the other despite the equal stresses placed on their microfibers every morning, a question that is the sole motivator in a text overtaken with the minutiae of the forensic imagination.

9. As Alan Liu notes, passages such as these are Gibson's hallmark; the "micro-physics of destruction," as Liu so cogently phrases it, are the counterpoint to the neon Cartesian ideal on display in Gibson's renderings of cyberspace. See Liu's *Laws of Cool* (Chicago: University of Chicago

The forensic imagination is no less active a modality in new media, especially at the fringe, in avant garde art enclaves, geek and hacker subcultures, and extreme research labs, all venues with the means and the motive to cultivate it. This is the forensic imagination as I have been pursuing it in this book. Crystallizing at the nexus of storage, inscription, and instrumentation, the forensic imagination stands in contrast to the medial ideology and screen essentialism that has held sway in the theoretical conversation's critical formative years for new media as a field. Yet these perspectives are perhaps not finally so much oppositional as cyclical. While it had been used as a display device since Braun's work at the end of the nineteenth century and deployed with radar systems in the years before World War II (notably England's Chain Home radar network), the cathode ray tube was initially known in computer science circles as a *storage* medium. The same properties that allow electrons to "paint" a phosphorescent coating and project an image on a screen can also be used to store and represent binary numbers, as was done in several early computing systems, most notably the Mark I developed by F. C. "Freddie" Williams and Alan Turing at the University of Manchester. These so-called Williams cathode ray tubes, which the team opted for instead of the mercury delay lines with which Turing had previously experimented (an alternative storage technology that relied on the time it took sound waves to travel through a conduit), enabled the implementation, in 1948, of the first actual stored program, written by their colleague Tom Kilburn—a short program to calculate the highest factor of an integer.

Press, 2004), 336–339. Still another example is provided by an artist's book printed by Nora Ligorano and Marshall Reese with text by the poet Gerrit Lansing, entitled *Turning Leaves of Mind*. The 8″ × 8″ book documents Spanish bookbinding from the thirteenth through the eighteenth century, and offers a visual essay on the subject with extreme close-ups that not only reveal intimate details of the book-objects but which also emerge as aesthetic formations in their own right. Decoupled from the normative expectations of scale, bindings and openings rise before the eyes like rock formations, their surfaces dense with marks of wear and friction, every mark a hidden history of contact, a forensic trace of history. From the flyleaf: "[photographic] images of early decorative, archival, and royal bindings are digitally manipulated, enlarged, and cropped to reconfigure the surface ornamentation and structural design of these early books." Two software packages, Adobe Photoshop and Adobe Illustrator, are named in the colophon. The digitized images are "manipulated, enlarged, and cropped" for aesthetic effect. This book about books is the product not only of (re)mediation but also extreme instrumentation.

Turing's biographer, Andrew Hodges, spins out a fascinating scene of the forensic imagination in the Manchester lab, resting upon the unique affordances then in play between storage, inscription, and display: "Physically, the Manchester computer was embodied in a scraggly jumble of racks and valves and wires, with three screens glowing in the gloom of a room with dirty brown tiles..." He goes on:

It was in fact the most obvious feature of the cathode ray tube storage system that one could actually *see* the numbers and instructions held in the machine, as bright spots on the three monitor tubes. Indeed, at this stage it was essential to see them for there was no other output mechanism.[10]

There had in fact been experiments with the tubes as storage devices at several venues, including the Moore School at Pennsylvania. A contemporary document surveying storage technologies underscores the advantage of the "visibility of storage" with a cathode ray tube.[11] The same document also goes into more detail about what one would actually see on that eerily glowing screen. The display was typically divided into a matrix or grid, and the presence or absence of a spot of light at a specific point on the grid corresponded to a binary 1 or 0. Williams, however, opted for a different configuration: his tubes used a dot and a line to differentiate between the two digits, in a manner directly analogous to Morse code. This was to become the signature of the Williams tube. Williams himself described the unruly play of colored lights on the monitor in their early, failed attempts to stabilize the program as a "mad dance" or a "dance of death," but then "one day it stopped and there, shining brightly in the expected place, was the expected answer" (quoted in Hodges; 392). Storage and output had thus converged, or collapsed, not only in the same material hardware configuration but also in the same range of affordances, or types of interaction, that computing made possible. In a manner anticipating later hacker argot, Turing referred to the practice of looking into the tube and interpreting the patterns of light he saw there as "peeping:" "He insisted that what one saw as spots on the tube had to correspond digit by

10. Andrew Hodges, *Alan Turing: The Enigma* (New York: Walker and Company, 2005), 391–392.

11. The document in question is an anonymous project report prepared for the National Bureau of Standards between 1950–1952, part of the Margaret R. Fox collection at the Charles Babbage Institute (housed at the University of Minnesota). Box 2, folder 27, pages 9–10.

digit to the program that had been written out" (Hodges 399).[12] (The instructions PEEK and POKE would become Apple BASIC's nomenclature for manually viewing and altering a byte of machine memory.)

The popular dramatization of forensics as criminalistics ("forensics noir" in Thomas Doherty's characterization[13]) is, I would argue, a mere caricature of the forensic imagination, which is finally—and profoundly—humanistic and generative. In a famous analysis, Carlo Ginzburg links the art historian Giovanni Morelli, who focused on the seemingly incidental details of portraiture (ear lobes and such) to ascertain whether the hand of the master was present, to Sherlock Holmes and Freud (who had himself read Morelli) and finds shared among them "an attitude oriented towards the analysis of specific cases which could be reconstructed only through traces, symptoms, and clues" (104).[14]

12. Brian Napper, maintainer of the *Virtual Museum of Manchester Computing*, offers further detail and distinctions: "Although the phosphor on the CRT would glow at charged points, in a way that might be distinguishable (between 0 and 1), the current contents of a CRT storage tube could not be viewed directly in practice. The front of the tube would be obscured by the pick-up plate. (At first this was a wire mesh, but later it was a metal plate.) Also the CRT had to be screened from outside electrical interference, e.g. local trams or close and aggressive motor cycles, so it was enclosed in a metal box. So typically the information on a Williams-Kilburn Tube would be displayed on a separate Display Tube, which would be updated synchronously with the refresh cycle of the Williams-Kilburn CRT Store. However the opportunity would also be taken to lay the values out in a manner most convenient to the onlooker." See http://www.computer50.org/kgill/williams/williams.html. Here storage and display mirror one another in two parallel devices rather than occupying the same physical device.

13. See Thomas Doherty in "Cultural Studies and 'Forensic Noir,'" *The Chronicle of Higher Education*, October 24, 2003, B15–16. He characterizes forensic noir thus: "Film noir is hard-boiled, resigned, and romantic; forensic noir is air-conditioned, tenacious, and scientific. Film noir is body heat; forensic noir is body stiff." He goes on: "Unlike the hero of the classic police shows, the rule-breaking maverick who played hunches and infuriated the by-the-book captain, the forensic cop is a clinical practitioner of the scientific method, at home amid the sinks, slabs, and scalpels of the morgue," and "The fixation on the body of the victim represents a telling shift away from the former site of detective work, the mind of the murderer. . . . Preferring pathology to psychology, the forensic detectives admit that human motives are beyond their ken" (B16–17).

14. See Carlo Ginzburg, "Clues: The Roots of an Evidential Paradigm" in *Clues, Myths, and Historical Method.*, trans. John and Anne C. Tedeschi (Baltimore: Johns Hopkins University Press, 1989): 96–125. John Lavagnino, in an early paper entitled "The Analytical Bibliography of Electronic Texts" (presented at the *ALLC-ACH '96* conference, University of Bergen), references this same passage in some similar contexts.

Coda

Ginzburg then adds a fourth and more primal figure to the tableau, a hunter kneeling on the trail to study the scat or track of his prey. This, according to Ginzburg, is our first reader of signs. Superimposed on the posture of that hunter I also see Alan Turing, leaning, straining, to "peep" the glowing spots and dashes in the Williams tube, marks inscrutable to most but as revealing to Turing as day-old prints on the forest floor. And superimposed over Turing, I would argue, is the familiar posture of today's computer user—shoulders hunched, head thrust forward, peering into the depths of the screen. Robert Markley's literal dismantling of his own screen is a brute force forensic intervention, a strikingly literal indulgence of the desire to glean something of the logic, of the processes of the machine, to transcend the system opacity that so vexed Michael Heim in his early encounter with the word processor. Nor is such exploration always exclusively located in the visual or haptic registers: here is how one of dozens of vintage Apple II cracker tutorials begins, with the injunction to *listen* to the sound of the disk drive: "To see how a disk is protected, first listen to the drive as it boots up the disk. Be prepared to know what a normal boot sounds like, then check for any differences. If you hear a 'swishing' or 'syncopated rhythm' the disk is proboably [*sic*] using nibble counting."[15] This is what Ginzburg describes as *venatic* lore, "the ability to construct from apparently insignificant experimental data a complex reality that could not be experienced directly" (103). In this he is echoed by Ordway Hilton, the questioned document examiner, who characterizes a document as "In its fullest meaning, any material that contains marks, symbols, or signs either visible, partially visible, or invisible that may ultimately convey a meaning or message to someone."[16] Much of what we call "materiality"

15.   Available at http://www.textfiles.com/apple/CRACKING/copyprog.app. Likewise, early programmers learned to debug their machines by *listening* to the sounds the mechanism made: "Circuits were opened and closed by relays—metal bars that were attached to springs that were raised by the pulling force of magnets. The thousands of relays being slapped into position in various sequences made a deafening racket at times, yet it was not merely random industrial noise. To the trained ear of a programmer, the repeated rhythm from one corner of the machine, signifying a program frozen in some calculating loop, was as dissonant as listening to a broken record. Later, when the next generation 701 Defense Calculator arrived, with its mute electronic switches instead of mechanical relays, Backus recalled feeling a twinge of panic. . . . 'How are we going to debug this enormous silent monster.'" See Steve Lohr, *Go To* (New York: Basic Books, 2001), 18.

16.   Hilton, *Scientific Examination of Questioned Documents*, 16.

in contemporary discussions of new media follows from the pursuit of this impulse.

Conclude with a mechanism, just the kind you would expect: procedures and variables, conditional branching, function calls, and object libraries. A mechanism is not a casual image for a book about new media. It is also not a particularly original one. Ellen Ullman, among others, has noted software's reliance on overtly mechanistic terms like *build*, *component*, and *assembly*. Ullman sees this as a way of rationalizing the process of translating human singularities into the stark arrays of machine-actionable procedure.[17] Mark Bernstein illustrates this as he describes the peculiar postindustrial labor of updating the Storyspace code to the latest iteration of the Mac OS: "Today was a big milestone. We had Storyspace completely disassembled, in parts spread all over the floor. We plugged in lots of new classes, mostly products of Tinderbox refactoring. We packed it all up again; today, we got a clean build in the new environment."[18] Software's developmental literature is filled with such accounts, the metaphors of the mechanism accumulating to a depth and granularity that makes them self-evidently more than metaphors.

The mechanism, as articulated in Gibson's poem, is the agent of irrevocable difference, the shutter of the camera "Forever/Dividing that from this." This is the very singularity whose mute evidence is incarnate on Leyton's deserted subway platform. That moment of division, like a dropout on a tape—the point at which the magnetic signal ceases to register above the tolerances of the read/write head—is a synecdoche for dropouts and gaps all over the present pasts of new media. To Alan Turing, peeping at the lights in his Williams tubes, and to the suburban software cracker listening to the clacking of the drive head as it skips over protected tracks, I would add whatever did or didn't happen as Kroupa and Templar hit the keys to upload "Agrippa" to Mind-Vox, or whatever "papers" of Michael Joyce's are not and never will be collected in the Michael Joyce Papers. Now that new media is being actively stored in archives and museums, as well as on the network—deliberately, as in the case of *The Agrippa Files*; socially, through abandonware sites; or automatically, through Google caches or the crawlers of the Wayback Machine—

17.   Interview with Ellen Ullman, "Of Machines, Methods & Madness," *IEEE Software* (May/June 1998). My thanks to Adriene Gesell for this reference.

18.   http://markbernstein.org/Jul0501/Storyspace25forMacOSXFirst.html.

such absences will become more palpable. We will feel the loss of what is already missing more keenly. And the forensic imagination will work on and work through all the mechanisms we make.

SAVE

SEND

Appendix

Hacking "Agrippa"—The Update

Given the importance of networks in the transmission history of *Agrippa*, I was immediately struck by the potential impact the launch of *The Agrippa Files* Web site might have on the work's reception and identity. "Inevitably (and also instantly)," I wrote in chapter 5, *"The Agrippa Files* themselves were and will be absorbed by the network constructs that surround them.... Thus *Agrippa* continues to reinvent itself and prove anew the chipped adage of textual scholar Randal McLeod: 'the struggle for tne text *is* the text." What I did not anticipate was that events precipitated by the launch of *The Agrippa Files* would become the catalyst for an immediate postscript.

On June 16, 2007, as I was awaiting proofs for this book, I and Alan Liu each received e-mail from an individual identifying himself as Rosehammer, one of the three pseudonymous hackers credited in Templar's original posting of "Agrippa" to MindVox. Rosehammer had found and read my narrative of "the hack" that I had written for *The Agrippa Files*, and he wanted to corroborate my account: "Since I was there, I can confirm the sequence of events of how the poem got published on the internet."[1] The exchange with Rosehammer quickly led to an e-mail contact and a phone conversation with Templar, who I had originally attempted to reach when I first began working on "Agrippa" four years ago almost to the very day. (We spoke for about half an hour; Templar was genial and outgoing.)

---

1. All quotations attributed to "Rosehammer" and "Templar" originated in e-mail to the author, June 16, 2007 12:39 PM and June 20, 2007 9:56 AM, respectively. All such quotations are used by permission.

Rosehammer and Templar provided additional details about "the hack," corrected a couple of errors of fact in my initial account, and addressed the discrepancy between Kevin Begos's recollection of what happened and Patrick Kroupa's. The salient points are these:

- Templar and Rosehammer had both been students in the Interactive Telecommunications program at NYU.[2] On December 9, 1992, a faculty member there was contacted by Begos, who wanted someone to coordinate the technical support at one of the events around town that night for the "Transmission." The faculty member told Rosehammer, who immediately tapped Templar and "Pseudophred" (Templar's significant other) to assist. According to Templar, it all happened very fast: "I was very excited, as I was a fan of William Gibson, and being a phone phreak and hacker from the 80s, instantly grasped the implications." Rosehammer concurs: "We just happened to be in the right place at the right time and understood the opportunity."
- The venue at which the surreptitious video recording was made ("the hack") was not the Kitchen, as I initially surmised, but the Americas Society on Park Avenue. Both venues, however, were part of the December 9 Transmission: the festivities began uptown at the Americas Society at 6:30 pm, and downtown at the Kitchen at 7:00 pm.[3]
- The hardware configuration that was the centerpiece of the hack arose from the complications of projecting an image of the poem onto a big screen for the audience at the Americas Society. According to Templar, "We didn't have a laptop with an external video port, so we grabbed a projector, a Hi8 camera, a handful of cables, (and my wife) and we jumped in a taxi and went uptown." Upon arrival (and with only minutes to spare) the trio pointed the camera at the laptop's screen and wired the camera's output to the projector, for display to the room at large. At this point, unknown to Begos, Templar also popped a tape into the camera and hit Record. While the camera rolled and the poem scrolled, a synchronized recording of Penn Jilette's voice reading the text was played for an audience of about forty. There was a brief question-and-answer

2. Templar and Rosehammer both corresponded with me using their real names, though they are not given here; both were indeed NYU film students at the time of the events in question; both provided details that no one who was not there could have furnished.

3. These timings are confirmed by a printed notice in *The New Yorker*, available from *The Agrippa Files*: http://agrippa.english.ucsb.edu/category/documents-subcategories/the-transmission/.

period afterward—but the whole thing didn't take long. Begos and artist Dennis Ashbaugh were present; Gibson was not.

- The text went up onto MindVox that same night and was also quickly posted to Usenet. Templar: "After the event, we rushed back to my office, and got down to work transcribing the video. I was the fastest typist, and did it straight through in one run. My wife [. . .] (Pseudophred) ran through it once looking for typos, but as it was late, I'm sure some got through." As for why MindVox, it was the natural destination for the poem; it was the Boing Boing and Slashdot of its day. "Pat and Bruce [Fancher] were friends of mine at the time, and I wanted it to go there first," said Templar. "Immediately afterwards, we sent the text to my attorney (Debacle), who posted it through a remailer onto Usenet. Unfortunately, due to a copy and paste error on my part, the end was cut off. I sent him the fixed text the next morning and he reposted it." (This is likely the "botched cut-and-paste job" I stumbled across during my own research.)

- The video that became *Re:Agrippa* was edited by Rosehammer not long afterward. It was designed to emulate the self-destructive behavior of the book and the encrypted diskette (a detail that does not appear to have been previously known). Rosehammer: "I had an edit system that was broken and made the video signal very unstable. I used that to create the piece with the idea that each time you played the tape, the signal would degrade, ultimately destructing itself." Templar adds: "I did some additional editing and titling on it, and we made a few 'masters,' in which we mangled the time code badly enough that we figured each tape would only last through a few showings before becoming unusable." Copies were sent to a handful of people, including Kevin Begos (whose copy became the source for the clip identified as *Re:Agrippa* on *The Agrippa Files*).

- Templar and Rosehammer's recollections vary on the subject of Kevin Begos's reaction, once it was known that the poem had been leaked out onto the network. Templar had the impression that, "I believe he thought we had violated the spirit of the challenge," whereas Rosehammer recollected that Begos seemed "excited" by the development and that there was a "wink-wink" quality to the whole affair. Not everyone felt that way in any case. "After we put it up on MindVox," recalls Rosehammer, "some people in the ITP department put two and two together and felt we had abused the opportunity. I didn't let it bother me." Templar concurs: "A hacker always takes the path of least resistance. And it is a lot easier to 'hack' a person than a machine."

Clearly the hack was the product of layer upon layer of personal and technological contingency, all deeply intertwined. The extreme remediation that is crystallized in the geometry of a Hi8 camera pointed at a laptop screen to project and record a video signal, the (edited and remixed) video footage of the event finding its way to Kevin Begos who many years later gives the tape to a university scholar for digitization and publication on the Web, at which point one of the original participants finds the Web site, watches the video, and elects to contact the researchers working to document the work's history—we know that contingencies and circumstances like these are inevitably the mechanisms of inscription, transmission, and preservation. The social life of information is again proven profoundly. Templar is right to say it is easier to hack a person than a machine, and in the end he and Rosehammer gave me leave to "hack" their individual memories, answering questions that the raw forensic evidence of network and archive could not.

There is one last contingency and circumstance worth remarking on. As Templar and Rosehammer's testimony establishes beyond a shadow of a doubt, the text of the poem as it circulates online today is *not* a digital copy whose bits were lifted from one of the project's diskettes, but rather the result of a manual transcription of a video cassette, with all of the potential for typist's errors that accompany the movements of eye and hand to screen and keyboard and back again. (Textual scholars have been aware of the patterns of such errors for decades.) Templar himself suggests that, "since it was retyped, it had, in essence, decayed by the time it reached the net." The cicadic motions of an active eye fixed on a static visual field (some 70 to 100 movements a second) produce dropouts and occlusions that are in their own way not so different from the nanoscale gap between the read/write head and the surface of a hard drive—not so different because this is where the formal and the forensic, allographic symbol and ineluctable embodiment, merge and fuse. This electronic text, last of the great pre-Mosaic Internet memes, survives today as the result of what was initially an act of scribal copying rather than any mechanisms of digital reproduction. Such was the nature of the event at the core of "Agrippa's" hack and transmission. And there is no legible trace of it outside of the written recollection of those who were there.[4]

4. As of the writing of this Appendix (July 2007), Rosehammer is attempting to locate the original Hi8 tape from the recording at the Americas Society. Readers are encouraged to check *The Agrippa Files*, http://agrippa.english.ucsb.edu/, for further developments.

Works Cited

The Works Cited list generally follows MLA style. Some works mentioned only in passing in the book's notes will not be listed here (for all works, however, the notes contain full citation information).

Archival materials from the Michael Joyce Papers at the Harry Ransom Humanities Research Center at the University of Texas at Austin are referenced in notes where they are cited. All citations to these materials appear by permission.

Stand-alone electronic content (on media such as CD-ROM or diskette) is cited in this section as usual. Regarding online materials, URLs and documentation for all online content is always available in the notes. Web sites, when referenced as such—as entities in their entirety, for example *The Agrippa Files*—are not listed here, nor are they generally below if their content does not benefit from being organized according to conventions of individual authorship; articles in electronic journals or other online publications *are* listed. Select, well-defined units of online content, such as individual e-mail messages, news items, or bulletin board postings, are also not listed here; again, full documentation for these is always available in the notes where they are referenced.

I have not included the usual dates of access for most online material, since in my view repeated and conspicuous emphasis on exactly when the source was checked is disruptive and serves to prejudice still-emerging perceptions of the stability (and reliability) of the medium. (One suspects these access dates are also too often only well-intentioned guesstimates—though the next generation of information management tools like del.icio.us and Zotero has the potential to change that with automatic record keeping.) Sometimes, however, online material is time-stamped to a specific posting day, allowing its publication date to be ascertained with more granularity than we are accustomed to with printed sources, and that information is included here.

All URLs are valid, and all content exists in the state it is referenced at the time of the book's printing. While 404s are inevitable, Google, Google Cache, and the Wayback Machine all offer recourse. Note too that the Wayback Machine can be useful in reconstructing the history of online material that may have been changed since the state in which it is referenced here. The same is true for *Wikipedia*'s page history function.

References

Aarseth, Espen J. *Cybertext: Perspectives on Ergodic Literature*. Baltimore: Johns Hopkins University Press, 1997.

Armstrong-Hélouvry, Brian. *Control of Machines with Friction*. Boston: Kluwer Academic Publishers, 1991.

Baker, Nicholson. *The Mezzanine*. New York: Vintage, 1986.

Bashe, Charles J., Lyle R. Johnson, John H. Palmer, and Emerson W. Pugh. *IBM's Early Computers*. Cambridge: MIT Press, 1986.

Benedikt, Michael, ed. *Cyberspace: First Steps*. Cambridge: MIT Press, 1991.

Blumenthal, Ralph. "College Libraries Set Aside Books in a Digital Age." *New York Times*, May 14, 2005.

Bolter, Jay David. *Writing Space: The Computer, Hypertext, and the History of Writing*. Hillsdale, NJ: Lawrence Erlbaum, 1991.

Bowers, Fredson. *Bibliography and Textual Criticism*. Oxford: Clarendon Press, 1964.

———. "Bibliography, Pure Bibliography, and Literary Studies." *Essays in Bibliography, Text, and Editing*. Charlottesville: University Press of Virginia, 1975.

———. *Principles of Bibliographical Description*, 2nd edition. Princeton: Princeton University Press, 1986.

————. *Textual and Literary Criticism*. Cambridge: Cambridge University Press, 1959.

Brown, John Seely and Paul Duguid. *The Social Life of Information*. Cambridge: Harvard Business School Press, 2000.

Brown, Nathan. "Needle on the Real: Technoscience and Poetry at the Limits of Fabrication." *Nanoculture*. Ed. N. Katherine Hayles. Bristol, UK: Intellect Books, 2004. 173–190.

Bryant, John. *The Fluid Text: A Theory of Revision and Editing for Book and Screen*. Ann Arbor: Michigan University Press, 2002.

Burnham, Van. *Supercade: A Visual History of the Video Game Age, 1971–1984*. Cambridge: MIT Press, 2001.

Caloyannides, Michael. *Computer Forensics and Privacy*. Norwood, MA: Artech House, 2001.

Campbell-Kelly, Martin. *From Airline Reservations to Sonic the Hedgehog: A History of the Software Industry*. Cambridge: MIT Press, 2003.

Ceruzzi, Paul E. *A History of Modern Computing*. Cambridge: MIT Press, 1998.

Clarke, Arthur C. "The Steam-Powered Word Processor." *The Collected Stories of Arthur C. Clarke*. New York: Tor, 2000. 930–934.

Clarke, Bruce and Linda Dalrymple Henderson, eds. *From Energy to Information: Representation in Science, Technology, Art, and Literature*. Stanford: Stanford University Press, 2002.

Clayton, Jay. *Charles Dickens in Cyberspace: The Afterlife of the Nineteenth Century in Postmodern Culture*. Oxford: Oxford University Press, 2003.

Coupland, Douglas. *Microserfs*. New York: HarperCollins, 1995.

Crain, Patricia. *The Story of A: The Alphabetization of America from* The New England Primer *to* The Scarlet Letter. Stanford: Stanford University Press, 2000.

Daniel, Eric D., C. Denis Mee, and Mark H. Clark. *Magnetic Recording: The First One Hundred Years*. New York: IEEE Press, 1999.

Delany, Paul and George P. Landow, eds. *Hypermedia and Literary Studies*. Cambridge: MIT Press, 1991.

DeLillo, Don. *White Noise*, Viking Critical Library. Ed. Mark Osteen. New York: Penguin, 1998.

Derrida, Jacques. *Archive Fever: A Freudian Impression*. Trans. Eric Prenowitz. Chicago: University of Chicago Press, 1995.

————. *Paper Machine*. Trans. Rachel Bowlby. Stanford: Stanford University Press, 2005.

Doherty, Thomas. "Cultural Studies and 'Forensic Noir.'" *The Chronicle of Higher Education* (October 24, 2003): B15–16.

Donadio, Rachel. "Literary Letters Lost and Found in Cyberspace," *New York Times Book Review* (September 4, 2005).

Douglas, Jane Yellowlees. *The End of Books—Or Books Without End: Reading Interactive Narrative*. Ann Arbor: University of Michigan Press, 2000.

————. "'How Do I Stop This Thing?': Closure and Indeterminacy in Interactive Narratives." *Hyper/Text/Theory*. Ed. George P. Landow. Baltimore: Johns Hopkins University Press, 1994. 159–188.

Drucker, Johanna. "The Future of Writing in Terms of its Past: The New Fungibility Factor." *Émigré* 35 (Summer 1995).

————. *The Visible Word: Experimental Typography and Modern Art, 1909–1923*. Chicago: University of Chicago Press, 1994.

Eaves, Morris. *The Counter-Arts Conspiracy: Art and Industry in the Age of Blake*. Ithaca: Cornell University Press, 1992.

Eco, Umberto. *Foucault's Pendulum*. Trans. William Weaver. London: Picador, 1989.

Edwards, Paul N. *The Closed World: Computers and the Politics of Discourse in Cold War America*. Cambridge: MIT Press, 1996.

Essick, Robert N. and Joseph Viscomi. "An Inquiry into Blake's Method of Color Printing." *Blake: An Illustrated Quarterly* 35, no. 3 (Winter 2001/2002): 74–103.

Farmer, Dan and Wietse Venema. *Forensic Discovery*. Upper Saddle River, NJ: Addison-Wesley, 2005.

Fuller, Matthew. *Behind the Blip: Essays on the Culture of Software*. Brooklyn, NY: Automedia, 2003.

Furness, Thomas A., III and Woodrow Barfield, eds. *Virtual Environments and Advanced Interface Design Design*. Oxford: Oxford University Press, 1995.

Garfinkel, Simson L. and Abhi Shelat, "Remembrance of Data Past: A Study of Disk Sanitization Practices." *IEEE Security and Privacy* (January–February 2003): 17–27.

Getting Started with Storyspace for Windows. Watertown, MA: Eastgate Systems, 1996.

Gibson, William. "Agrippa: A Book of the Dead." New York: Kevin Begos Publishing, 1992. Available online—everywhere.

———. *Burning Chrome*. New York: Ace, 1986.

———. *Virtual Light*. New York: Bantam Spectra, 1993.

Ginzburg, Carlo. "Clues: The Roots of an Evidential Paradigm." *Clues, Myths, and Historical Method*. Trans. John and Anne C. Tedeschi. Baltimore: Johns Hopkins University Press, 1989: 96–125.

Gitelman, Lisa. *Always Already New: Media, History, and the Data of Culture*. Cambridge: MIT Press, 2006.

———. *Scripts, Grooves, and Writing Machines: Representing Technology in the Edison Era*. Stanford: Stanford University Press, 1999.

Gitelman, Lisa and Geoffrey R. Pingree, eds. *New Media 1740–1915*. Cambridge: MIT Press, 2003.

Gomez, Romel, A. A. Adly, I. D. Mayergoyz, and E. R. Burke. "Magnetic Force Scanning Tunneling Microscopy: Theory and Experiment," *IEEE Transactions on Magnetics* 29 (November 1993): 2494–2499.

Gomez, Romel, E. R. Burke, A. A. Adly, I. D. Mayergoyz, J. Gorczyca, and M. H. Kryder. "Microscopic Investigations of Overwritten Data," *Journal of Applied Physics* 73.10 (May 1993): 6001–6003.

Goodman, Nelson. *Languages of Art: An Approach to a Theory of Symbols*. Indianapolis: Hackett, 1976.

Graves, David. "Second Generation Adventure Games." *The Journal of Computer Game Design* 1, no. 2 (August 1987): 4–7. Also available online at http://teladesign.com/tads/authoring/articles/graves1.html.

Greenblatt, Stephen. *Shakespearean Negotiations: The Circulation of Social Energy in Renaissance England*. Berkeley: University of California Press, 1988.

Greetham, D. C. "Textual Forensics." *PMLA* (January 1996): 32–51.

Greg, W. W. "Bibliography—An Apologia." *Collected Papers*. Ed. J. C. Maxwell. Oxford: Oxford University Press, 1966: 239–266.

————. "The Rationale of Copy Text," *Studies in Bibliography* 3 (1950–1951): 19–36.

Guillory, John. "The Memo and Modernity." *Critical Inquiry* 31 (Autumn 2004): 108–132.

Gumari-Tabrizi, Sharon. *The Worlds of Herman Kahn*. Cambridge: Harvard University Press, 2005.

Gutmann, Peter. "Secure Deletion of Data from Magnetic and Solid-State Memory." *Sixth USENIX Security Symposium Proceedings*, San Jose, California, July 22–25, 1996. Also available online at http://www.cs.auckland.ac.nz/~pgut001/pubs/secure_del.html.

Hancher, Michael. "*Littera Scripta Manet*: Blackstone and Electronic Text." *Studies in Bibliography* 54 (2001): 115–132.

Haraway, Donna J. "A Cyborg Manifesto: Science, Technology, and Socialist-Feminism in the Late Twentieth Century." In *Simiams, Cyborgs, and Women: The Reinvention of Nature*. New York: Routledge, 1991. 149–181.

Haugeland, John, ed. *Mind Design II: Philosophy, Psychology, and Artificial Intelligence.* Cambridge: MIT Press, 1997.

Hawthorne, Nathanial. *Fanshawe.* Ed. Fredson Bowers. Centenary Edition. Columbus: Ohio State Press, 1964.

Hayes, Brian. "Terabyte Territory," *American Scientist* 90 (May–June 2002): 212–216.

Hayles, N. Katherine. "Flickering Connectivies in Shelley Jackson's *Patchwork Girl*: The Importance of Media-Specific Analysis." *Postmodern Culture* 10, no. 2 (2000), http://www.iath.virginia.edu/pmc/text-only/issue.100/10.2hayles.txt.

———. "Virtual Bodies and Flickering Signifiers." *Electronic Culture: Technology and Visual Representation*, ed. Timothy Druckrey. Romford, England: Aperture, 1996: 259–277.

———. *Writing Machines.* Cambridge: MIT Press, 2002.

Heim, Michael. *Electric Language: A Philosophical Study of Word Processing*, 2nd edition. New Haven: Yale University Press, 1999.

———. *The Metaphysics of Virtual Reality.* New York: Oxford University Press, 1993.

Hill, William C., James D. Hollan, Dave Wroblewski, and Tim McCandless. "Edit Wear and Read Wear." *CHI '92 Conference Proceedings*. Reading, MA: Addison-Wesley, 1992. 3–9.

Hillis, W. Daniel. *The Pattern on the Stone: The Simple Ideas That Make Computers Work.* New York: Basic Books, 1998.

Hilton, Ordway. *Scientific Examination of Questioned Documents.* Revised Edition. New York: Elsevier, 1982.

Hodge, James J. "Bibliographic Description of *Agrippa*." *The Agrippa Files*. 6 November 2005 〈http://agrippa.english.ucsb.edu/hodge-james-bibliographic-description-of-agrippa-commissioned-for-the-agrippa-files/〉.

Hodges, Andrew. *Alan Turing: The Enigma.* New York: Walker and Company, 2005.

Johns, Adrian. *The Nature of the Book: Print and Knowledge in the Making*. Chicago: University of Chicago Press, 1998.

Johnson, Steve. *Everything is Bad is Good For You*. New York: Riverhead Books, 2005.

Jonas, Gerald B. "The Disappearing $2000 Book." *Cyberreader*. Ed. Vitctor J. Vitanza. Second edition. Boston: Allyn and Bacon, 1999, 287–289.

Joyce, Michael. *Afternoon: A Story*. First edition. Self-published, 1987.

———. *Afternoon: A Story*. Third edition. Watertown, MA: Eastgate Systems, 1990.

———. *Afternoon: A Story*. Fifth edition (for Windows). Watertown, MA: Eastgate Systems, 1992.

———. *Of Two Minds: Hypertext Pedagogy and Poetics*. Ann Arbor: University of Michigan Press, 1995.

Kiehne, Thomas, Vivian Spoliansky, and Catherine Stollar. "From Floppies to Repository: A Transition of Bits. A Case Study in Preserving the Michael Joyce Papers at the Harry Ransom Center." Unpublished paper, May 2005.

Kirschenbaum, Matthew G. "Editing the Interface: Textual Studies and First Generation Electronic Objects." *TEXT* 14 (2002): 15–51.

———. "Virtuality and VRML: Software Studies After Manovich." *Electronic Book Review* (August 29, 2003), http://www.electronicbookreview.com/thread/technocapitalism/morememory.

———. "The Word as Image in an Age of Digital Reproduction." *Eloquent Images: Word and Image in the Age of New Media*. Eds. Mary E. Hocks and Michelle R. Kendrick. Cambridge: MIT Press, 2003. 137–156.

Kittler, Friedrich A. *Discourse Networks 1800/1900*. Trans. Michael Metteer. Stanford: Stanford University Press, 1990.

———. *Gramophone, Film, Typewriter*. Trans. Geoffrey Winthrop-Young and Michael Wutz. Stanford: Stanford University Press, 1999.

———. *Literature, Media, Information Systems*. Ed. John Johnston. Amsterdam: G+B Arts, 1997.

Knapp, Steven and Walter Benn Michaels. "Against Theory." *Against Theory: Literary Studies and the New Pragmatism*, ed. W. J. T. Mitchell. Chicago: University of Chicago Press, 1985. 11–30.

Kozierok, Charles M. *The PC Guide*, http://www.pcguide.com.

Kraus, Kari M. "Conjectural Criticism: Computing Past and Future Texts." Dissertation. University of Rochester, 2006.

Kruse, Warren G., II and Jay G. Heiser. *Computer Forensics: Incident Response Essentials*. Boston: Addison-Wesley, 2002.

Kunzru, Hari. *Transmission*. New York: Dutton, 2004.

Latour, Bruno. *Science in Action*. Cambridge: Harvard University Press, 1987.

Lenior, Timothy, ed. *Inscribing Science: Scientific Texts and the Materiality of Communication*. Stanford: Stanford University Press, 1998.

Lesk, Michael. "How Much Storage is Enough?" *Storage* 1, no. 4 (June 2003). Available online at http://www.acmqueue.org/modules.php?name=Content&pa=showpage&pid=45.

Levy, David. *Scrolling Forward: Making Sense of Documents in the Digital Age*. New York: Arcade, 2001.

Leyton, Michael. *Symmetry, Causality, Mind*. Cambridge: MIT Press, 1992.

Liu, Alan. *The Laws of Cool: Knowledge Work and the Culture of Information*. Chicago: University of Chicago Press, 2004.

Lok, Coire. "Nano Writing." *MIT Technology Review* (April 2004): 77.

Lohr, Steve. *Go To*. New York: Basic Books, 2001.

Love, Harold. *Scribal Publication in Seventeenth-Century England*. Oxford University Press, 1993.

Works Cited

Lowood, Henry. "The Hard Work of Software History." *RBM: A Journal of Rare Books, Manuscripts, and Cultural Heritage* 2, no. 2 (Fall 2001): 141–161. Also available online at http://www.ala.org/ala/acrl/acrlpubs/rbm/backissuesvol2no/lowood.PDF.

Manovich, Lev. *The Language of New Media.* Cambridge: MIT Press, 2001.

Markley, Robert. "Boundaries: Mathematics, Alienation, and the Metaphysics of Cyberspace." *Virtual Realities and Their Discontents.* Ed. Robert Markley. Baltimore: Johns Hopkins University Press, 1996.

Masten, Jeffrey, Peter Stallybrass, and Nancy J. Vickers, eds. *Language Machines: Technologies of Literary and Cultural Representation.* New York: Routledge, 1999.

Mayergoyz, I. D., C. Tse, C. Krafft, and R. D. Gomez. "Spin-Stand Imaging of Overwritten Data and Its Comparison with Magnetic Force Microscopy," *Journal of Applied Physics* 89 (June 2001): 6772–6774.

McCaffery, Larry. *Storming the Reality Studio.* Durham: Duke University Press, 1991.

McGann, Jerome J. *The Romantic Ideology.* Chicago: University of Chicago Press, 1983.

———. *The Textual Condition.* Princeton: Princeton University Press, 1991.

McKenzie, Donald F. *Bibliography and the Sociology of Texts.* London: The British Library, 1986.

———. "Printers of the Mind." *Studies in Bibliography* 22 (1969): 1–75.

McLeod, Randall. "From 'Tranceformations in the Text of *Orlando Furioso.*'" *New Directions in Textual Studies.* Ed. Dave Oliphant and Robin Bradford. Austin: University of Texas Press and Harry Ransom Humanities Research Center, 1990. 61–85.

———. "Information on Information." *Text* 5 (1991): 240–281.

Montfort, Nick. "Continuous Paper: The Early Materiality and Workings of Electronic Literature." Available online at http://nickm.com/writing/essays/continuous_paper_mla.html.

———. *Twisty Little Passages: An Approach to Interactive Fiction.* Cambridge: MIT Press, 2004.

Morris, Mitchell E. "Professor RAMAC's Tenure." *Datamation* (April 1981): 195–198.

Negroponte, Nicholas. *Being Digital*. Cambridge: MIT Press, 1995.

Nickell, Joe and John F. Fischer, *Crime Science: Methods of Forensic Detection*. Lexington: University Press of Kentucky, 1996.

Nöth, Winfried. *Handbook of Semiotics*. Bloomington: Indiana University Press, 1990.

O'Gorman, Marcel. "Friedrich Kittler's Media Scenes—An Instruction Manual." *Postmodern Culture* (September 1999), http://www3.iath.virginia.edu/pmc/text-only/issue.999/10.1.r_ogorman.txt.

Osborn, Albert S. *Questioned Documents* (Second Edition). Albany: Boyd Printing Company, 1929.

Patterson, Dave and Jim Gray. "A Conversation with Jim Gray." *Storage* 1.4 (June 2003). Available online at http://www.acmqueue.org/modules.php?name=Content&pa=showpage&pid=43.

Peckham, Morse. "Reflections on the Foundations of Modern Textual Editing." *Proof* 1 (1971): 122–155.

Poster, Mark. *The Mode of Information: Poststructuralism and Social Contexts*. Chicago: University of Chicago Press, 1990.

Pugh, Edmund W., Lyle R. Johnson, and John H. Palmer. *IBM's 360 and Early 370 Systems*. Cambridge: MIT Press, 1991.

Quan, Margaret. "Holographic Storage Nears Debut," *EE Times*, April 26, 2001. Available online at http://www.eetimes.com/story/OEG20010423S0113.

Rabinow, Jacob. "The Notched-Disk Memory," *Electrical Engineering* (August 1952): 745–749.

Raley, Rita. "Interferences: [Net Writing] and the Practice of Codework." *electronic book review* (September 8, 2002), http://www.electronicbookreview.com/thread/electropoetics/net.writing.

Ratner, Mark and Daniel Ratner. *Nanotechnology: A Gentle Introduction to the Next Big Idea*. Upper Saddle River, NJ: Prentice Hall, 2003.

Rogers, Shef. "How Many Ts Had Ezra Pound's Printer." *Studies in Bibliography* 49 (1996): 277–283.

Ronell, Avital. *The Telephone Book: Technology—Schizophrenia—Electric Speech*. University of Nebraska Press, 1989.

Ryan, Marie-Laure. "Cyberspace, Virtuality, and the Text." *Cyberspace Textuality: Computer Technology and Literary Theory*. Ed. Marie-Laure Ryan. Bloomington: Indiana University Press, 1999. 78–107.

Salomon, Frank. *The Cord Keepers: Khipus and Cultural Life in a Peruvian Village*. Durham: Duke University Press, 2004.

Sampson, Geoffrey. *Writing Systems*. Stanford: Stanford University Press, 1985.

Schwenger, Peter. "*Agrippa*, or the Apocalyptic Book," *South Atlantic Quarterly* 92.4 (Fall 1993): 617–626.

Sconce, Jeffrey. *Haunted Media: Electronic Presence from Telegraphy to Television.* Duke University Press, 2000.

Sellen, Abigail J. and Richard H. R. Harper. *The Myth of the Paperless Office*. Cambridge: MIT Press, 2001.

Shannon, Claude and Warren Weaver. *The Mathematical Theory of Communication*. Urbana, IL: University of Illinois Press, 1949.

Slade, Robert M. *Software Forensics: Collecting Evidence from the Scene of a Digital Crime*. New York: McGraw Hill, 2004.

Smith, Abby. "Preservation in the Future Tense," *CLIR Issues* 3 (May/June 1998): 1, 6.

Sterling, Bruce. *Shaping Things*. Cambridge: MIT Press, 2006.

Stille, Alexander. *The Future of the Past*. New York: Picador, 2002.

Tanselle, G. Thomas. "Bibliographers and the Library." *Literature and Artifacts*. Charlottesville: Bibliographical Society of the University of Virginia, 1998. 24–40.

———. "The Life and Work of Fredson Bowers." *Studies in Bibliography* 46 (1993): 1–154.

Taylor, Gary. "c:\wp\file.txt 05:41 10-07-98." *The Renaissance Text: Theory, Editing, Textuality*. Ed. Andrew Murphy. Manchester: Manchester University Press, 2000. 44–54.

Thibodeau, Kenneth. "Overview of Technological Approaches to Digital Preservation and Challenges in the Coming Years." *The State of Digital Preservation: An International Perspective*. 2002. Washington DC: Council on Library and Information Resources, http://www.clir.org/pubs/reports/pub107/thibodeau.html.

Turing, Alan. "On Computable Numbers, With an Application to the *Entscheidungsproblem*." *The Essential Turing: The Ideas That Gave Birth To the Computer Age*. Ed. B. Jack Copeland. Oxford: Oxford University Press, 2004. 58–90.

Tuthill, Harold. *Individualization: Principles and Procedures in Criminalistics*. Salem, OR: Lightning Powder Co., 1994.

von Neumann, John. "General and Logical Theory of Automata." *Collected Works*, volume 5: *Design of Computers, Theory of Automata and Numerical Analysis*. Ed. A. H. Taub. Oxford: Pergamon Press, 1963. 288–328.

Wiener, Norbert. *Cybernetics* (Second edition). Cambridge: MIT Press, 1964.

———. *The Human Use of Human Beings: Cybernetics and Society*. New York: Doubleday, 1956.

Williams, Roberta and Ken Williams. *Mystery House*. Los Angeles: Sierra On-Line, 1980, 1987. Available online at ftp://ftp.apple.asimov.net/pub/apple_II/images/games/adventure/.

Worth, Don and Pieter Lechner. *Beneath Apple DOS*. Quality Software, 1985.

Works Cited

Index

Index

Index

Index

Smith, Oberlin, 6n14

Social theory, 162

Software, 17
  digital preservation and, 3–4
  formal materiality and, 142–156
  IBM's unbundling of, 14
  as industry commodity, 14–15
  marketing of, 176–177

Software forensics, 209–210

Sondheim, Alan, 230–231, 235

Sony, 3

Soresi, Filippo, 161n4

Spimes, 108

Spoliansky, Vivian, 209n81

Spolsky, Joel, 242–243

Stark, David, 241n64

"Steam-Powered Word Processor, The"
  (Clarke), 36–37

Stephenson, Neal, 6n13

Sterling, Bruce, 108, 224

Stevenson, Adlai, 79

Stille, Alexander, 1

Sting, 60n63

Stoll, Clifford, 49

Stollar, Catherine, 209

Storage, 251–252
  Agrippa codework and, 233
  archival issues and, 21–22, 96–109
  cathode ray tube and, 254–258
  CD-ROMs and, 32
  Clearing and Sanitization Matrix, 26–
    27, 58, 70–71, 160
  computer forensics and, xi–xii, 15–17,
    30, 45–69 (*see also* Computer
    forensics)
  costs of, 49–50, 98
  data standards for, 17
  digital preservation concept and, 3–4
  digital watermark and, 14
  floppy disks, 32–34, 69, 84, 164
  forensic imagination and, 249–259
  hard drives, 74 (*see also* Hard drives)
  Harry Ransom Humanities Research
    Center and, 20, 164, 207–211
  High Bias recording and, 6n14
  historical perspective on, 5–9, 76–86
  holographic, 96
  impact of, 4–5
  infinite, 107
  information objects and, 3–4
  inscription and, 58–69, 74–109 (*see
    also* Inscription)
  instrumentation and, 58–69
  iPods and, 4–5
  JPEG format and, 142–149
  khipu and, 28
  libraries and, 100
  machine readability and, 27–31
  magnetic tape, 6n14, 74, 81–82
  marketing of, 82–86
  materiality and, 9–15 (*see also*
    Materiality)
  media convergence and, 6
  as medial ideology, 36–45
  Memex and, 80–81, 101
  memory sticks and, 5
  Moore's Law and, 74
  MP3, 5
  notched-disk doughnut and, 80–81
  obsessive-compulsive, 97–102
  online, 98–108
  paper and, 31–32
  processing and, 5–6
  RAM, 5, 13n22, 42, 49–52
  screen essentialism and, 27–35
  security issues and, 25–27 (*see also*
    Security)
  show header function and, 13
  as suspended animation, 97
  system opacity and, 40–41